THE LOUISIANA SCALAWAGS

RECONSTRUCTION!
AS IT SHOULD BE
AS IT IS!
Grand March
BY
CHARLES YOUNG.
New Orleans

THE LOUISIANA SCALAWAGS

POLITICS, RACE, AND TERRORISM DURING THE CIVIL WAR AND RECONSTRUCTION

FRANK J. WETTA

Louisiana State University Press
Baton Rouge

Published by Louisiana State University Press

Manufactured in the United States of America
First printing

DESIGNER: Michelle A. Neustrom
TYPEFACE: Ingeborg
PRINTER: McNaughton & Gunn, Inc.
BINDER: Dekker Bookbinding

FRONTISPIECE: Charles Young. *Reconstruction! Grand March.* Johns Hopkins University, Levy Sheet Music Collection, Box 095, Item 076.

LIBRARY OF CONGRESS CATALOGING-IN-PUBLICATION DATA

Wetta, Frank Joseph, 1942–
The Louisiana scalawags : politics, race, and terrorism during the Civil War and Reconstruction / Frank J. Wetta.
p. cm.
Includes bibliographical references and index.
ISBN 978-0-8071-4746-7 (cloth : alk. paper) — ISBN 978-0-8071-4747-4 (pdf) — ISBN 978-0-8071-4748-1 (epub) — ISBN 978-0-8071-4749-8 (mobi)
1. Louisiana—Politics and government—1861–1865. 2. Louisiana—Politics and government—1865–1950. 3. Reconstruction (U.S. history, 1865–1877)—Louisiana. 4. Whites—Louisiana—Politics and government—19th century. 5. Louisiana—Race relations—History—19th century. 6. Terrorism—Political aspects—Louisiana—History—19th century. 7. Republican Party (La.)—History—19th century. I. Title.
F374.W47 2012
976.3'05—dc23

2012005568

The paper in this book meets the guidelines for permanence and durability of the Committee on Production Guidelines for Book Longevity of the Council on Library Resources. ♾

In memory of T. Harry Williams (1909–1979)

CONTENTS

ACKNOWLEDGMENTS

I am deeply grateful to my colleague John J. Guthrie (1955–2000) for his friendship. John and I had intended to write this book as coauthors when I was serving as an academic vice president. His passing was a great loss to the profession.

Particular thanks are due to Terry Seip, F. Wayne Binning, Howard Nichols, E. Russ Williams, and Richard Hume for their advice and generous sharing of research material.

I wish to record my appreciation of Joan Hyatt, former librarian at Galveston College, Texas, for her courtesy and helpfulness. Many thanks as well to Michael and Phyllis Ward, whose generosity made my research trip to Washington, D.C., such an enjoyable one.

This study was born as a dissertation at Louisiana State University. T. Harry Williams was my major professor. Those on the graduate committee who kindly read and criticized the manuscript back then were Drs. John Loos, Anne Loveland, Burl Noggle, and Gary Crump.

I am also indebted to Rand Dotson of the LSU Press for his encouragement and support for the project.

Of course, this career would be no fun at all without going to the "the Southern" each year with the LSU Boys—Joseph G. Dawson, George Rable, Terry Seip, Marius Carriere, Larry Hewett, Eric Walther, and Roger Spiller.

Finally, I owe a special gratitude, as always, to my wife, Jean, who kept saying, "I really liked that story about the scalawags and the riot. When are you going to write the book?"

THE LOUISIANA SCALAWAGS

INTRODUCTION

> Louisiana to-day is Paradise Lost. In twenty years it may be Paradise Regained. It has unlimited enchanting possibilities. Now . . . a gigantic struggle is in progress. It is the battle of race with race, of the picturesque and unjust civilization of the past with the . . . leveling civilization of the present.
>
> —EDWARD KING, *Scribner's Monthly,* December 1873

Nothing in Louisiana is ordinary. Bayous and alligators, Creoles and Cajuns, jambalaya and file gumbo, the French Quarter and the Garden District of New Orleans, zydeco festivals and Mardi Gras characterize an extraordinary land and people—*Laissez les bons temps rouler* (Let the good times roll). And Louisiana's political history is as fascinating as its environment and culture. Along with the enchantment, however, there has existed a heavy atmosphere of injustice and violence. Reconstruction provides an example.

The Mardi Gras parade of 1866, the first since the Civil War began in 1861, reflected the contested political culture of postwar Louisiana. Battle-hardened ex-Confederates were now determined to regain control of politics and race in the state. The Fat Tuesday parade offered a premonition of things to come. The Mistick Krewe of Comus was composed of masked Confederate veterans and their sympathizers—"recently grim visaged warriors, who had played conspicuous parts in the recent sad scenes of havoc and slaughter." The theme of the parade was "The Past, the Present, the Future." The Rebels were once again on the march, their way lighted by an escort of torchbearers. This time their nemesis was not the Union army but the agents of Reconstruction—southern white Republicans (the scalawags) and their black allies.[1]

"Scalawag" and "carpetbagger" are idioms that evoke the rough politics of the post–Civil War American South. Today the term "scalawag" has lost its bite. Nationally, you can find "Scalawag" fish-and-chip shops, golf courses, Celtic folk singers, amusement-park pirate characters, even pet boutiques. But in Reconstruction Louisiana and across the defeated South, the term was a vicious slur often used with deadly intent.

The etymology of "scalawag" is obscure. The word may have originally referred to a type of dwarf cattle raised in the Shetland Islands. As early as 1848, it served as a common epithet in western New York for a rogue or rascal. By 1866, "scalawag" had acquired its specialized southern tenor: "Whenever a white man appeared to vote" in Alabama, the *Washington Morning Chronicle* informed its readers, "every one of these infuriated devils . . . sets up a yell, calling him 'white negro,' 'low trash,' 'scalawag,' 'mean white,' etc." The slur was applied primarily to those with a particular political profile: southern white Republicans in positions of influence and leadership, or those native white men identified as voting the Republican ticket. In other words, the "scalawags" were those seen by the opposition as traitors to conservative political and racial interests. In this study, the scalawags also include northern-born and foreign-born whites who settled in the South before the Civil War and who later joined the radical movement: southerners by choice, not birth. In the years before the war, these men were absorbed into southern life and became identified with the establishment through social, economic, and political ties. Whether native-born or adopted southerners, the scalawags were distinct from northerners, the "carpetbaggers," who came to Louisiana after the Civil War. The scalawags fit the classification defined by Richard L. Hume and Jerry B. Gough in their survey of the radical constitutional conventions of 1868. They recognize that any classification necessarily involves "a degree of irreducible arbitrariness." Nevertheless, they divide white Republicans in the postwar South into two types: outside white men who came to the South after the war (the carpetbaggers) and white men who lived in the South before the war (the scalawags).[2]

In Louisiana, the scalawags also differ from the carpetbaggers in that the success of Reconstruction in Louisiana depended not only on the new black southern voters and effective federal intervention (no matter what size the force) to prevent a counterrevolution of conservative whites, but also on effective native white southern leadership. If Reconstruction was to be a success, it needed a substantial base of southern white support. Yet, as Eric Foner concludes for Reconstruction as a whole, corruption, factionalism, and "the failure to develop an effective long-term appeal to white voters made it increasingly difficult for Republicans to combat the racial politics of the Redeemers."[3] Republican success could not rest on black votes, "outside whites," and the intervention of Federal troops alone. In the long run, a lasting, sustained settlement that could ensure black rights and a true political reconstruction based on Unionist principles needed a solid, enduring foundation of economic and political reformation led by southern white leaders, leaders who could sustain basic changes in southern government and race relations. It needed a leadership that could bring white voters into support for Reconstruction.

Identifying the southern white Republicans in Louisiana can help to explain the failure of the first Reconstruction of the 1860s and 1870s and to define the nature of scalawagism: Who were the leading scalawags and the lesser functionaries? What were their geographical, economic, social, and political origins? What distinguished them from their political associates, the carpetbaggers? In what did they believe? What role did they play in the Federal occupation of New Orleans? What happened to the scalawags in the New Orleans Riot of 1866? What role did they play in the founding of the Republican Party and its internecine political wars? How deep was their commitment to racial justice and political reform? How did they navigate the currents and eddies of Louisiana politics during the fifteen years of Reconstruction in Louisiana? What was the effect of white terrorism and intimidation on the scalawags? Finally, what is the scalawag legacy? Therefore, the role of the southern white men who challenged the restoration of the antebellum political and social order, the struggle over the future of Louisiana in the 1860s and 1870s, the interplay of politics and race, and the resultant terrorism are the subjects of this book.

1

THE SCALAWAGS IN "THE LAND OF JUBILEE"

MYTH, MEMORY, AND THE HISTORIANS

> Patrick Quinn acknowledged that there's a fine line between an entrepreneur and a vulture. Borrowing a term coined during Reconstruction, he allowed that there was a question whether he was a hero or a "scalawag"—a son of the South exploiting a chaotic and defeated region.
>
> —GARY RIVLIN, "Après Le Deluge, Moi: One Man's Flood Is Another Man's Opportunity"

At the close of 1877, Charles Etienne Gayarré, a Louisiana historian and politician, surveyed the course of southern Reconstruction. "All the honesty and intelligence of the country were driven out of sight into nooks, corners, and rat-holes," he wrote, "and the Southern States were delivered to the merciless legislation of ignorant negroes, acting blindly under the guidance of white leaders, the majority of whom will be eternally gibbeted in history under the appellations of carpet-baggers and scalawags." For Gayarré, himself impoverished by the Civil War, the natural order of things had been reversed: "the social body was inverted; the feet were up and the head down." The masters had become the servants, the servants the masters. "There was such a bubbling up of scum to the surface of the boiling caldron," he lamented, "as had never been seen before, and Swift's fictitious story of the Yahoos became a reality." In Gayarré's view, the Southland became a Yahoodom at the point of Federal bayonets, and an orgy of corruption and misrule ensued. Gayarré, a southern patrician, saw his world destroyed not by some heroic revolutionary impulse; rather, it was a "kitchen uprising of impish dwarfs, of creeping things used to the chains of servitude, crouching under the flagellation of centuries and relying for their support on outside power." Conditions had been particularly bad in South Carolina and Louisiana: "In these two states there was such a topsy-turvy condition of things as to baffle description and defy belief." Abolition destroyed a benign institution and the subsequent attempt to force equality in political and social affairs upon an unwilling South resulted in "a reign of insane power." With the withdrawal of federal support for the radical governments in the South, he prayed that the final "solution to the free-negro question" would be "left entirely to those who best understand the difficulties." From Gayarré's perspective, America's experiment in racial democracy had been a tragic mistake.[1]

Gayarré's account of Reconstruction and its principal participants was an expression of what became the traditional or orthodox interpretation of life and politics during the postwar years in the South. A central character in the orthodox version is the villainous scalawag—the traitorous southern white who joined with ex-field hands and carpetbaggers in an unholy trinity.

The white southern Republican was identified more precisely from the unreconstructed Louisiana perspective in "Pen Picture of a Scalawag," an editorial on the front page of the *Alexandria Caucasian* of June 6, 1874. The piece described the southern white man who entered the Republican ranks as "an artificial structure, two parts greed and one part insensibility to shame." A traitor to his race and section, the scalawag had all "the sanguinary and ferocious instinct of a hyena." Bowing low before "the shrine of negro worship," the scalawag allied with the radical "gang of unprincipled scamps, and their ignorant black followers" in their plunder of the defeated South. Although he might pretend to be "a gentleman and a patriot," the scalawag and his progeny to the third and fourth generations would carry the indelible mark of his apostasy. The editorialist concluded his attack with the prediction that "even beyond the grave memory of such a man would be held up to public execration."

Another portrait of the scalawag appeared in the November 1874 edition of the *Southern Magazine*. The author, Herbert Barnes, flailed those white southerners who cooperated with "Sambo," charging them with race treason: "He [the scalawag] goes beyond the *pale* in the selection of his associates; voluntarily places himself on a level with beings of a vastly inferior order; would erase, if he could, all the natural distinctions which a wise creator has established between the white man and the black, and would bury and conceal his own shame beneath the universal wreck of Southern society." Barnes depicted the scalawags as "poor white trash," "human vermine," Sabbath-breakers, debauchees, and persons who had treated the blacks with contempt and cruelty during the antebellum years. Although Barnes conceded that the scalawag ranks might include "a few men of liberal education, good moral training, and withal scions of respectable families," these well-bred scalawags had abandoned their class, as well as their race, to unite with the carpetbaggers and blacks.

The scalawags, Barnes charged, were oblivious "to all the horrors of negro domination." Race traitors were the guiding force in the creation of the black-based Republican Party in the South: "These people have all along existed as reckless and abandoned individuals," he wrote, "but it was not till the institution of Loyal Leagues and the enfranchisement of the blacks that, fired with the prospect of holding office, they became known as a class—with less morality than the negro, but more intelligence, and thus the duty of organizing the Republican Party in the South devolved upon them."

Following the creation of the party, however, the influence of the scalawags declined as black men gained power and self-confidence. Barnes described the scalawags as disappointed with their loss of influence and unwilling to accept the full implications of radical political and social legislation. Now, he said, southern white Republicans had begun a migration back to the "white-man's party." Barnes professed a willingness to accept them provided they were "deodorized"—purified in a sort of racial purgatory. In his conclusion, the author hoped that the history of that degenerate class of southerners known as scalawags would remain unwritten out of deference to the reputation, hopes, and traditions of the white race.[2]

In essence, these three crude diatribes (written without a speck of genuine humor or introspection) contain all the elements of what would become the traditional or orthodox view of Reconstruction in general and the scalawag in particular. In time, such images became embedded in the dominant Lost Cause narrative—in southern folk memory, popular histories, professional histories, novels, and film, most famously (or infamously) in the second half of D. W. Griffith's three-hour film epic

Birth of a Nation (1915). The meaning of Reconstruction history was no obscure historiological debate among scholars but a view of history that had real-life consequences—many of them violent.

Damnation of the scalawags continued into the twentieth century in words and images no less harsh than those uttered by the scalawags' enemies in the 1870s. It was a view particularly associated with the Columbia University historian William A. Dunning and the authors of various state histories following his lead. Scholars of Reconstruction, writing in the early twentieth century and applying the Dunning template, produced a range of studies recounting the postwar history in individual states of the former Confederacy. Two historians, John Rose Ficklen, in *History of Reconstruction in Louisiana (through 1868),* and Ella Lonn, in *Reconstruction in Louisiana after 1868,* unsurprisingly, took a dismal view of the carpetbag-scalawag-Negro regimes; both shared the pervasive racial and class prejudices of their generation. Ficklen taught at Tulane University but died before the publication of his pejorative analysis in 1910. He was the son "of an old and sturdy family of Virginia" who was "colored by that indefinable tint of gentility that is the precious heritage of such an ancestry." Lonn, born in the North, was a professor at Grinnell College in 1918, when she sought to "disentangle the complicated story of Reconstruction in Louisiana."

In the preface to his book, Ficklen argued that the victors in the Reconstruction struggle were better able than the defeated to write an objective history of the period: "The story of Reconstruction in the South should be told by writers of the South, for to the South was given the final victory in this conflict; and it is beginning to be acknowledged by writers of the North that Reconstruction of the congressional type was a gigantic blunder—if not a political crime." Ficklen made no attempt to study the social and political background of the southern white Republicans. Nor did he attempt to analyze their motives in any depth. Ficklen's Louisiana scalawags were stereotypes—political adventurers and demagogues—southern defectors who incited the "darkies" into demanding social and political equality with their former masters. These southern white collaborators, with the aid and encouragement of northern radicals, lifted "an inferior race . . . to a dizzy height of political power." The radical southerners, according to Ficklen, distributed illustrated campaign literature that provided "easy catechisms" for the political education of "the darkies." He pointed for an example to Michel Vidal, a St. Landry Parish scalawag who, he claimed, enticed the freedmen with visions of an integrated promised land: "An orator named Vidal . . . was heard declaring to the crowd of negroes that he was 'raised' in France where social equality of races existed. He told the negresses present that in that country they would be received like white women. He added that as the negroes were in the majority in Louisiana, they should control everything." To counter this intolerable situation, Ficklen continued, the decent white people of Louisiana had to resort to terroristic methods to restore white supremacy. The Ku Klux Klan and the Knights of the White Camellia grew out of the white citizens' "instinctive revulsion to forced political equality for blacks and to its natural corollary—racial equality. Southern whites were determined to "overthrow negro domination." Ficklen quoted approvingly novelist Thomas Dixon, the author of *The Clansman* (1905), the book that inspired *Birth of a Nation*: the Klan "was a magnificent conception" that "deserved success."[3]

Ella Lonn continued where John Ficklen ended.[4] Lonn considered southern white Republicans a mischievous, dangerous element: "men who pursued no occupation, but preyed on black and white alike, as gamblers and tenth-rate politicians, drinking and swaggering at the bar, always armed with knife and revolver, shooting negroes now and then for excitement." This notorious crew "was recruited, largely, from the descendants of the old overseer and negro-trader of ante-bellum days," she contended. The importance of this group, Lonn reasoned, lay in the fact that the scalawags had "just enough education to enable them to dazzle the negro by a political harangue." Accordingly, the scalawags "were both disliked and feared by decent white people." The failure to crush these disreputable politicians was the chief reason for the fifteen years of black rule. A central theme in Lonn's study was the manipulation of the ignorant freedmen by the more intelligent, but unscrupulous white Republicans, the puppeteers of the black vote. Lonn saw the freedmen as the central element in the political alliance, but an element controlled by whites. She contended that the ex-Rebels were quite willing to accept a fair and reasonable peace, but to place white southerners under the heel of black rule was simply intolerable. She chastised white Republicans for inflicting upon white Louisianians rule by the "especially vicious negroes" of the Gulf States region, who "were on the average less intelligent than in most of the former slave States." According to Lonn, it took white talent to mold the turbulent mass of ex-slaves into a viable political force.[5] The scalawags and later the carpetbaggers would provide the talent; the freedmen would provide the votes. Despite or perhaps because of the obvious Democratic bias and antiblack prejudice, Lonn's volume long remained a standard treatment of Louisiana Reconstruction—like the other Dunningite treatments, they were more interested in dishing out the dirt than producing a nuanced understanding of a complex history. This was the gospel according to Dunning.

In 1929, the Literary Guild of America published the most influential popular history of Reconstruction, *The Tragic Era: The Revolution after Lincoln.* Written by Claude G. Bowers, an Indiana Democratic politician, diplomat, historian, and biographer, this brilliantly crafted, though historically unsound book presented the story of Reconstruction in colorful and lurid detail. Bowers's treatment of Reconstruction in Louisiana was representative of the tenor of his work. He cast a supercilious eye on men and events in New Orleans as typical of Reconstruction governments. Mechanics' Hall, the meeting place of the radical legislature, is pictured as "a monkey house." The blacks and their white allies in the state assembly inhabit a political "zoo" to which the better elements come to view the antics of the Republicans with disgust and fascination. Corruption, drunkenness, and ignorance characterize the new government, which was, according to Bowers, typical of the radical governments in the "land of jubilee." Over the radical legislature, he noted, presided a scalawag by the name of Mortimer Carr, "a shrewd, unscrupulous, audacious youth of twenty-six." Outside the chamber, the "lobbies teem with laughing negroes from the plantations, [and] with whites of the pinch-faced, parasitic type."[6]

In the Literary Guild's monthly brochure for September 1929, *Wings*, Carl Van Doren, a nationally prominent historian and member of the Guild's editorial board, praised *The Tragic Era* as combining "the art of the dramatist no less than the science of the historian."[7] At least in the first sense he was right, and the public responded warmly to the melodramatic story. This is the stuff of which much popular history is made, and the volume made its author, according to Kenneth Stampp, "the chief disseminator of the traditional picture of Reconstruction."[8] But racism and historical myopia aside, it was not difficult to exaggerate the exotic atmosphere of wartime and postwar Louisiana and the wild politics of New Orleans, the "Great Southern Babylon."

Politicians as well as historians of the conservative persuasion found a mother lode of stories from Louisiana to enrich the enduring myth of Reconstruction. The white southern memory of Reconstruction, for example, was called on by one legislator in response to the Supreme Court's *Brown* decision of 1954. The chairman of the Joint Committee to Maintain Segregation of the Louisiana State Legislature warned his colleagues that to vote against segregation was "an open invitation to the carpetbaggers and scalawags and the National Association for the Advancement of Colored People to integrate our schools."[9]

In the 1959 edition of his widely used textbook *Louisiana: The Pelican State,* Edwin Adams Davis, a professor emeritus at Louisiana State University, embedded the Dunning interpretation in the story of Louisiana Reconstruction—what he labeled the "Military Occupation" of 1862–77. "Carpetbaggers," he instructed the students, "were persons from outside Louisiana who packed their belongings in a carpetbag and came to the state to win political power and make personal gains." The "scalawags were Louisianians who joined the Radicals for reasons of personal profit." The 1976 edition of the text repeated the charge that the scalawags were out for personal profit. Davis described the Louisiana blacks as a mass of political simpletons who were led by their collective noses through the Reconstruction years by the more intelligent but unscrupulous carpetbaggers and scalawags. Thus, the black Republicans "should not be too seriously blamed for the part they played during the tragic period," Davis stated. He justified the terrorism of the Ku Klux Klan and the Knights of the White Camellia. "Loyal Louisianians had to operate outside the law to preserve order," he reasoned. In view of this lack of law and order in Louisiana, the Klan and other white secret societies "did much good until they came under the control of revengeful leaders and had to be disbanded."[10] Davis's Louisiana text was not unique; it matched what was taught across the nation's high schools in the North as well as South. As Frances FitzGerald observed in her survey of the history of the "textbook business," *America Revised,* the traditional view of Reconstruction and its Republican villains—carpetbaggers, scalawags, and ignorant blacks—was, despite easily accessible, if not dominant, academic revisionism, the common "textbook wisdom" until late in the twentieth century.[11]

The southern conservative bias, one-dimensional characterizations, and "lazy generalizations" make the textbook description of the horrors of Reconstruction and the white counterrevolution read like a Democratic broadside of 1876.[12] The texts also reveal the remarkable staying power of the Redeemer interpretation of Reconstruction as an abnormal, desperate, and tragic affair. The radicals were pictured as a gang of political troglodytes emerging from the ruins of the Civil War to victimize and brutalize the defeated South. The staying power of the traditional interpretation, however, was due as much to the outlandish drama of Louisiana politics itself as to the prevailing conservatism of the age.

W. E. B. Du Bois, the famous black historian, biographer, sociologist, and essayist, attempted to rehabilitate the image of the scalawags in arguing that Reconstruction was a true revolutionary experience that included an alliance of poor white people and freedmen that looked to a new economic and racial order in the South.[13] This black–white brotherhood, Du Bois praised as a revolution from the bottom up. T. Harry Williams, however, raised serious doubts about the existence of either a common white–Negro coalition or a southern white proletariat during Reconstruction. According to Williams, "the great mass of the whites were yeomen farmers who thought in terms of racial supremacy instead of class solidarity." He also maintained that "the overwhelming mass of the people—the yeomen farmers, middle-class whites, and poor whites—were fiercely opposed to Negro suffrage and to any condition of equality for the Negro."[14] Drawing from the theories of the social psychologist Kimball Young, Williams held that the southern caste system effectively prevented poorer whites from cooperating with the freedmen. Williams actually stood Du Bois's visionary interpretation on its head when he pointed out that the planter-business classes in Louisiana, not the poor whites, were the ones who sought an alliance with blacks. Concerned about the dangers to property that the black vote entailed, the planters and businessmen sought to ally with the blacks in order to control their votes in the interest of economical government—that is, low taxes. The planter-business interests tried to manage the black electorate first by supporting black candidates for office, then by openly joining the Republican Party, and, finally, by attempting to organize political organizations outside the Republican and Democratic Parties. In Louisiana, this plan—the Louisiana Unification movement—found support among "the flower of the wealth and culture of New Orleans and South Louisiana." The movement failed because the economic interests of the planters and the freedmen were diametrically opposed. Further, the planters could not convince the "common whites" to join the movement.[15]

In his revisionist survey of Louisiana Reconstruction, Joe Gray Taylor held that some southern white Republicans in Louisiana seemed to have come from the ranks of the defunct Whig and Know-Nothing Parties. He did not pursue the question further, noting simply that "a study of the scalawags, the native white Republicans in Louisiana, is badly needed."[16]

When Kenneth M. Stampp published his history of Reconstruction in 1965, he assigned most scalawags to one or more of the following categories: (1) Unionists who aimed to control their states through the disenfranchisement of the ex-Confederates but who were reluctant to accept black suffrage; (2) a minority of the poor whites and yeomen farmers located in areas where the black population was small; (3) businessmen and those living in eastern Tennessee, western Virginia, North Carolina, and northern Alabama who saw the possibilities of economic development of their resource-rich areas through such Republican policies as a national banking system, the protective tariff, and federal support for internal improvements; and (4) upper-class Whigs who saw the Republican Party as the heir of Whig traditions and who aimed to control the black bloc votes in their own interest.[17]

Eric Foner's *Reconstruction: The Unfinished Revolution, 1865–1877* (1988) is the latest and, at this point, definitive survey of the era. He argues that southern political leaders were too moderate and too weak to effect a fundamental transformation of southern society. Further, he judges in reference to the scalawag leaders that "factualism and corruption . . . undermined their claim to legitimacy and made it difficult for them to respond effectively to attacks by resolute opponents."[18]

For his part, William C. Harris focuses on Abraham Lincoln's desire for a "restoration" of the Union but one "shorn . . . of the spirit of disunion and the institution of slavery." To this end, he states, Lincoln looked to southern Unionists to effect a quick reunion through self-reconstruction that would not "overturn the Southern social order." In the case of Louisiana, the trouble was that the southern Unionists were not united. From the embryonic stage of Reconstruction, systemic factionalism served to undermine the efforts either to restore without fundamental social change or to reconstruct the state along more radical lines, reflecting a dysfunctional political movement. Perhaps things would have been different if Lincoln had lived. Perhaps, Harris argues, he would have greatly adjusted his restoration policies in the face of the then "unforeseeable contingencies, such as terror campaigns sure to undermine black freedom and loyal control."[19] Lincoln was a master politician, and one can hardly imagine him making the kinds of mistakes that his successor, Andrew Johnson, made. Yet Lincoln miscalculated in thinking there was a dependable base of white Unionism in Louisiana. Here, those attempting to reconstruct (or restore) the political system on the basis of Unionism were "unsuccessful in marshalling significant numbers of southern whites to the Republican cause."

In his search for the elusive scalawag, James Alex Baggett identifies 742 southern white Republican leaders and compares them to 666 of their redeemer Democratic opponents during the Reconstruction years. His is a "collective biographical approach" that reveals the scalawags' geographical, social, economic, ideological, and political antecedents across the South and within three Southern regions—the Upper South, the Southeast, and Southwest.[20] With variations, this study of Louisiana's southern white Republican leadership largely agrees with Baggett's conclusions about the course of scalawag history, but especially with his emphasis on Unionism as a key to understanding scalawag motivation.

2

BACKSTORY

THE ORIGINS OF THE LOUISIANA SCALAWAGS

I was no thug.
—R. F. DAUNOY, 1866

Men on the Make

It took an exceptional southern white man to be a Republican in Louisiana during the Civil War and Reconstruction. You needed courage or idealism or ambition or all three. This did not necessarily mean that you needed an elevated moral character, but a southern man capable of imagining his role in a new social and political order was remarkable. Such a man had to step outside the norms of white society and face the hostility of the majority of his neighbors. White Louisiana was visceral in its dislike of Yankee reformism and dogged in its commitment to white supremacy; further, to collaborate with the northern enemy and associate with black men was to subject yourself to ostracism and real danger—you were a "scalawag." Few were willing to take on the burden of scalawagism, but those who did played a critical role in the story of Reconstruction and the struggle for mastery of the state that began in 1862.

The following profiles focus on the geographical, educational, occupational, political, and ideological background of the Louisiana scalawags: native-born, northern-born, and foreign-born. Louisiana attracted ambitious men, men on the make, men who saw in the cosmopolitan city of New Orleans or the rural parishes a new land of opportunity. Here, Alecia P. Long describes the attractions of the "Great Southern Babylon" during the post–Civil War years and beyond: "While the city has always had a reputation for difference and decadence, between 1865 and 1920

New Orleans began to exploit that reputation in order to profit from it and draw people to the city. As the states of the former Confederacy struggled to come to terms with Emancipation and a new postslavery economic order, New Orleans underwent a profound transformation. The city ceased to be the nation's largest slave market and most important port. Instead it became a tourist destination that encouraged and facilitated indulgence, especially in prostitution and sex across the color line."[1]

No evidence exists that the scalawags were lured by the exotic or sensual pleasures of New Orleans. More important were the exhilarating possibilities inherent in the collapse of the old regime and the creation of a new economic and political order. For some, it was the economic attractions of the Crescent City. For others, it was the cotton and sugar lands of the rural parishes. For still others, it was the new political landscape. The scalawags were men of ambition. Some were born in Louisiana; others came from the North or foreign lands before the war. They were a diverse lot in an environment open to economic and political exploitation. Consider the following representative men.

Dramatis Personae

JAMES G. BELDEN, physician.[2] Although his birthplace is unknown, Belden, a nephew of the famous American lexicographer Noah Webster, was a descendant of one of the first settlers of western New York State. A graduate of the New York College of Physicians and Surgeons, he practiced medicine in New Orleans for fourteen years prior to the Civil War. Belden was, according to the *New York Times,* a slaveholder and a southerner by "feeling and adoption."[3] But he "converted" to emancipation during the Civil War.[4]

WILLIAM JASPER BLACKBURN, newspaper editor.[5] Few southern white Republicans in Louisiana were as outspoken and as consistent in their support of the radical cause as this scalawag journalist. Born in Randolph County in northeastern Arkansas on July 24, 1820, he received his primary education both at home and in the local public schools. For two years (1838 and 1839) he studied at Jackson College in Columbia,

Tennessee. When he returned to Arkansas in 1839, Blackburn became a printer in Batesville. He moved to Little Rock in 1845 and to Fort Smith in 1846 before settling in the town of Minden in the hill country of north Louisiana about 1848. Here he established the *Minden Herald.* Ten years later, he moved to Homer, a trading center in Claiborne Parish. His second journal, the *Homer Iliad,* openly championed the Union during the secession crisis and during the war. With the advent of Reconstruction in Louisiana, Blackburn's little weekly paper (he estimated the circulation in 1868 at about 250 persons) stoutly defended the radical movement. In 1867, Michael Hahn, a fellow scalawag, testified to Blackburn's Unionism in a letter recommending the editor for a position with the Internal Revenue Service: "W. Jasper Blackburn . . . was a true, fearless and talented advocate of the Unionist cause throughout the late rebellion and since the ending of the war has constantly and earnestly contended in his paper . . . for a reconstruction of the Southern state governments." Thomas Jefferson Durant, a prominent scalawag attorney, also recommended Blackburn on the basis of his "able and fearless" devotion to the Union during the rebellion. The editor, Durant claimed, "was more than once placed in circumstances of great peril by reason of his devotion to the Union." Indeed, someone at the Treasury Department scribbled across the back of the letter of recommendation—"Too radical to live."[6]

GEORGE WASHINGTON CARTER, educator, preacher, lawyer.[7] Carter was a man of some accomplishment and no little ambition. He was a Methodist minister and president of a woman's college in Oxford, Mississippi, and later in Texas. He also served as a Confederate cavalry commander during the Civil War. In 1867, he defended Henry Clay Warmoth in Galveston, Texas, after Warmoth was charged with embezzling twenty-one thousand dollars. Warmoth was acquitted, and Carter moved to New Orleans from Houston and joined the Republicans after Warmoth became governor of Louisiana. Carter's politics were flexible. (In 1867, he advocated that blacks in Houston vote the Conservative Party ticket.) Described as "old and deaf," yet "shrewd and wiley," he fit the stereotype of the scalawag, offering this explanation for Louisiana's reputation for corruption: "There seems to be something in the climate here that affects both parties."

THOMAS GREEN DAVIDSON, schoolteacher, lawyer, civil servant, sugar planter, cotton planter, politician.[8] Davidson was a Democrat among the Republicans. He became a radical in practice, if not in name, and he deserves to be included in the scalawag ranks. He was born in Jefferson County, Mississippi, of middle-income parents, Thomas J. Davidson and Mary Shank, on August 3, 1803, and was raised in that area of Louisiana known as the Florida Parishes (an area inhabited principally by white Anglo-Saxon Protestants). There he read law under the direction of Martin G. Penn (of Covington), "the most influential politician and [Democratic] political boss in St. Tammany Parish." Following his apprenticeship, Davidson moved to Montpelier (St. Helena Parish) sometime before 1828. Here Davidson opened a law office in partnership with James M. Bradford, "which changed [Davidson] from a 'poor self-made' man into a man of wealth and political power." By 1850, Davidson's financial condition was more than sound. The census reported the value of his estate at $88,500 (including sixty-one slaves, 300 acres of land, livestock, and other property). In 1860, the estimated value of his estate had increased to $100,000 (including ninety-one slaves and 600 acres of cotton-producing land). His biographer concluded, "Davidson could well afford the luxury of a full political life, and during the antebellum period it was quite apparent that he enjoyed his public involvement and did everything in his power to retain his position." Davidson's prewar political career began in 1826. In 1833, he received an appointment from the Jackson administration as a register of the United States Land Office (located in Greenburg, St. Helena Parish). This was a plum for his endorsement of three prominent Louisiana Democrats, Martin G. Penn, Judge Larry H. Moore, and Colonel William Breed. In that same year, Davidson also secured a seat in the Louisiana state legislature, a position he held from 1833 until 1846. For nine to ten years following his service to the legislature, Davidson concentrated on his law practice in the Florida Parishes in southeastern Louisiana. But he also remained politically active "by making frequent appearances at barbecues on behalf of Democratic candidates in election years." Davidson came back into public office as a United States congressman (March 4, 1855, to March 3, 1861). The Whigs were outraged by Davidson's success. James Moore attacked Davidson in a letter to T. C. W. Ellis, an old Davidson enemy: "How can the South expect to be regarded with respect when she sends such crippled Satans to Congress to advance her interests and give character to Southern institutions and reputation of minds that budded and blossomed in the South? Is old *Crutch* [Davidson] a model specimen of a Southern Statesman? Do the Democrats suppose that the old tub of quack and trite vulgarisms will be heard in Congress where there are God-fearing *honest* men?"

Thus, Davidson's politics were controversial even before Reconstruction. In 1857, he opposed the Democratic Party candidate for the judgeship of the Eighth Judicial District in favor of Martin G. Penn, then running as an independent against the regular candidate. When Davidson himself sought and won reelection despite heated opposition from many regular Democrats, including Governor Robert C. Wickliffe, he attributed his victory to support by Senator John Slidell and Emile Le Sere (Slidell's chief lieutenant). Davidson's erratic behavior, however, caused him to be "the disruptive feature in the party until secession in 1861." On the national scene during the crisis decade of the 1850s, Davidson vigorously defended the South and its peculiar institution with "frequent dashes of humor, ready repartee, and spontaneous eloquence." He attacked the new Republican Party as a "tad-pole" organization of "ultra-Abolitionists." When the secession crisis began, Davidson, along with the other members of the state's congressional delegation, signed a joint letter to the Louisiana Secession Convention of 1861 urging an immediate withdrawal from the Union. Despite his support for the secession movement, he later claimed to have actively opposed secession. Davidson held no office under the Rebel state government, and he apparently gave only lukewarm support to the Confederacy. As the Federal hold on Louisiana tightened, Davidson saw his chance and moved closer to the Unionists in the state and eventually into the arms of the Republicans. E. Russ Williams concludes that Davidson was "a devious and scheming individual with the capability of turning everything to his advantage." To his enemies, he was a "scalawag."

ANTHONY PAUL DOSTIE, dentist.[9] Born in Saratoga County, New York, the son of a barber of French descent, he received his early education in the local public schools. At the age of nineteen, Dostie married a young woman from Cazenovia, New York, Eunice Hall. After her death six years later, Dostie never remarried. Young Dostie moved (ca. 1840) to Amsterdam, New York, where he studied dentistry under J. C. Duell, a locally prominent doctor. Before he settled in New Orleans in 1852, Dostie traveled through the Midwest (he lived in Chicago, Illinois, and Marshall, Michigan) and the South (he resided in Texas for six years). Along with his successful dental practice, Dostie was also active in two fraternal secret societies, the Odd Fellows and the Masons.

Because of his Jacksonian persuasion and his outspoken commitment to the Union, he refused to take an oath of loyalty to the Confederacy. The Rebel authorities in New Orleans then forced him to leave the city on August 21, 1861. On his way north, Confederate officials imprisoned him briefly at Nashville, Tennessee. Dostie's wartime experience left him with a deep-seated bitterness toward the Louisiana Rebels. Dostie later complained that the Confederates had "wrecked" his dental practice and his property when they forced him to become a refugee. After a short stay in Chicago during his exile, the French-speaking Dostie came back to New Orleans when the Union army captured the city in 1862. Upon his return, Dostie launched a new and controversial career in politics that ended with his murder in 1866. In the view of the conservatives of the Reconstruction years and the traditional historians, Dostie was the Robespierre of the scalawags—a "half crazed orator."

THOMAS JEFFERSON DURANT, lawyer.[10] "Tall, thin, sallow, cadaverous," this scalawag attorney played a vital role in the early stage of Louisiana Reconstruction. Born in Philadelphia on August 8, 1817, to John Waldo and Sarah Heyliger Durant, he received his primary education in the local common schools. He attended the University of Pennsylvania, but moved to New Orleans in 1834 before completing his degree. Durant worked for a time in the post office, then studied law and opened a law office in New Orleans.

Early in his career, he developed a keen interest in social reform and politics. Durant was especially attracted to the teachings of the eccentric, but influential, French social critic and utopian philosopher Charles Fourier. There was a bizarre element to Fourier's ideas. He contended, for example, that a powerful telescope would enable earthlings to observe a harmonious civilization existing on the planet Jupiter. Apparently, what impressed Durant and the other American Fourierites, however, was not the crackpot dreams of this utopian socialist, but his critical insights into the problems of society and his ingenious plans for a new world order. A series of letters from November 1844 to June 1847 reveal Durant's involvement with utopian reformism. "I have read [in French] Fourier's New Industrial World with care," he wrote on November 14, 1844, "and am thoroughly convinced of the truth of his views and principles." Yet, he adopted Fourierism with a certain critical remoteness. In a letter (dated June 4, 1847) to Robert Wilson, a fellow Fourierite from Franklin, Louisiana, Durant criticized the impractical methods by which Fourier envisioned the advance of his system. It was naïve, Durant suggested, to believe that lectures and sample phalansteries (a close-knit series of harmonious communities of approximately 1,600 to 1,800 hundred people each) alone would convert the masses to the principles of association.

Two days later, he wrote to Albert Brisbane, an energetic socialist instrumental in establishing more than forty Fourierite communes in America, concerning the quixotic elements in Fourier's schemes. Durant rejected as nonsense the idea that, once the Fourierites established a single trial phalanx, the world would quickly become convinced of its benefits, and there would follow a chain reaction that would result in a brave new world of happy phalanxes. It was not Fourier's objectives, but the methods that Durant questioned. He saw Fourier's belief in an almost instantaneous new harmonious society as a sheer physical impossibility. Durant held that the cause of utopian socialism in the Fourier mold could best be advanced not through proselytizing and a simple-minded reliance upon imitation, but through hard-headed practical reform and common sense. In the same letter, and in the same vein, he attacked the famous editor Horace Greeley (a Fourier disciple who advanced the cause in his *New York Tribune*) as a faddish crusader insistent upon identifying the movement "with one of the two political parties, with anti-renters, forced temperance, and many other peculiarities."

Durant also communicated with George Ripley (the Unitarian-Transcendentalist-Fourierite and guiding light of the Brook Farm experiment in communal living) and subscribed to the *Harbinger,* the Fourierite journal. "I feel deeply concerned," he wrote to the editors at West Roxbury, Massachusetts, on January 13, 1847, "in the propagation of the doctrines you uphold and the success of the paper as the only vehicle of them in this country." Yet in the same letter he criticized the editors for allowing anti-renters to publish articles in the journal, thereby leading "some to imagine that the disciples of association reason in the same way." His criticisms apparently had no direct influence upon Fourierite thought in America. His letters, nevertheless, do suggest that he attempted to infuse an element of realism into what was essentially an endearing, but hopelessly naïve system. If Durant ever saw the contradiction in his desire for practical reform and Charles Fourier's curious and impractical designs for the restructuring of society, it was not evident from his surviving papers.

On the issue of slavery Durant also took an unorthodox position. His views on the South's peculiar institution, in fact, resemble closely the antislavery and free-labor arguments of the future Republican Party. In a letter to John D. Wilkins in December 1844, Durant declared that "one of the great causes for the decline and retrogradation of agriculture south of the Potomac" was that it was "carried on almost exclusively by slave labor." He held, too, that free labor was "a necessary step in the progress of the race." He wrote to Robert Dale Owen in 1847 that unless one or both of the two contending forces in the slavery controversy be utterly mad, a compromise had to be reached. When the Wilmot Proviso provoked debate on slavery in 1846, Durant attacked the measure as premature and unnecessary. On the other hand, he considered John C. Calhoun's pro-slavery resolutions as "incendiary in their character, and founded on a Constitution solecism." "You ask me should we or should we not attack slavery openly and strongly as one of the giant evils of civilization," he wrote in response to an inquiry from Albert Brisbane (the leading American Fourierite and founder of a New Jersey phalanx), "or had we better try and cultivate the South?" Durant's answer was an appeal for patience and moderation. "Have some confidence in the reformers of the South," he wrote, "believe that the Southern people are men and brothers, not altogether unmindful of the evils of their social institutions, not altogether ignorant of the condition of their circumstances by which they are surrounded." Yet he continued, "I would have you speak freely of slavery as an evil affecting the white race even more than it does the black, but speaking of it I would not have you forget that you are an American citizen bound in honor by the Constitution by gentlemanly feeling not to insult, bound by common sense to know that no man can be cured of his error but by kind treatment." Durant also advised Brisbane to "treat slavery as a Philosophical Philanthropist should treat all subjects. Slaveholders here do not hold slaves for the mere love of the system itself, but because they have not, or they are not yet convinced that they have a better mode of making labor effective, convince him that there is another and better mode, and you may be sure [the slaveholder] will adopt it." He believed that others in the South shared his moderate views on slavery. In a letter (dated December 27, 1844) to Henry G. Langley, Durant stated that "the people here are highly sensitive; yet in New Orleans at least we are not in the main any more pro-slavery fanatics than the mass of northern people are anti-slavery fanatics."

But Durant was as interested in practical politics as he was in utopian socialism and the economics of slavery. He allied with the Democratic Party. In early 1844, Durant was an active member of the Democratic state committee that managed the Louisiana campaign of James K. Polk. On the eve of the election, Durant wrote optimistically about the prospects for his party in Louisiana. "The political horizon," he claimed, "never looked more clearly for the Democratic Party, than it does at the present, and our friends in [New Orleans] and around it were never in better spirits." Indeed, Durant and his political allies should have been optimistic. As Perry Howard, an authority on Louisiana political patterns, notes: "The year 1844 proved to be pivotal in the history of political parties in Louisiana, for it was in this year that the Democratic Party had wrested political power from the Whigs in a close and heated presidential election." As a member of the state campaign committee, Durant played an important role in the triumph of the Louisiana Democrats. For the sources of his political philosophy he looked back to the old Democratic-Republicans. "I am glad to see you admire so much John Taylor of Caroline," Durant wrote to a friend late in 1844. Taylor and Jefferson were his "political instructors."

In 1846, Durant received the Democratic nomination for a seat in the state senate. On New Year's Day of that year, he wrote to his mother concerning his future in politics. His election was a matter of doubt, Durant reported, but the fact of his nomination alone placed him "in a very excellent position with the Democratic Party." He noted, too, that his service to the party would be of great benefit to him in the future. His Jeffersonian idealism was tempered with a measure of self-interest.

When the Democrats defeated the Whigs in the state election of 1846, Durant again wrote to his mother concerning the campaign and his commitment to the Democrats. The state contest "has resulted in the complete triumph for the Democratic Party," he stated, "to which you know I have been ardently attached ever since I first comprehended a political principle. I was one of four candidates selected by our party in New Orleans to be supported for the State Senate, and was elected by a very handsome majority, exceeding the vote of the highest Whig candidate by Three Hundred and Fifty-One." Thus, at the age of twenty-nine, Durant saw his life changing for the better, and he was pleased and flattered by his success. "I trust that this may be the first step in a more successful path than that which I have hereto trod in life," he continued, "for it really has been a hard one, calling for all the firmness and courage I possess to meet and overcome its difficulties." The future looked even more promising to the young lawyer-politician when later, as a reward for his service to the party, President Polk appointed him a United States district attorney.

His interest in politics also extended outside of Louisiana. In 1847, Durant wrote to a friend in Mississippi for advice on that state's politics. Durant reasoned that the Whigs were about to nominate a "war candidate" for the office of governor, especially someone who had seen action in Mexico. Durant suggested that the Mississippi Democrats counter this move by nominating a war hero of their own. He suggested "the Colonel of the first Mississippi Regiment, Jefferson Davis." Durant said that if Davis were a Louisianian, "no man in our state could make a stronger run."

By the eve of the Civil War, Thomas Jefferson Durant had become part of the southern establishment. A prosperous lawyer, reformer, successful politician, and a slave owner (despite his professed free-labor ideology), he had a reputation for honesty and integrity. He was, no doubt, a man to be reckoned with in law and politics in Louisiana. Yet there was a side to Durant's antebellum career that clearly placed him outside the mainstream of southern thought. At a time when most southern whites viewed social reform with alarm, Durant embraced Fourierism, one of the most colorful and oddest follies of the age. At a time when southerners resented any criticism of their domestic institutions and strongly defended slavery as a positive good, Durant wrote openly in favor of free labor as a superior economic system. In a sense,

Durant was an anomaly whose career in important ways ran counter to the common order of southern life. His attraction to reform and his free-labor views conditioned him to welcome the disruption of southern society and the political opportunities created by the Civil War in Louisiana.

Durant's ardent and consistent Unionism also set him apart from the majority of his fellow Louisianans. In 1860, he openly supported Abraham Lincoln for the presidency despite his own Democratic background and despite the fact that in Louisiana Unionists supported Stephen Douglas or John Bell, and virtually no one supported the "Black Republican" candidate, Lincoln. During the short-lived Confederate regime in New Orleans, Durant withdrew from public life. During the Federal occupation in 1862, Durant reappeared in the political arena as the head of a movement designed to reorganize Louisiana as a free state. Durant brought to the Free State and radical movements talent, wide political experience, and a keen sense of the constitutional issues of the day.

EDWARD HENRY DURELL, lawyer.[11] No Louisiana scalawag had a more impressive family tree. His grandfather, Nicholas Durell, commanded a troop of Patriot cavalry during the Revolutionary War. His father, Daniel Meserve Durell, was graduated from Dartmouth in 1797 and served in the Tenth Congress (1807–9) and in the New Hampshire House of Representatives for one year (1816). From 1816 until 1821, the elder Durell served as chief justice of the State District Court of Common Pleas. Later, during the Andrew Jackson administration, he was the United States attorney for the District of New Hampshire (1830–34). E. H. Durell's mother, Elizabeth Wentworth, belonged to a well-to-do, prominent New England family. A remarkable clan, the Wentworth family included Puritan leaders, Patriots and Tories, merchants and lawyers, governors and legislators, jurists and journalists. The family story reads like a history of New Hampshire itself. E. H. Durell, the third son and sixth child of his parents, was born in the Wentworth ancestral mansion in Portsmouth on July 14, 1810. He attended Phillips Exeter Academy and was graduated from Harvard in 1831. His contemporaries at Harvard included Wendell Phillips, Charles Sumner, and Oliver Wendell Holmes. Following his graduation, Durell read law under his father's direction, then moved to Mississippi. The young lawyer finally settled in New Orleans in 1837.

Durell became active in a variety of community affairs. A city booster, he secured election as an alderman in 1854. During his tenure, Durell devised various plans to improve the municipal tax system, city finances, and the public school system. He reorganized the faction-ridden and inefficient New Orleans fire department and introduced the first steam fire engine into service. He also worked to improve the city streets, sewer service, and drainage system. Perhaps his greatest success as a city father was to secure the adoption of a new city charter in 1856. This reform document, which he composed, introduced a whole range of municipal improvements principally involving real estate laws and taxation. When Durell reentered public life during the occupation, he brought ability and wide experience to the Republican cause in Louisiana. Durell was a man of uncommon talent and education. His "commonplace book" reveals a man of wide interests. He claimed to have read more than 1,400 books on a variety of subjects, including history, drama, law, literature, philosophy, science, and poetry. He could read German, French, and Latin. His "Catalogue of Books Read" shows that he was familiar with the biographies of Robert Burns, Oliver Cromwell, Lorenzo de Medici, Lord Byron, John Milton, Jonathan Swift, Napoleon, John Dryden, and others. His own publications included *New Orleans as I Found It,* a travel guide to the Crescent City published in 1845. Also in 1845, he compiled a statistical pamphlet designed to encourage a close economic and political relationship between the South and the West. Durell, a Democrat and an ardent and outspoken Unionist, refused to condone the secession movement. When William Lowndes Yancey made an inflammatory speech in New Orleans during the secession crisis, Durell openly denounced the "fire-eater" and was driven out of public life for the duration of Rebel control as a southern turncoat and northern sympathizer. Educated, literate, and experienced, Durell, like most white politicians who allied with the new Republican order, was not unfamiliar with power and public life. He brought to the Republican Party in Louisiana a good measure of talent and energy.

BENJAMIN FRANKLIN FLANDERS, teacher, journalist, railroad executive, politician.[12] This southern Yankee was born in the town of Bristol in Grafton County in western New Hampshire on January 26, 1816. He was graduated from Dartmouth in 1843 and moved to New Orleans one year later. Flanders then studied law under Charles M. Emerson, a fellow Dartmouth graduate, in New Orleans in 1843. He did not pursue a legal career, but became a teacher in the public schools (1844–45). For a brief time, he published and edited the *Tropic,* a short-lived newspaper. From 1848 until about 1852, Flanders served as an alderman representing the Third Municipal District of New Orleans. In 1852, he returned to teaching. In that year Flanders also became the secretary and treasurer of the Opelousas and Great Western Railroad Company. He remained in that position until January 1862. When the Civil War broke out, Flanders's Unionist sentiments forced him to flee to the North until Federal troops captured the Crescent City. Flanders cooperated closely with the military government. General Benjamin F. Butler appointed Flanders city treasurer for New Orleans (he held this office from July 20 to December 10, 1862). "A more reliable or better Union man cannot be found," Butler informed Lincoln. In 1863, Secretary of the Treasury Salmon P. Chase appointed Flanders the supervising special agent of the Treasury Department for Louisiana, Mississippi, and Texas. His collaboration with the military and Federal authorities led to his involvement in Republican politics. When he allied with the Louisiana radicals, he brought with him significant political experience.

MICHAEL HAHN, lawyer.[13] He was short, with a dark complexion, a broad, square face and dark, curly hair, and a limp so severe that he was forced to use a crutch. He was born Georg Michael Decker, the son of a widow in the Bavarian village of Klingemunster. Shortly after the child's birth, Mrs. Hahn (née Decker) immigrated with her five children to New York City. The family then moved to Texas and finally settled in New Orleans in the city's large German community about 1840. One year later, Hahn's mother died of yellow fever. Orphaned and thrown upon his own resources, young Hahn completed his elementary and high school education. At the age of nineteen he began reading law under the direction of Christian Reselius, one of the city's most prominent attorneys. Hahn also studied law at the University of Louisiana. Following his graduation from law school in April 1851, he entered quickly into the civic and political life of New Orleans. Elected at the age of twenty-two to the city school board, Hahn served for several years as either a school director or as president of the school system. In politics, the young, ambitious attorney allied with the Louisiana Democrats, following the leadership of Pierre Soule, the head of the anti-Slidell faction of the party. In 1856, Hahn and the other Soule Democrats opposed the nomination of James Buchanan for the presidency. During the 1860 presidential race, Hahn served on the state committee that ran Stephen Douglas's campaign in Louisiana. The secession crisis saw Hahn emerge as an outspoken Unionist. At a mass meeting held in Lafayette Square on May 8, 1860, Hahn made a strong antisecessionist speech and offered a series of pro-Union resolutions. During Confederate rule in New Orleans, he refused to take the oath of allegiance to the Rebel government. When Federal control returned, Hahn became a collaborationist. He organized Union associations and worked closely with the Union authorities in the city. Here again was a man familiar with public life and political in-fighting.

WILLIAM HENRY HIRE, physician.[14] The records of the Royal College of Surgeons of England show that Hire came from the West Indian island of Bermuda to study medicine in London. Following his successful completion of the oral and written examinations in anatomy, pathology, and physiology, he became a Fellow of the College on July 7, 1843. Two years later, Hire settled in New Orleans. Here he opened his medical practice and also worked as a chemist. According to his own account, Hire worked hard to combat the yellow fever epidemics that ravaged the city in 1845 and 1853. "I have fought vigorously on every battlefield against Bronze John . . . since 1845, and was brevetted on the field of battle in 1853 by being appointed City Physician on recommendation of the Board of Health," he claimed in a letter dated March 15, 1890. When the war came, Hire remained loyal to the Union, and during the occupation under Generals Butler and Banks he served as secretary of the Board of Health and head surgeon at the Marine, St. James, and Barracks Hospitals. His commitment to Unionism led to his association with the Republican Party in New Orleans. Hire "has been a Consistent Republican," a testimonial addressed to President Chester A. Arthur stated in 1881, "and very active in party politics, was an original Union man and served his profession in charge of large hospitals under military appointment during the whole time the Army was in [New Orleans]."

* * *

JAMES LONGSTREET, professional soldier.[15] He was no "Union man" during the Civil War. When the Federal wooden frigates and gunboats under Admiral Farragut arrived at New Orleans on April 24, 1862, Longstreet was half a continent away in command of a division of Rebel troops on the lower peninsula of Virginia. The Confederate forces west of Richmond stood on the defensive, and Longstreet's superior officer, Joseph E. Johnston, anticipating a strong Union offensive, prepared to retreat from the Yorktown line. A major general as of October 2, 1861, Longstreet had a reputation for steady competence. Partially deaf, he appeared laconic to his companions, and yet, until the tragic death of three of his children in 1862 from scarlet fever, he was outgoing and sociable.

In his classic study of the Confederate commanders in the eastern theater, Douglas Southall Freeman paints this portrait: "Blunt and roughly bantering, he is not ill-natured. If he is not brilliant, in strategy or in conversation, he is solid and systematic. Ambitious he is, also, but not disposed to pick quarrels. In height he is about 5 feet 10½ inches, age 40 [in 1861]. He is slightly deaf, but a dignified, impressive man known to his soldiers as 'Old Pete.' The secret of his power is his incredible nervous control. He never gets tired."[16] Here is Michael Shaara's sketch from his Civil War novel *The Killer Angels:* "A large man, larger than Lee, full-bearded, blue-eyed, ominous, slow-talking, crude. He is one of the first of the new soldiers, the cold-eyed men who have sensed the birth of the new war of machines."[17]

Longstreet was the son of James and Mary (Dent) Longstreet, and thus a cousin of Julia Dent, wife of Ulysses S. Grant. He was the nephew of Augustus Baldwin Longstreet (1790–1870), the Georgia jurist, educator, and author noted for his humorous and realistic sketches of life in the Old Southwest and for his fervent defense of states' rights. Born on January 8, 1821, in the Edgefield District of South Carolina, James Longstreet grew up near Augusta, Georgia, where his father worked a farm until his death in 1833. His widow then moved the family to Sommerville in Morgan County in northern Alabama. In 1838, Longstreet entered West Point, where his classmates included the future Union generals Irvin McDowell, William Tecumseh Sherman, Henry W. Halleck, George H. Thomas, and Ulysses S. Grant. When he was graduated in 1842, he ranked fifty-fourth in a class of sixty-two cadets. During the next four years, the young infantry lieutenant served at Jefferson Barracks, Missouri; Natchitoches, Louisiana; and St. Augustine, Florida. During the Mexican War, Longstreet fought under Zachary Taylor in northern Mexico and under Winfield Scott during the march on Mexico City.

Like many other southern-born officers, Longstreet (in 1861 a major in the paymaster department) resigned from the "old army" to serve the Confederacy. Commissioned a brigadier general on June 17, 1861, he acquired one of the most distinguished, active, and controversial war records in the southern army. He served the southern cause from First Manassas, to Yorktown, Williamsburg, Seven Pines, the Seven Days' Battles, Second Manassas, Antietam, Fredericksburg, the "Suffolk Campaign," Chancellorsville, Gettysburg, Chickamauga, Knoxville, the Wilderness, and the defense of Richmond. But as the structure of the Confederacy began to collapse, and especially after the terrible defeat at Gettysburg, Longstreet's faith in the cause collapsed too. Despite his disillusionment, however, Longstreet remained loyal to the very end. When the time came to surrender, Longstreet told Robert E. Lee, "General, unless [Grant] offers us honorable terms, come back and let us fight it out."[18]

Despite Longstreet's dedicated service to the southern cause, his place in southern memory remains encased in controversy. He was never considered among the pantheon of Confederate heroes, like one of those giant figures hacked out of the northeast wall of Stone Mountain in Georgia. In the context of Reconstruction and the myth of the Lost Cause, southerners never felt compelled to erect a monument to scalawags: Longstreet's alleged slowness at Gettysburg, his criticism of the sainted Robert E. Lee, and his political metamorphosis from Rebel to Republican in 1867 sent hard-line southern conservatives into a state of apoplexy. David Blight notes that Longstreet was among those ex-Confederates (including the Virginian John S. Mosby) who "embraced the new economic development and acted with a spirit of Unionism to resist Lost Cause mythology."[19] But, as we will see, Longstreet's motives, whatever his economic philosophy or idealism, were not free of either nostalgia for the old order or self-interest.

JOHN THEODORE LUDELING, lawyer.[20] He was born on January 27, 1827, in New Orleans to John and Françoise Lorette de Salnave Ludeling. His maternal grandfather, a coffee planter in Spanish Santo Domingo, and most of the de Salnave family were murdered in January 1801 during the slave uprising led by the Haitian liberator Toussaint L'Ouverture. His mother, then only three years old, and his grandmother managed to escape to New Orleans. Françoise grew up in New Orleans and there married John Ludeling, a French immigrant. When Ludeling died, she remarried. Her new husband, Bernard Hemken, then moved the family to Monroe in the planter parish of Ouachita in north Louisiana. At the age of twelve, John Theodore Ludeling enrolled on July 18, 1839 in St. Louis University, the Jesuit school founded in 1818 in Missouri. John and his brother Frederick registered under their stepfather's name, Hemken. Ludeling followed the "classical" course of instruction. This program included mathematics, geography, English, history, Greek, Latin, and French. An able student, the young scholar ranked near the top in his class. In 1841 and 1842, his name appeared on a list of those who had distinguished themselves in the annual examinations. He remained at the university until 1843 and left without completing the six-year baccalaureate program. When he returned to Louisiana, he read law under Isaiah Garrett, a Monroe attorney. Following his admittance to the bar, Ludeling married Maria Copley, the daughter of Enoch Copley. In politics, Ludeling allied with the Republican Party. Although his two brothers served in the Confederate Army, Ludeling remained loyal to the Union.[21]

PHILIP HICKEY MORGAN, lawyer, jurist, diplomat.[22] Born in Baton Rouge in 1825, Morgan was educated at the University of Paris (1841-1846). He served as a first lieutenant in the Mexican-American War. He married Beatrice Leslie Ford in 1852. They had nine children. Morgan practiced law in Baton Rouge with his father (1848–1853) and then moved to New Orleans, where he continued his legal work (1853–70s). He also served on the Second District Court of Louisiana (1853–57). During the secession crisis, Morgan refused to support the Rebel cause. He opposed abolition by peaceful means, he told a New Orleans crowd gathered on Canal Street in 1861, but, he would remain loyal to the Union. He warned them that if they fired on the "Stars and Stripes," they would lose the war and, as a consequence, the slaves would become their "political masters." In response to his oration, he was hanged in effigy. Around the neck of the straw-stuffed image, the mob strung a placard that read: "P. H. Morgan—Traitor."

JOHN RAY, lawyer.[23] This scalawag was born in Washington County, Missouri, on October 14, 1816. His grandfather, an associate of the frontier explorer Daniel Boone, had immigrated to Missouri and served in the state's first constitutional convention. Educated in Kentucky at Augusta College and Transylvania University, John Ray migrated to Ouachita Parish following his graduation. In Monroe, he read law and was admitted to the bar in 1839. Already a member of the Whig Party when he came to Louisiana, Ray became involved in state politics. He served in the lower house of the state legislature (elected 1844) and the state senate (elected 1850). Twice Ray sought the position of lieutenant governor (as a Whig in 1854 and as a Know-Nothing in 1859), but failed to win the elections. His second defeat was at the hands of W. W. Farmer, a Democrat from Union Parish. In Ouachita Parish, Ray's home, the candidates tied (229 to 229), but the state totals gave the victory to Farmer (17,729 to 15,721). The election did not put an end to Ray's political ambitions. "But as would be amply demonstrated in his post-war career," E. Russ Williams states, "Ray's thirst for political participation and power remained unquenched."[24] Ray's Unionist sentiments are evident in his support of the Bell Everett ticket in 1860, when he served as an elector for the Constitutional Union Party. Until 1863, when Monroe came again under United States control, Ray maintained a discreet support for the Union cause. In 1863, however, he openly affirmed his loyalty to the Union. "Throughout the civil war Mr. Ray was a consistent Unionist," according to one source, "and at its close he favored the plan of reconstruction that was advocated by the Republican Party."[25] When Ray allied with the new Republican organization, he was a man well-trained and tried in the tough in-fighting of Louisiana state politics.

JAMES GOVAN TALIAFERRO, lawyer, judge, planter.[26] Born on September 28, 1798, in Amherst, Virginia, Taliaferro was the son of Zacharias Taliaferro, a lumberman, mill owner, and small planter who migrated to Mississippi and then to Catahoula Parish in 1815. Young Taliaferro attended Transylvania University, where he remained to study law following his graduation. Admitted to the bar in 1820, Taliaferro returned to Louisiana with his bride, Elizabeth Williamson of Lexington, Kentucky, and opened a law office in Harrisonburg, a village in central Louisiana. Early in his career he showed an interest in local and national politics.

In 1824 and 1828, he supported John Quincy Adams for the presidency. Taliaferro's dedication to National Republican principles was so strong that he named one son John Quincy Adams Taliaferro and another son Daniel Webster Taliaferro. When the National Republican Party evolved into the Whig Party, Taliaferro continued to be an active party member in Catahoula Parish and on the national level. In 1840, Taliaferro enthusiastically supported Harrison's "Log Cabin and Hard Cider" campaign. In fact, he was so confident of a Whig victory over Van Buren that he bet one thousand dollars with one Ditto L. Nuttall. The amount of the wager was a measure of Taliaferro's wealth. From 1834 until 1847, Taliaferro served as the parish judge of Catahoula. In 1859 and 1860, he won election as president of the Harrisonburg Police Jury. At the 1852 constitutional convention, Taliaferro opposed a plan to base representation on the total population. Although a Whig and a slaveholder himself, Taliaferro stood against the Black Belt, white-planter scheme to count the slaves as population rather than property and thus increase the number of representatives from the planter parishes. Mills claims that Taliaferro's controversial stand reveals his dedication to principle rather than expediency. Mills's study presents Taliaferro as a liberal statesman who "believed that equality and fairness in government should be based on republican principles rather than aristocratic principles." And his speeches, she contends, "reflect his confidence in the voice of the people." Other evidence indicates, however, that Taliaferro may have been motivated as much by political expediency as by a devotion to the "voice of the people" and "republican principles." Although he was an ardent Whig, his political base was strongly Democratic. In 1828 and 1832, Catahoula Parish voted overwhelmingly for Andrew Jackson, and the average presidential Democratic vote from 1836 to 1860 ran from 50 to 59.9 percent. The average gubernatorial Democratic vote reflected the same figures. During the secession winter of 1861, Taliaferro came to the Baton Rouge secession convention as an outspoken and intense Unionist. Here again he reflected the interests of his parish; in 1861, the vote for secession in Catahoula was less than 40 percent.

In addition to his law practice and his planting and political activities, Taliaferro owned and edited the *Harrisonburg Independent,* a weekly journal published by his bachelor son John Quincy Adams Taliaferro. He continued to edit the newspaper until May 1861, when he sold his interest. Taliaferro had wide intellectual interests, including classical studies, science, history, geology, and Indian folklore. His personal library contained 340 volumes in addition to his collection of law books. The census records of 1850 and 1860 reveal a man of considerable wealth. In 1850, he owned real estate valued at $10,000. In 1860, the value had increased to $87,000. His father owned four slaves in 1820. By 1860, Taliaferro owned twenty-seven slaves. Thus, on the eve of Reconstruction, he was a man of some wealth and influence, a Unionist, a planter, and a man of wide political experience. He, too, was familiar with the world of power and politics. "A man of Judge Taliaferro's education and professional training was a rare phenomenon in those days, especially in a small town like Harrisonburg," Mills concludes.

MICHEL VIDAL, newspaper editor.[27] Born in the medieval fortress town of Carcassonne in the province of Languedoc in southern France on October 1, 1824, Vidal attended college and then immigrated to Texas about 1845. Soon after the annexation of Texas, he moved to Louisiana and engaged in "literary and scientific pursuits" for two years. A sort of minor Tocqueville, Vidal made a study of American political institutions and for several years toured on foot a large part of North America. If Vidal scribbled down his impressions of the new land, they have been lost. During this period, Vidal worked as an associate editor at various times for the *New York Courrier-Des-Etats-Unis,* the *New York Messenger,* the *Quebec Journal,* and the *New Orleans Picayune.* As a journalist, a delegate to the convention of 1867–68 (sometimes called by the enemies of the radicals the "Black and Tan Convention," or "Bones and Banjo Convention") and as a state and federal office holder, Vidal would make a valuable contribution to the radical movement in Louisiana.

RUFUS WAPLES, lawyer.[28] Born in Millsboro, Delaware, he was the descendent of Peter Waples, who settled in that region in about 1690. Waples received a common school education and attended Milton Academy in Delaware. He was graduated from Louisiana University in 1852 with a degree in law and began practice in New Orleans in 1853 with his brother Stephen H. Waples. In 1855, Waples formed a law partnership with James B. Eustis, a future United States senator from Louisiana. Waples lived in New Orleans for twelve years before the outbreak of the Civil War, but remained a firm Unionist. When the Confederates took control of Louisiana, Waples fled to Washington, D.C., where he remained until the reestablishment of Union authority. In May 1863, Lincoln appointed Waples United States attorney for the Eastern District of Louisiana. He served in that office until October 30, 1865. Waples played an important role in Unionist politics and in the creation of the Republican Party in Louisiana.

JAMES MADISON WELLS, planter.[29] A native of Louisiana, Wells was born twelve miles north of Alexandria in the planter-dominated Rapides Parish on January 8, 1808. The family traced its origins in America to Samuel Levi Wells I, an Irish immigrant and civil engineer who settled in Louisiana about 1760. On June 20, 1764, Wells's Creole wife (a woman of "high social standing") gave birth to a son, Samuel Levi Wells II, near Manchac in West Florida. Spanish judicial records show that the elder Wells owned a plantation in that region in 1780. Sometime later the family moved to south central Louisiana near Ville Platte. In 1785, the restless Wells clan resettled in the El Rapido territory (now Rapides Parish). Samuel Levi Wells II worked as a civil engineer and surveyor for the Spanish government. His first wife, "Miss Bonner," gave birth to two boys, Willis and Randolph. The former son moved to Mississippi. Bonner died shortly after the births of Willis and Randolph, and Samuel remarried in 1794. The second Mrs. Wells (Mary Elizabeth Calvit of Adams County, Mississippi) claimed to be the granddaughter of Frederick, the sixth Lord Baltimore. The newlyweds lived in Natchez for a brief time and then returned to Louisiana in 1795. By 1800, Wells had established a plantation home, New Hope, on the Bayou Rapides, fifteen miles upstream from the Red River in the sugar-producing region. Nine years later, following the death of his wife, Mary, Wells moved his residence to Prospect Hill, a second plantation home near the town of Lecompte.

Over the years, Samuel Levi Wells II created a minor financial empire based on sugar and indigo production and land survey commissions. His wealth brought power and influence. Elected several times to the Orleans territorial legislature, Wells also served as a delegate from Rapides to the first state constitutional convention and as a member of the new Louisiana state legislature during the War of 1812. When he died at the age of fifty-two at Prospect Hill, he left eight children and several plantations. Three of the sons became prominent in the Rapides area, Monfort Wells, Thomas Jefferson Wells, and James Madison Wells.

Orphaned at the age of eight, James Madison Wells lived with his aunt, Mrs. John Classon (née Emily Clementine Wells). Young Wells attended primary school in Rapides, and then, despite the family's strong Episcopalian orientation, he enrolled in St. Joseph's College, a Jesuit institution in Bardstown, Kentucky. Later he attended Alden Partridge's American Literary, Scientific, and Military Academy in Middletown, Connecticut, and the Cincinnati School of Law in Ohio. Wells also read law under the direction of the famous Ohio lawyer and journalist Charles Hammon. A strong nationalist and rabid abolitionist, Hammond possessed a razor-sharp legal mind. The combined influences of Alden Partridge and Charles Hammond must have had a profound impact upon the young Louisianian. In his study of Wells's political career, Lowrey notes that "the early influences of his life were driving young Wells away from his family's church, slaveholding planter ideas, and the doctrine of states' rights held by most Southerners." Thus, when Wells returned to Louisiana in 1830, "he had been away for several years of the most formative period of his life, all spent in an atmosphere distinct from that of his homeland."

Whatever his nationalist proclivities were at this stage, Wells partook of the powers or the pleasures of the southern planting life. Following his marriage to Mary Ann Scott, an Anglo-French belle of Rapides, on May 11, 1832, the young couple lived at Gravel Hill, Wells's plantation near Colfax. His other plantations in the same area included Kateland, Duroc, and Glencoe. He also purchased a plantation twelve miles south of Alexandria. In 1850, Wells bought a beautiful summer home as a present for his wife. Located in the pine hills south of Lecompte, Jessamine Hill became the family residence during the hot, humid summer months from 1850 until 1862. Near the resort was "Bear Wallow," Wells's huge private swampland hunting preserve.

The census records of 1850 and 1860 provide evidence of the steady growth of Wells's fortune. In 1850, his real estate was valued at $15,000, and by 1860, the value of his real property had increased more than ten times. By 1860, he owned $164,000 in real estate and $236,000 in personal property (including 200 milk cows, evidence of a thriving dairy business). His slaves numbered ninety-five in 1860, placing Wells among the largest slaveholders in the South.

Even before the rapid increase in his wealth, Wells acquired political power. In 1839, A. B. Roman, the Whig governor of Louisiana, appointed him sheriff of Rapides Parish. In 1841, Wells won election as a Whig to the state legislature. Although the Whig tradition remained strong within him, during the election of 1860 he supported the northern Democrat, Stephen Douglas. "I voted for Mr. Douglas in the struggle to avert war," he claimed, "not that I endorsed his doctrine. [Douglas] had struggled against Lincoln in Illinois, and having a great prominence in the West I thought that if we could elect such a man we could avert war; and for that reason I voted for him."

When the planters of the South led their section into war, Wells actively opposed secession. At first, he used political tactics to delay appropriations for the defense of Rapides Parish. Later, Wells led a band of Unionist guerrillas that attacked Confederate wagon trains. When the pressure from the Rebel forces in Rapides became too great, Wells periodically retreated to Bear Wallow, where from 30 to 160 Unionist sympathizers stood guard against Confederate counterattacks. Wells claimed that his band of "Jayhawkers" came from the poorer whites of the district. "I had the poorer people with me," he declared with obvious pride, "the people who had no slaves. People who had been taxed largely to build up the levees upon lands that had been bought for ten bits, and which were made worth $100 to $125 an acre by the levees. Those were the men that were with me—men that had no negroes."

A prosperous planter-slaveholder, the possessor of rich agricultural lands, a connoisseur of fine race horses (the Lecompte plantation was name after one of his horses), a local magistrate possessed of a sense of noblesse oblige, he was, in short, the Complete Planter. Now he allied with Unionists and made himself an outlaw in his own parish. His family and planter friends found his behavior outrageous. Many saw him as a traitor to his race, to his class, and to his section.

As the Rebel authorities moved in on his hideout, Wells fled to the Federal lines aboard the gunboat *Choctaw* on November 7, 1863. A pass signed by General Nathaniel P. Banks ensured that Wells would find safety and hospitality with the forces of occupation. When Wells arrived in New Orleans, he found the city in a state of ferment as the Federal authorities and their Unionist collaborators began the process of Reconstruction. Wells would play a decisive role in that process.

Other Players

As for other southern white Republicans in Louisiana, they, too, represented eclectic origins. Here are the bits and pieces of their lives, as examples.

The Geographic Origins

The Louisiana native sons included men from Natchitoches Parish in the central pine-hill region of the state: Simeon Belden, a future Speaker of the state House of Representatives and attorney general, and Alexander Breda and his brother J. Ernest Breda. Two white southern Republicans, William Cooley and Oscar Jeffrion, came from Pointe Coupee Parish in the south Louisiana planter section. Charles Delery was a native, it is believed, of St. Charles Parish (also located in the south Louisiana planter section). Robert J. Caldwell was "a native born citizen of the State of Louisiana." Arnaud Commagere, one of the founders of the Republican Party in Louisiana, was also a native Louisianian.[30] Those who were born in the urban center of New Orleans included Benjamin Bloomfield, R. F. Daunoy, Charles Leaumont (born 1836), J. R. G. Pitkin, S. R. Snaer, and Eugene Staes.[31] Some Louisiana scalawags were born in the South but outside Louisiana or they came from the Border States. Napoleon Underwood migrated from Mississippi. Gilderoy Snider moved to Louisiana from South Carolina. William B. Phillips, a native Alabamian came to Louisiana at the end of the Civil War. Richard C. Downes claimed to be "by birth and residence a Southern man."[32] The Border State scalawags included Robert Ray, the younger brother of John Ray, who was born in Missouri and migrated to Louisiana when he was seventeen years old. Thomas Crawford was a Kentuckian, as were George Dearing and John Dinkard. L. W. Baker was from North Carolina.[33]

Not all Louisiana scalawags originated in the South. As Peter Kolchin notes regarding the mobility of Americans in the nineteenth century and the definition of a "scalawag," those who moved to the South as children were "more likely to feel and act as a southerner than as a northerner by 1870." But, he argues, "the start of the war is a far more useful dividing point because it separated those who committed themselves to living in the slave South from those who migrated as part of the war or the postwar effort to change the South."[34] The former group includes Louisiana's "southern Yankees," men of northern birth who made the South their home well before the Civil War and who became associated with the southern establishment through politics, business, or professional affairs. In his essay on the role of the Yankee in the Old South, Fletcher M. Green notes this large number of northern-born men and women who contributed to the society of the antebellum South. In 1850, for example, 9,461 of the 40,000 American-born whites living in New Orleans were of northern origin. Although some northerners came to the South only to return to their northern homes, by 1860, 360,000 northerners were still residing and assimilated in the southern states and engaged in a great variety of occupations, including doctors, lawyers, politicians, artisans, merchants, bankers, and planters.[35]

These northern-born Louisiana scalawags fit Green's description of southern Yankees. Four came from New York. William R. Crane, the "war-horse of the Republican Party" in Louisiana, was born in New York, as were Chauncey Kellogg and Joshua Fisk. A. W. Faulkner, an associate of the carpetbagger Henry Clay Warmoth, came from Ohio, but lived in the South (Mississippi and Louisiana) for eighteen years prior to the Civil War. James H. Veazie, in a letter to Secretary of the Treasury George S. Boutwell in 1869, claimed to be a southern man by choice. "I am a native of Massachusetts," he stated, "but have lived thirty-two years in the South. I married here and here my children were born."[36]

A final category includes southerners of foreign birth. Like their Yankee counterparts, these men saw the South as a new frontier. They were similar to those northerners described by Green: "some were children [when they came]; and others, probably a majority, were young men . . . who sought opportunity in a new land."[37] Maximilian Ferdinand Bonzano was born in the city of Ehingen on the Danube River, in the kingdom of Württemberg, Germany. He came to America with his father and mother in 1835. The family lived in east Texas for a time and then settled permanently in New Orleans. Louis Dupleix (born to Yoes and Marguerite Lawalle Dupleix) came from the ancient seaport of Bordeaux in southwestern France to the United States in 1841. In 1843, he married Clemence Dugas, a native of Lafayette Parish, Louisiana. William Henry Hire, a British subject, came to New Orleans in 1845. Bartholomew Leahy Lynch, an active supporter of the Republican Party in Louisiana, was born in Ireland, but came to the South fifteen years before the outbreak of the Civil War. Frederique "Fred" Marie was born in France and settled in Terrebonne Parish, where he ran a hotel.[38] As Gerald M. Capers observes, some were "Yanks for the money," but many showed a genuine commitment to their adopted communities.[39]

Despite their identification with or adoption by the South before the Civil War, the men born outside the South but identified with their adopted communities were more inclined to collaboration than the majority of native whites. Collaboration implied, it seems, no disloyalty in their minds; rather, it represented new opportunities and commitment to change. They were a minority, but an important one to consider in making sense of Louisiana Reconstruction and the lure of scalawagism.

The Educational Background

The Louisiana scalawags were, by the educational standards of the nineteenth century, among the elite. And they were especially well educated by southern standards. In an age when having more than three or four years of formal schooling was uncommon, a high school or college degree was truly exceptional. Some Louisiana scalawags apparently attended college without graduating but received professional training. Alexander Breda, a physician and surgeon in Natchitoches, received a common school education and then attended the Western Military Institute at Drennon Springs, Henry County, Kentucky. A yellow fever epidemic forced the institute to close in 1853, and Breda returned home. Two years later, however, he began to study medicine under the direction of his father, Dr. John P. Breda, a native of France and a graduate of the Baltimore Medical College. Alexander Breda then studied medicine at the University of Louisiana, where he was graduated in 1859.[40] Charles Leaumont, a scalawag judge in Orleans Parish, studied at Jefferson Academy in New Orleans. He later attended St. Louis University "but was withdrawn by his parents when about nineteen years of age on account of the ill-treatment he received at the hands of one of the professors of said university." Following his withdrawal from the university, young Leaumont attended a school run by Louis Duffan on Dauphine Street, "for the sole purpose of learning the French language, which he had nearly forgotten whilst in the University at St. Louis." He then read law under a Mr. LeGarden and opened a practice in 1858.[41] R. F. Daunoy attended college in France. In testimony before a congressional committee in 1866, Daunoy stated: "Before [the Civil War] I had come from college at Paris. I never learned the English language well. I was raised in Paris." Ten of the Louisiana scalawags received professional educations or training. Simeon Belden studied law under the direction of "John B. Smith, a talented lawyer who was very fond of him." M. F. Bonzano was an apprentice chemist and pharmacist in a drugstore for a time and then became a medical doctor following his residency at New Orleans Charity Hospital.[42]

The Occupational Background

The scalawags were men who had made a place for themselves in the economy of nineteenth-century Louisiana. The white southern Republican leadership included farmers, pharmacists, preachers, schoolteachers, bankers, grocers, custom house brokers, hotel keepers, clothing merchants, jewelers, carpenters, sea captains, dentists, lawyers, newspaper editors, mechanics, planters, physicians, bankers, and one house painter.[43]

Politics has always attracted lawyers, and Louisiana was no exception: Simeon Belden, J. Ernest Breda, John Barrett, Robert J. Caldwell, William H. Cooley, William R. Crane, Thomas Crawford, Josiah Fisk, Ezra Hiestand, Wade H. Hough, Chauncey Kellogg, George S. Lacey, Charles Leaumont, James R. Lewis, B. L. Lynch, Robert Ray, and James H. Veazie all made their livings as attorneys.[44]

Alexander Breda opened his medical office in 1859 in Natchitoches and continued his practice as late as 1890. John Vandergriff, a member of the Radical "Black and Tan Convention" of 1868, was a physician. George M. Wickliffe (of East Feliciana Parish) practiced dentistry at a time when dentistry was emerging as a true profession.[45]

Charles Delery, W. E. Maples, Frederick Otto, S. R. Snaer, and John S. Walton were merchants. Delery owned a business in Monroe before the secession. Maples worked as a cotton factor and later as a commission merchant in Shreveport in 1877. Otto "was doing business in Baton Rouge at the beginning of the rebellion." In 1866, Snaer, then twenty-two years old, operated a "commission store" in partnership with his brother. Walton, "an old citizen" and businessman in New Orleans, became president of the Louisiana Savings Institution in 1869. Joseph H. Oglesby, "an outspoken, square Republican," was president of the Louisiana National Bank in New Orleans as of March 27, 1870. Other occupations were represented by L. H. Panza (New Orleans river pilot and ship captain), Nathan Schwab (jeweler), Gelderoy Snider (mechanic), Andrew Demarest (house painter), and John Dinkard (grocer). Those identified as farmers include William B. Phillips (Rapides Parish), Charles Dearing (Rapides Parish), and Edward Fielding (Avoyelles Parish).[46]

The Antebellum Party Affiliations and Experience

The Louisiana scalawags were not political adolescents, men new to politics and public affairs. When these southern whites joined the Republican Party, they brought with them political experience gained on the local, state, and federal levels during the antebellum years.

Among the Louisiana scalawags were Whigs, Democrats, Know-Nothings, and those associated with the Constitutional Union Party in 1860. The ex-Whigs included J. G. Beauchamp, Alexander Breda, J. Ernest Breda, Chauncey Kellogg, Robert Ray, and Louis Dupleix and others. In a letter to Henry Clay Warmoth, dated June 12, 1868, the young carpetbag editor Emerson Bently reported on the politics of J. G. Beauchamp, a St. Landry–based scalawag: "Beauchamp is an old-line Whig . . . a Republican although not quite as Radical as some would desire. He has fought the Democratic Party for many years; and it was the desire of many that he should have been placed on the last parish ticket, in order that his political talents might have given strength to the ticket; . . . No members of the Radical party here would be offended if he should obtain an appointment, although his Taliaferro proclivities may to some have a bad odor. Beauchamp would be a person of considerable executive ability." Alexander P. Breda, of Natchitoches Parish, "was formerly an Old Line Whig, and voted with that party until 1856, and since 1868 he has been an ardent Republican." Breda's brother, J. Ernest Breda, according to the same source, "was formerly a Whig in his political views, but is now a staunch Republican." When Chauncey Kellogg applied for a position with the Treasury Department in 1889, the petition, endorsed by Henry Clay Warmoth and J. Q. A. Fellows, among others, described Kellogg as "a Whig and Unionist before and during the war . . . and . . . a zealous Republican." Robert Ray was a Whig before the Civil War "like his father and brothers." Louis Dupleix, an active Natchitoches Republican and former Whig, received an appointment as registrar of the United States Land Office at Natchitoches from President Ulysses S. Grant in 1872.[47]

Democrats also joined the Republican movement in Louisiana. M. F. Bonzano, although he claimed to have no political interests before the war, received a patronage position as melter and refiner of the United States Mint at New Orleans from the Democratic President James K. Polk in 1848.[48] E. L. Pierson, a lifelong resident of Natchitoches, was an antebellum Democrat but changed his allegiance with the triumph of the radicals after the war.[49]

A fellow Know-Nothing, R. F. Daunoy (he was elected coroner for the City of New Orleans in 1847 and served as a clerk in the New Orleans Customs House in 1870) also belonged to the party in the 1850s. "I was a know-nothing," Daunoy admitted defensively to a congressional committee in 1866, "but I was no thug."[50]

The election of 1860 saw two scalawags, Andrew Hero and the versatile John Ray, allied with the Constitutional Union Party. A pamphlet published in 1886 stated that Hero, then the chairman of the Republican Congressional Committee for the Second Congressional District in Louisiana, "never was a Democrat," so he did not desert his party at the close of the war. Hero, an editorial in 1886 claimed, "opposed the Bourbon Democrats before the war; he was against the irreconcilables during the war, and he had opposed them ever since the close of the war." In 1860, Hero had voted the Bell-Everett ticket and "was pronounced in declaring his attachment to the Union and the Constitution."[51]

Other future scalawags were also active in prewar local and state politics. This group includes Robert J. Caldwell (district attorney),[52] Richard E. Downes (judge and state representative),[53] George S. Lacey (New Orleans city attorney),[54] James Monroe Porter (state legislator in 1845),[55] and J. D. Watkins (district attorney).[56]

These and the other identifiable Louisiana scalawags were men with a stake in the community of the South. They were not new to politics. They were not raw or unsettled men, men without form or foundation. The white southern Republicans in Louisiana were essentially no different from those men who have always controlled American government on the national, state, and local level. In fact, "government leaders are seldom recruited from the masses. This is true in the case of top cabinet officials and presidential advisors; of congressmen, governors, and state legislators; even of mayors and city councilmen. [They] are recruited primarily from the well educated, prestigiously employed, successful and affluent upper and upper middle class." The Louisiana scalawags were much like the white southern Republicans described by Joel Williamson in his study of Reconstruction in South Carolina: "A fair proportion of the scalawag leadership had been accepted in the elite circle of their own communities before becoming Republicans."[57] Nor were they different from either northerners or their fellow white southerners when it came to capitalistic and materialistic values.[58] They did, however, differ significantly in their politics from the majority of white southerners during Reconstruction. In this sense, they were outside the mainstream of the southern persuasion.

3

"THE RAINBOW OF HAPPINESS"

THE SCALAWAGS' UNIONIST CONNECTION

> Please accept the accompanying case of pistols in token of the gratitude I feel for your coming here, and the re-establishment of Federal rule in place of the tyranny practiced by Jeff Davis and his followers.
>
> —A "UNION MAN" to General Benjamin F. Butler, 1862

The Whigs and the Scalawags

Although historians, including David Donald, have argued that persistent Whiggery was the foundation of white Republicanism in the South, there is little evidence that ex-Whigs as a group played an important role in Louisiana Republicanism. True, some Louisiana scalawags had been Whigs, but no significant Whig-Republican alliance existed in the state during the era of Reconstruction.[1]

As Reconstruction was coming to an end, the Republicans were, in fact, still seeking to bring those attracted to the principles of Henry Clay, Daniel Webster, and William Henry Harrison into the party. In a pamphlet published in March 1876, for example, J. R. G. Pitkin, a New Orleans scalawag and corresponding secretary of the Republican State Central Committee, issued a last, desperate call for the old Whigs of Louisiana to leave the Democrats, "which whenever they [the Whigs] have affiliated therewith at all, they have usually been unable wholly to dismiss from mind a historic and honorable prejudice." Pitkin reminded the old-line Whigs that the Republican Party had inherited the Whig principles. "I respectfully invite your attention," he wrote, "to the Declaration of Principles emitted by the Republican State Central Committee of Louisiana, as the basis of the Republican organization. You will discover that it is simply a re-affirmation of tenets to some of which the party has adhered since as a Whig organization it re-adopted in 1856 its original title of National Republicans." As evidence of the modern Republicans' Whig principles, Pitkin pointed to the federally funded internal improvements program in Louisiana, especially "in relation to the Mississippi outlet and divers bayou improvements." He also assured the old Whigs that the Republican Party opposed any inflationary monetary policy that would "prejudice the industrial and commercial interests of the country." It must have been obvious, he continued, that "the Republican Party seeks not to cripple business by retiring the greenback dollar but by gradual efforts to assure thereto the value of a hundred cents and thus befriend business." With such arguments, Pitkin hoped to lure the former Whigs away from the "mongrel Democratic party, whose passion is disorder and whose highest principle is jealousy of color," and into the arms of the Louisiana Republicans. He contended in a poker-faced bluff that this appeal to the Whigs was not being made from a position of weakness. "This suggestion," he stated, "is made not because the Republican Party is numerically impotent to maintain its control, for the recent census reveals a majority in its favor of about 20,000 voters." Rather, he argued that people were leaving the Democrats because of the "dishonesty of the Democratic chiefs" and their "corps of place hunters."

Pitkin admitted that the Republican Party contained its quota of political adventurers and spoils men, but, he argued, this was all the more reason for the Whigs to join the radicals. "It is to be deplored that some individual Republicans have . . . cast reproach upon their sect and the good fame of the State," the scalawag conceded, "but let the Whigs of Louisiana come with their ancient fervor for reform into that sect or measurably cooperate with it as censors upon its members while those members are candidates, not simply after they shall have been elected." In addition to their honesty and proclivity for reform, the Whigs would bring to the Republican Party their talent and education. Pitkin argued, "Were the Whigs of the State . . . to contribute of their intelligence and seek with those less fortunate [the less-educated blacks] in the past than themselves, to supply the parochial trusts with more efficient servants, wherever such may be needed, there is reason to believe that better accord and administration might be assured."

Pitkin went on to remind the Whigs that the Democrats remained their ancient enemy and that the Whig-Democrat alliance was an unnatural association. "It must be clear to the Whigs," he insisted, "that the Democracy is no less their enemy to-day than in years gone by; cherishes all its old prejudices against them and declares tacit armistice only while they choose to vote its ballots."

The Reconstruction amendments to the Constitution, Pitkin told the Whigs, made blacks a part of the political system. The Whigs, he felt, would surely recognize the new realities of political life and support and defend the Constitution: "It is submitted that the question of color having been adjudicated by the American people and the negro being the civil and political equal of the white by constitutional guarantee, it cannot be less honorable to a Whig than it was twenty years ago, to insist that the Constitution should be jealously maintained against all assaults upon it by its old enemy the Democracy."[2]

Based on the appeal of the Pitkin pamphlet, it is obvious that the Republicans in Louisiana still hoped as late as 1876 to lure the Whigs away from the Democrats. Federal aid for internal improvements, promises of fiscal responsibility, and appeals to the Whigs' loyalty to the Constitution: this was the bait. But few old Whigs were willing to bite.

Three of the most prominent scalawags (John Ray, James Govan Taliaferro, and James Madison Wells) were former Whigs, but few other Louisiana Whigs followed their lead. Still, the hope remained that the old-line Whigs could be lured into the party. In 1889, twelve years after the end of Reconstruction, Chauncey S. Kellogg, a former Whig and active Republican during the radical years, wrote to W. H. H. Miller, the attorney general in Benjamin Harrison's cabinet, concerning the revival of Republicanism in Louisiana and the possibility of attracting old Whigs to the party standard. As a result, he predicted, the Republicans would carry Louisiana in 1892. He assured Miller that the "leading businessmen of [New Orleans], and planters, including bankers, factors, wholesale merchants and manufacturers, who are at heart Republicans, but have not heretofore voted the Republican ticket" now supported the Republicans. It was a political homecoming because "the old Whig doctrine of protection to American industries being the same as that advocated by the Republican Party has aroused the old Whigs to return to their old faith." This persistent scalawag argued that the Whigs had never been happy as Democrats and that they now were eager to join the Republicans under the right circumstances: "Why! Mr. Attorney General, many citizens who were old Whigs, and several Democrats even, said to me 'President Harrison is an old Whig, and he is good enough for me.' Old Whigs would add: 'I never was a Democrat.' I venture the assertion that there cannot be found in the State of Louisiana to-day, one old Whig who will admit that he is, or ever was, a Democrat in principle. They are all proud of having been Whigs . . . although they have heretofore voted the Democratic ticket." Kellogg concluded his letter with the suggestion that blacks be excluded from office holding and the leadership of the party. Only then, he contended, could whites be attracted to the party. Kellogg envisioned a new Republican coalition in Louisiana composed of white men of "irreproachable character," wartime Unionists, and former Whigs.[3] Thus, twenty-four years after the founding of the Louisiana Republican Party, the organization was still trying to coax the Whigs into the party and, in this appeal, at the expense of loyal Black Republicans.

Further evidence of this activity is found in a letter of May 1, 1889, from Cuthbert Bullitt, an old Unionist and conservative Louisiana Republican, to John W. Noble, the secretary of the Interior, concerning the future of the party. "When I had the pleasure of seeing you in St. Louis," he stated, "I told you, candidly, that our party in New Orleans lacks respectability & I say so now, & to gain strength we must have good men in office." These men, Bullitt suggested, would come from the ranks of the former Whigs: "The old Whig element is still strong & eager to join our party, but not under the rule of Scalawags & Carpetbaggers."[4]

If, as Taylor points out, "The Old Whigs . . . found it distasteful to sleep in the same bed with Democrats,"[5] they apparently found it even more distasteful to sleep with scalawags, carpetbaggers, and blacks. Although the marriage between the Whigs and the Democrats during the Reconstruction years was an unhappy one, it was far more satisfying from the Whig perspective than the kind of political miscegenation proposed by the Louisiana radicals.

The Pitkin pamphlet (written at the close of Reconstruction) and the letters from Kellogg and Bullitt (written at the time of the ascendancy of the Bourbon Redeemers) indicate that the Republican Party, at least in Louisiana, never attracted a Whig constituency with any success. More important as a factor in the transition to postbellum Republicanism than the survival of Whig principles or the memories of the prewar

Whig-Democratic battles was the spirit of Unionism. This (along with simple ambition or opportunism) was the vital link between prewar, wartime, and Reconstruction politics for the scalawags.

The Unionist Connection

Unionist sentiment in wartime and postwar Louisiana reflected the degree of individual complicity in the rebellion, genuine patriotism, and self-interest. James O. Fuqua, a Confederate veteran and Baton Rouge attorney, in a letter dated June 8, 1865, to James G. Kilbourne, a planter and ex-Rebel, lashed out at those who, now that the war was over, were eager to profess their loyalty to the Union and discount any contributions they had made to the southern cause:

> Tell *everybody,* proclaim it on the house tops, publish it from Dan to Beersheba, that nobody can take the oath [of loyalty to the U.S. Constitution and the Union] here, that the military are [*sic*] waiting official instructions, and that as soon as the operation *does* commence they can take it just as well at home as here [Baton Rouge]. . . . I ask this for my own protection for my office is constantly thronged with would be loyal citizens "wanting to know you know" how it is to be done, and wanting me as I "know em all" to introduce them to "the General [Philip H. Sheridan] and see if . . . they can't take some kind of oath" to save their . . . [*sic*]. And then the sneaking hound must tell me how they opposed the war, and how (Solomons that they were) they "knowed all the time jest how it would turn out," and then what they have done, which generally amounts to, "only this and nothing more"—they never done noth'n. This agreeable conversation is occasionally varied with the inquiring "Squire what do you thin is gwine to be done with the nigger."

Fuqua ended with this warning: "Keep these [amnesty seekers] away or I shall do them a mischief. Or if they *must* come, warn them to keep away from me. I am armed, and am dangerous—have got a knife, a big stick, and a little nigger to collect brickbats."[6]

No doubt, as the letter implies, many professions of Unionist sympathy were entirely self-serving. As the Confederate cause collapsed, many who had been active adherents of the rebellion now proclaimed that they had never supported the Rebels, or, at least, that they had never willingly given aid and comfort to the enemy. Scalawags like Robert J. Caldwell, R. F. Daunoy, Wade H. Hough, B. L. Lynch, James Monroe Porter, Robert Ray, and J. D. Watkins all insisted that, despite their Confederate records, they never really intended to aid the Confederacy. "Robert J. Caldwell," John Ray wrote in 1868, "is a worthy man and in 1860 & 1861 an ardent opponent of Secession and was in feeling [although he served as a private in the Rebel army] a union man during the war and since has been an active Reconstructionist."[7] Caldwell himself claimed that he entered the Confederate army "under the pressure of circumstances," but that he was "quiet during the war and since the Surrender . . . has been an ardent union man" who "favored Reconstruction under the Reconstruction Acts and aided in Reconstruction." (The petition for the removal of Caldwell's "political disabilities" also carried the endorsement of Louisiana's carpetbag governor Henry Clay Warmoth.)[8] R. F. Daunoy, a thirty-six-year-old, Paris-educated New Orleans scalawag, admitted in 1866 to having served ninety days in the Confederate militia. "I did not want to go into it," he insisted. "I asked Governor [T. O.] Moore [the Confederate governor of Louisiana] whether if I served ninety days he would release me; he said he would, and I went voluntarily without being sworn in; I was never mustered in, and never required to take any oath." With the Federal seizure of New Orleans, however, Daunoy insisted upon being discharged. "As soon as the city was taken I applied to my captain to be relieved," he testified; "he [Daunoy's captain] said the confederate congress had passed a law declaring all under forty-five years of age to serve during the rest of the war. I told him if he did not give me a discharge I would go over to the enemy on the first occasion." Daunoy claimed that his refusal to serve in the Rebel army and his Unionist sympathies caused him to be labeled a turncoat by his fellow southerners: "I came here [to New Orleans] and took the oath of allegiance, and now all that population here have turned their back upon me . . . and called me a 'damned traitor.'"[9]

John Ray (in a petition to Congress dated June 23, 1868) testified on behalf of Wade H. Hough, a fellow scalawag. Ray stated in the document that Hough "actively sympathized with the union men—[and]—after he left the [Confederate] army he did all he could to assist men to keep out of the army—and since the close of the war . . . he has been a strong union man [who] has zealously supported reconstruction under all the plans proposed by Congress."[10] Michael Hahn also supported Hough and recommended that Congress remove his political disabilities: "He was a member of the Secession Convention of this State, but voted against and never signed, the ordinance of secession. Although drawn somewhat into the rebel service I am satisfied he never sympathized with the rebel cause."[11] Hough (in a letter to President Grant dated August 20, 1871) admitted to his participation, but claimed, nevertheless, to have been a strong Unionist from the start. "In 1860 I was a Union Man," he wrote, "and opposed with all my zeal & ability the Secession of my State from the Federal Union." Hough admitted his "unwilling participation in the Rebellion," but now claimed to have "accepted and advocated the adoption of the reconstruction measures of Congress adopted in 1867." During the presidential campaign of 1868, Hough stated that he actively and at a great personal risk supported the candidacy of Ulysses S. Grant. "I was the first man," he wrote to the president, "among the old citizens of the country of any political standing that openly & avowedly advocated your Election."[12]

Irish-born scalawag Bartholomew Leahy Lynch claimed to have supported the rebellion only reluctantly. "I was a Lieutenant in the unarmed mob called the Louisiana State Militia after the secession of Louisiana," he admitted in a letter to Benjamin F. Butler in March 1869, "and up to the occupation of New Orleans by the troops under your command, I was *forced* into that so called militia as a private but subsequently I voluntarily accepted a . . . commission from Gov. Moore for the purpose of getting out of the companionship and association of the miserable dregs of humanity among whom I was thrown." And, Lynch insisted, "I was then at heart as bitter an enemy of the rebellion as I have been ever since."[13] This limited participation in the rebellion, Lynch stated in another petition, was the "sum and substance" of his "political sinning."[14]

James Monroe Porter, a St. Landry Parish scalawag, was a colonel of the parish militia by appointment of Governor Moore. Porter's petition for the removal of his political disabilities (referred to the Senate Judiciary Committee on February 15, 1869) stated that Porter served as a colonel in the St. Landry Parish militia. He claimed that he had to serve in the militia "or go into the Confederate States Army." Porter also admitted to serving as a recruiting officer for the Rebel army between May 26, 1861, and April 17, 1862. On the latter date, however, "he left the Parish of St. Landry with his family and servants and proceeded to the State of Texas." When Porter returned to Louisiana in the summer of 1862, he "was arrested by order of Capt. J. M. Taylor then enrolling officer, and was ordered into the regular Confederate States Army." Later Porter arranged to get a special assignment to a noncombat position as deputy marshal and deputy collector of customs at Opelousas. He then obtained a "leave of absence and permission to go to Texas for his family and servants and left about the 1st November 1864 and returned 31st May 1865."[15]

The obituary notice for Ouachita Parish scalawag Robert Ray in 1899 noted that Ray "became a soldier in the Third Louisiana [Confederate] Cavalry, Col. Harrison's regiment, but his heart was on the other side and he was not a very effective soldier."[16] Napoleon Underwood, a member of the 1868 "Black and Tan Convention," was another southerner whose heart, it seems, was on the other side. In a letter to President Grant (dated April 6, 1869), Theodore E. Rovee, the secretary of state of Louisiana, described Underwood's rebel service: "Mr. Underwood joined the 'Beauregard Honor Guards' and upon the passage of the fleet went with them (as did many other Union Men) to Camp Moore. Here in company with other Union Sympathizers, he deserted, fled to the woods and returned to his family and friends." From 1866 on, Underwood, Rovee stated, "took up the cudgel in opposition to the Democratic party." An ardent and active Unionist and Republican, he worked for the election of Grant and Colfax in 1868 "in the face of the most violent opposition and at the peril of his life."[17]

John D. Watkins, a Claiborne Parish scalawag, also claimed to have served the Confederate cause, but without enthusiasm. In a petition to Congress (July 22, 1868), Watkins stated that "he both in public speeches and on all occasions in 1860 & 1861 opposed Secession and was a Union man." In the early part of 1861, he continued, he "made an effort to sell his property & remove to California a loyal State but could not affect a sale." He insisted, to avoid direct service himself and "to avoid opposing the United States Government contrary to his views of right he furnished a substitute." Later, however, Watkins became an enrolling officer for Ouachita Parish. In November 1864, he became the commander of a battalion of Confederate reserves; and in February 1865, he was ordered to act as judge advocate in the Trans-Mississippi theater of operations. Despite all this, Watkins stated that he unwillingly became a Rebel soldier. His acts, he said, "were controlled by circumstances," and he "never for one hour had any hope or desire for the defeat of the U.S. & the Success of the Confederacy." Watkins's petition bore the endorsements of Unionists James G. Taliaferro and Michael Hahn.[18]

It is difficult to gauge the sincerity of these statements and others like them. Many honest "Union men" had served the Rebel cause under pressure. Others suddenly discovered their Unionist principles at the time of the Union victory in 1865. Yet some scalawags admitted openly to having supported secession and the Confederacy and were accepted eagerly by the Republicans, evidence that there was little need to exaggerate one's wartime sympathies. Dr. Alexander P. Breda "was [in 1862] filled with a natural desire to assist the Confederacy and enlisted in Company 'C,' Second Louisiana Cavalry, under Co. W. G. Vincent . . . as a medical assistant." He later received a commission as assistant surgeon of the Seventh Louisiana Cavalry. Nevertheless, after 1868, Breda became "an ardent Republican."[19] His brother, J. Ernest Breda, also a scalawag, joined the Beazeale Battalion of the Natchitoches [Confederate] Rangers on August 9, 1862, and served throughout the war. Breda was without doubt a committed Rebel. "We must submit cheerfully to all the vicissitudes entailed on us by that terrible curse to humanity (the *infamous Yankee*)," he wrote on July 25, 1864, "and bear a smile on our countenances as all persons who cherish truly Southern Principles should do while we conceal within the sufferings of the bitterest pangs of adversity we have chosen to suffer for our cause."[20] In November 1864, Breda complained that he was ill and would soon return home. "All of this [suffering]," he wrote, "I owe to our *friends* the *Yankees* whom I will never, never forgive as long as I live. I believe that if Lincoln is reelected, so that we must have war 4 years more or submit, submission is a thing that is impossible with true Southerners. Over the ashes of desolated home, and the wreck and ruin laid before them, *Rebels* do not tamely lick the hand that strikes them; but, driven back, exiled from the scenes of happy days they cherish their sufferings, their humiliations, their wrongs and labor for revenge with all the energy and powers of body and mind given them by their Creator and will it be to the end."[21] Yet, in June 1865, Breda took the amnesty oath and in time became "a staunch Republican,"[22] despite the social ostracism and threats of violence from the conservatives of Natchitoches.

George W. Carter, one of the most prominent Louisiana scalawags, organized a regiment of Rebel cavalry and served as an officer in the unit. "The regiment," Henry Clay Warmoth reported in his memoirs of the Civil War and Reconstruction years, "was especially armed . . . with revolvers and Bowie knives."[23]

New Orleans scalawag Andrew Hero served with distinction in the famous Washington Artillery, a Rebel unit composed of "wealthy and prominent" New Orleans citizens.[24] Hero rose through the ranks from sergeant to major. Promoted for "gallant and meritorious service," he was seriously wounded during the Antietam campaign.[25] In 1888, the Louisiana *Standard* described this former Rebel and scalawag as a "brave and gallant ex-Confederate, loyal to the 'Lost Cause' who was no less true and loyal to the Republican Party, whose faith he long ago espoused and to whose advancement he . . . devoted his whole energy and his well-known superior abilities."[26] Hero supported the Unionist-Republican cause, taking the amnesty oath on September 9, 1869.[27] In a letter of recommendation (dated June 30, 1868) to Warmoth, Republican James Graham noted that Hero demonstrated "a praiseworthy desire to see the efforts of Congress to restore the State to her place in the Union carried into effect, and notably so as regards the Reconstruction Laws." This letter carried the endorsement of Thomas Jefferson Durant, a prominent southern Unionist-Republican.[28]

Other Louisiana scalawags, however, served the Union cause during the rebellion. George W. Mader, a New Orleans resident, was forced "to participate in the rebellion for a short time." With the occupation of the city by troops, however, he joined the United States Signal Corps. Mader remained in the service until June 29, 1865. "I rendered important service to the Army and Navy in the siege of Mobile," he claimed in a letter to carpetbagger William Pitt Kellogg, "and refer you to the report of Maj. Genl. E. R. S. Canby then [commanding] the Army against Mobile." Mader also claimed to be "one of the first white men in [Louisiana] after the war who advocated the Reconstruction Laws of the United States and the principles of the Republican Party."[29] In 1870, the *New Orleans Republican* reported that without Mader in its ranks "the Republican Party would be a feeble organization."[30]

Frederick Otto (a longtime resident of Baton Rouge) also served in the Union ranks during the war. "Mr. F. Otto," Major J. M. Magee, the commander of the Third Massachusetts Cavalry wrote to Captain G. B. Halsted at Port Hudson on November 4, 1863, "is a good *loyal Union man.* He went with my company all through the Teche Company, and when we came to Port Hudson he lay in the 'Rifle Pits.'" Otto, Magee informed Halsted, "is thoroughly posted as to the nature of the country and can give you some valuable information."[31] In 1869, Michael Hahn recommended Otto for a position with the Treasury Department on the basis of his Unionism and his Republicanism. "He was doing business in Baton Rouge at the beginning of the rebellion," Hahn wrote, "but immediately on the arrival there of the Union army he abandoned his business, joined the army, served on the staff of one of our officers, [and] rendered important service from his knowledge of the country." Otto's loyalty and service to the Union earned him, Hahn wrote, the bitter hatred of the ex-Rebels, and Otto now found it "impossible to regain a business standing among them." Hahn urged George Boutwell, the secretary of the Treasury under Grant, to provide this southern Unionist with a position in the Internal Revenue service. Otto, Hahn concluded, is "competent, honest and modest, a true Republican."[32]

Virginia-born scalawag Philip Pendleton was an officer in the Volunteer Artillery of West Virginia. He "was in the field during [John] Pope's Retreat [Second Bull Run] . . . and during the Campaign in Maryland under [George B.] McCellan."[33] In March 1869, Pendleton wrote to President Grant regarding his war record. "At the breaking out of war," he claimed, "I promptly took sides with the National Government and served as a First Lieutenant through some of the severest battles of the war."[34]

James Ready, an "active Union man and Republican,"[35] also supported the cause during the war. "I neither aided, abetted or assisted the Rebellion, in any shape or form by sword, deed or action," he stated in a March 15, 1869, letter to Boutwell, "and was the first to volunteer to head a committee of twenty-seven original Union Citizens of Louisiana to hoist the United States Flag over the City Hall at New Orleans on the 7th day of June 1862. Said Flag I afterwards carried to Washington and presented it to the Revenue Department on the 2nd day of April 1866."[36] Ready also claimed to have aided in the defense of New Orleans in 1863. "During the siege of Port Hudson when Genl. Banks was cut off from all communication with New Orleans by a Rebel Raid which threatened to burn the city," he stated, "I raised a regiment consisting of nine hundred of the best Colored citizens of New Orleans, armed, equipped and marched them into the field ready for service."[37]

The most prominent scalawag to oppose the Confederates openly and actively was James Madison Wells. As described above, Wells led a band of Unionist partisans in Rapides Parish during the early stages of the Civil War in Louisiana.

Other identifiable scalawags who expressed Unionist sympathies during the secession crisis and the war included W. Jasper Blackburn, M. F. Bonzano, Elias Carter, A. P. Dostie, William D. Downey, Thomas Jefferson Durant, E. H. Durell, Benjamin Franklin Flanders, Michael Hahn, Peter Harper, Ezra Hiestand, William Henry Hire, Thomas Hudnall, Charles Leaumont, John Theodore Ludeling, J. R. G. Pitkin, John Ray, James Govan Taliaferro, James H. Veazie, John S. Walton, and Rufus Waples. Some openly expressed their Unionist principles despite great pressure from their Rebel neighbors, some withdrew from public life, and some fled north and did not return to Louisiana until the federal government reestablished its authority in the state.

In 1860, W. Jasper Blackburn, despite the "hissings and scoffs" of the people of Homer, supported Stephen Douglas for the presidency over the southern pro-slavery-rights candidate John C. Breckinridge. Angered by his outspoken Unionism during the war, the Rebels forced Blackburn to suspend publication of the *Iliad*. "My paper was suppressed," he testified in 1867, "and I had to take refuge in the woods."[38] Ezra Hiestand, a New Orleans lawyer, was also an ardent Unionist who, despite the threat of Rebel retaliation, collaborated with the occupiers. He filled important judicial stations under the military government and was "one of the most out-spoken and fearless friends of the Union during the rebellion," according to T. R. Clay (a delegate to the Republican National Convention in 1868).[39] When Monroe, Louisiana, fell to the Federal forces under Brigadier General John D. Stevenson, John Ray contacted one of the Yankee officers and proclaimed his loyalty to the Union. "This action endangered his life," E. Russ Williams writes, "as Confederate sympathizers plotted to assassinate him. He narrowly averted death when a local Catholic priest warned him of the conspiracy against his life."[40] Thomas Hudnall of Morehouse Parish also found the life of a Unionist difficult. In an affidavit dated September 4, 1868, he testified to his troubles: "I was a strong Union man during the late rebellion. I was much persecuted then on account of my sentiments. I remember that once in 1862 ten men on horseback rode up to my house and attempted to arrest me; they would have shot me had they laid hands upon me." Hudnall claimed that, after this attempt to murder him, he fled to Texas and did not return until 1866.[41] Nevertheless, he remained consistent in his Unionist persuasion and, as we will see, in 1868 he was again visited by men on horseback.

Those men who withdrew from public affairs rather than risk ostracism or violence because of the Unionist sympathies included Michael Hahn, Thomas Jefferson Durant, Edward Henry Durell, and James G. Taliaferro. In 1860–61, Hahn campaigned against secession and refused to take the Confederate oath of allegiance (required of notary publics). "At a time when a public exhibition of Union sentiment meant martyrdom," Amos E. Simpson and Vaughn B. Baker contend, "he kept silent but did not abandon his unionist views."[42] Durant supported the Republican ticket in 1860. "A conscientious and consistent Unionist," Durant "fought strenuously against secession, and when that became a reality he remained in New Orleans, but during the Confederate regime abstained from all political activity."[43] When Ben Butler commanded in New Orleans, he informed Edwin M. Stanton, the secretary of war, that Durant was among the "gentlemen who enjoy the confidence of the community . . . and who you know to be well-disposed to the Union."[44] Edward Henry Durell was another Unionist who retreated from public affairs during the Confederate era in New Orleans: "He was a pronounced Unionist, strenuously opposed the ordinance of secession, and on its adoption in 1860 retired for a time from public life."[45] When New Orleans fell to the Federal forces, Durell became a collaborationist and worked closely with the military authorities. In 1862, he designed a plan, later adopted by the military government, to reorganize the municipal government in New Orleans and received an appointment as "president of the bureau of finance" for the city. In 1863, the military appointed Durell mayor of occupied New Orleans. Late that year, Lincoln made him a federal judge for the Eastern District of Louisiana. In 1864, Durell went to Baltimore as a delegate to the Republican National Convention.[46]

The Unionism of scalawag James Govan Taliaferro is also well documented. On October 8, 1856, he warned Louisianans of the dangers and illegality of secession in his newspaper, the *Harrisonburg Independent.* "Secession," he argued, "can only exist as a revolutionary right. It can never exist as a peaceful remedy." Adherence to such a theory, Taliaferro prophesied, "would inevitably lead to war and bloodshed."[47]

The winter of 1861 saw Taliaferro still firmly in support of the Union. As a delegate from Catahoula Parish to the secession convention, Taliaferro openly opposed the secession resolution. He argued that secession was wrong on practical, as well as ideological, grounds. This is seen in Taliaferro's "Protest against the Ordinance of Secession," originally delivered to the convention on January 26, 1861, and later published in the *New Orleans Daily Crescent*[48] and as a broadside. Taliaferro contended that (1) southern rights could still be adequately protected under the Constitution of the United States; (2) the current situation did not justify such an extreme southern reaction as secession; (3) the Border States would not join the secession movement; (4) little support for secession existed outside the Deep South; (5) secession was impractical, unconstitutional, and dangerous; (6) secession would endanger the very institutions (e.g., slavery) that it ought to preserve; (7) secession would forfeit southern claims to the national public domain; and (8) only the people (not the convention) had the right to undertake such a revolutionary action.[49]

His opposition to secession aroused such anger that Taliaferro had to cease publication of the *Harrisonburg Independent.*[50] He was imprisoned briefly for several days in Alexandria in retaliation for his outspoken Unionist sentiment. His sons tried to convince their father to seek refuge within the Union lines. The elder Taliaferro, however, remained at Harrisonburg for the duration. "Judge Taliaferro," Wynona Gillmore Mills writes, "had done everything to prevent Louisiana from leaving the Union, but failing, he accepted defeat and retired to his home to wait for the inevitable Confederate defeat."[51]

M. F. Bonzano, A. P. Dostie, Benjamin Franklin Flanders, and Rufus Waples fled north when the Confederates took power. An officer in the United States Mint at the time of secession, Bonzano fled to New York

City, along with the foreman of the mint's coining department. Before leaving, Bonzano and his foreman destroyed "all the coining dies remaining on hand, thus preventing the possibility of their use" by the Rebels.[52] On June 7, 1862, Bonzano returned to New Orleans to reopen and repair the mint facilities. In that same month, Bonzano became a leader in the Unionist movement in New Orleans.[53] When Benjamin Butler commanded during the occupation of New Orleans, he was informed of Bonzano's useful loyalty: "Dr. B. was a faithful among the faithless. He had an intimate knowledge of men in N.O. and the South West generally—a man of learning and well tried integrity." Further, "You can trust him to death and will . . . find him an excellent auxiliary in subduing the Rebellion.[54]

The Rebel authorities forced the outspoken A. P. Dostie to leave New Orleans on August 21, 1861, when he refused to take the oath of allegiance to the Confederate government. In a letter to Dr. J. C. Duell, Dostie expressed his passionate devotion to the Union:

> Two days afterward [April 21, 1861] I departed from what had been my beautiful and genial home, to come where I could once more see the old banner wave "o'er the land of the free and the home of the brave." For six months it had been shut out of my sight. I felt during that time despondent and gloomy, and almost ashamed of being an American and not with the battling hosts of my country, helping to raise that sacred ensign upon the parapets from which it had been so causelessly and ignominiously torn. I was resolved, if need be, to enlist, but thanks to the inborn patriotism of the people, I found on arriving here, there was no lack or need of men. They have gone forth in plentiful numbers, unfaltering in their determination to conquer back the Union, or die gloriously fighting for Freedom's hope. We will not despair, the sky is brightening, the rainbow of happiness will soon appear. A little while and it will be visible, welcomed by the gladdened hearts of a glorious nation.
>
> "May God save the Union, grant it may stand
> The pride of our people, the boast of the land;
> Still, still, 'mid the storm, may our banner float free,
> Unrent and unriven, o'er earth and o'er sea.

"May God save the Union, still, still may it stand,
Upheld by the prayers of the patriot band;
To cement it our fathers ensanguined the sod,
To keep it we kneel to a merciful God."[55]

Dostie returned to New Orleans when the Union army captured the city. Dostie, Willie Malvin Caskey writes disdainfully, "like others of Union sentiments, had returned with his fellow soldiers of fortune—but not, it seems, to practice dentistry."[56]

When the Confederates seized power in New Orleans, Benjamin Franklin Flanders, who "like a large proportion of the prominent men in the South . . . [lived] there so long as to be generally considered a native," also chose to move North.[57] "He is a Southern Loyalist," Rufus Waples claimed in 1877, "and was such throughout the late war, persecuted for his opinions in 1861."[58] Flanders went to New York. He had been "driven out of the city New Orleans . . . by a body of Rebels styling themselves a Vigilance Committee, for his devotion to the Union. He made his way to Cairo [Illinois] and Columbus [Ohio], barely saving his life, and returned with Butler."[59]

At the outbreak of the rebellion, Rufus Waples fled to Washington, D.C., and, like Bonzano, Dostie, and Flanders, eventually returned to New Orleans.[60]

The foregoing stories demonstrate that most of the major scalawags in Louisiana and many of the lesser Republican functionaries were Unionists during the secession crisis and the war or, if we can believe them, Unionists by principled conversion at war's end. Thus, persistent Unionism rather than persistent Whiggery provides a clue to the ideological basis of the Republican Party in Louisiana. These white southerners were much like those scalawags in South Carolina identified by Joel Williamson: "The single quality found in the background of most native white Republican leaders was a spirit of Unionism deeper than that of their neighbors."[61] This is especially evident when one looks at the period of 1862–65.

What exactly did "Unionism" mean? For some, it was choosing the winning side out of greedy opportunism. For others, it was "a path to personal power" as in the type of religious conversion described by writer Fay Welton: "When all of a sudden it seems the other side is singing the best tunes, over you go."[62] And for still others, it was real patriotism. After all, to be devoted to the Union did not exclude seeking the main chance. As Gary W. Gallagher states: Unionism "represented the cherished legacy of the founding generation, a democratic republic with a constitution that guaranteed political liberty and afforded individuals a chance to better themselves economically."[63] In Louisiana, the motives of the Unionists were as mixed as the ingredients of the region's rich gumbo. It was scalawagism that gave Louisiana Unionism its unique flavor. And it was these Unionists who played the leading role in the organizations and activities that led directly to the creation of the Republican Party in Louisiana. Whatever it was that converted them to Republicanism, it was Unionist tunes they were singing now. It would prove impossible, however, to get the rest of white Louisiana to sing along with the scalawags.

4

"MINDS AND HEARTS"

THE SCALAWAGS, UNIONISM, AND THE MAKING OF THE REPUBLICAN PARTY IN LOUISIANA

The Union people who remained at home and fraternized with the Union Army, who attended the balls and receptions of the military commanders and participated in the social life of the times, were especially objects of the resentments of the returned Confederates.

—HENRY CLAY WARMOTH, *War, Politics, and Reconstruction: Stormy Days in Louisiana*

The Unionist Collaborators

"Soon after the capture of [New Orleans], a few noble men undertook to arouse and organize the Union sentiment," the carpetbagger George S. Denison wrote to his uncle, Secretary of the Treasury Salmon P. Chase, in November 1862.[1] "Among these were Mr. Flanders, Judge Hiestand, Judge Howell . . . [and]," Thomas Jefferson Durant, whom Denison described as one of the best lawyers in the state.[2] Despite threats of violence and ostracism, Denison claimed, the New Orleans Unionists "persevered, called meetings, made speeches—organized Union associations—Union home guards, etc. These men have borne the heat and burden of the day and have redeemed this City."[3]

Unionists such as Durant, Flanders, Hiestand, and A. P. Dostie provided the leadership for the activities and organizations out of which the Republican Party in Louisiana emerged. An important step in the mobilization of the Louisiana Unionists took place at the end of May 1862, with the establishment (at the instigation of Major General Benjamin F. Butler, the commander of the Federal occupation troops in the city from May to December 1862) of a Union Association. This organization aimed at creating a coordinated movement directed by the Executive Committee of the association. The committee would arrange for prominent pro-Union men to speak at regularly scheduled meetings. To become a member of the association, one had to take an oath: "I, ________, do solemnly swear [or affirm], that I will true and faithful allegiance bear to the United States of America, and shall support and maintain to the best of my abilities, the Union and the Constitution thereof. So Help Me God."[4]

The association program began with a series of rallies at the Lyceum Hall, "for the purpose of stimulating and cultivating a spirit of Unionism under the protecting wings 'of the Union forces.'"[5] During July, Unionist rallies were held weekly and sometimes more frequently. Well-known Unionists appeared at the meetings. "These men were pointed to as so many living indexes of a latent Union sentiment in the state," Willie Malvin Caskey writes."[6]

A. P. Dostie was one of the most prominent Unionists on that index. "Among the arrivals by steamer was Dr. Dostie, an eminent dentist of this city, who was compelled to leave last August, on account of his bold expressions of Union sentiment," the *New Orleans True Delta* of August 20, 1862, informed its subscribers. "Dr. Dostie has been welcomed by a large circle of friends. He is a fluent and earnest speaker, and we hope, will be heard by our Union citizens at their meetings."[7] Indeed, Dostie would be heard. "I have come back after one year's absence from my loved home to die for the cause of liberty; if by such sacrifice it shall receive one impetus," he announced grandly upon his arrival in New Orleans on August 20, 1862.[8] Four years later Dostie would, in fact, die for the cause.

Dostie was typical, if perhaps more outspoken than most, of the Louisiana Unionists. An early and active supporter of Federal policy in New Orleans, Dostie worked closely with Butler. Dostie spoke, for example, to various Unionist assemblies, and he served, along with Hahn and Flanders, on Butler's reorganized New Orleans school board.

Butler sought, as an early objective, to exorcise pro-Confederate spirits in the New Orleans school system through the appointment of the Unionists. As a result, Butler hoped to bring about a political and educational reformation. "Dr. Dostie," Emily Hazen Reed (Dostie's biographer) claims, "was the animating soul in that reformation."[9]

In March 1863, the new Unionist school board adopted a series of resolutions that called for the teachers "to counteract the evil [i.e., Rebel] tendencies of the time, and to infuse into the minds of their pupils ideas in relation to public affairs which will be equally consistent with true patriotism and sound morality." The board also ordered the teachers "to make the singing of patriotic songs, and the reading of appropriate passages from the addresses of patriotic men, a part of the business of each day."[10]

The need for a Unionist indoctrination program seemed obvious. According to Fred H. Harrington: "Reared in Southern homes, taught by states' rights teachers, New Orleans youngsters recited the deeds of Stonewall Jackson and P. G. T. Beauregard, sang Confederate songs [including "Dixie" and the "Marseillaise"], [and] mocked men in Union uniform."[11] Flag presentation ceremonies were an important part of the Unionist indoctrination program. The ceremony held in March 1863 at the Madison School, an elementary school where a Rebel demonstration had occurred, was typical. At the assembly, the students sang the "Star-Spangled Banner," and a troop of little girls recited a patriotic address. "We dedicate to the Madison School this 'Star-Spangled Banner,'" they chanted, "the emblem of our own native land, as a tribute to patriotism. Long, long may it wave over our school dedicated to union, science and liberty." Dostie appeared at the meeting and delivered, on behalf of the school board, the manifesto of the educational objectives of the Unionist reformers. The dentist spoke of the necessity of winning the "minds and hearts" of the young people of New Orleans. "As we cast our eyes over this great Republic," he boomed, "and behold the causeless and furious civil war now desolating our once peaceful, happy and glorious land, filling, as it does the patriot's heart with terrible apprehensions for the future of this most sacred gift—self-government—to whom are we to look for hope of salvation, but to you this rising generation, educated as, we pray the Father of Nations may be, in the just and beneficent principles of Republicanism, of unity, peace and fraternity. Then our dear country will not know the Arnolds . . . , Calhouns, or Davises any more." Dostie went on to speak of the young George Washington ("remember he could not *lie*"), and of the essential duty of the public schools to instill Americanism in their young charges. "Had the youths of the rebellious portions of our country been the recipients of the blessings of this munificent institution," he informed the children, "'grim-visaged war,' with its concomitants—famine, pestilence and death, would not now be blighting our once happy and homogeneous people."

At that point, Dostie introduced "Little Mary Murray," who presented a United States flag to the school on behalf of the four hundred students at the school. Dostie intoned, pointing to the national ensign: "That beautiful emblem of our glory and power that a Washington triumphantly bore through the revolutionary struggles; that a Jackson won a halo of undying glory upon the Plains of Chalmette; that a Taylor so heroically bore aloft at Buena Vista; that a Scott reveled within the halls of Montezumas; that a Farragut carried by Forts Jackson and St. Phillip in a flame of lightning; that Butler, the indomitable, unfurled from the ramparts of our treason-bound emporium; that will victoriously float over Liberty's Dominions, when the "Stars and Bars" will be buried in oblivion."[12] The attempt to convert the little Rebels and their teachers to the principles of Unionism met with stiff opposition. Principals and instructors were fired, and, at one point, one-half of the school system's eight thousand students boycotted classes for a time in protest against the board's requirements that the pupils sing Unionist songs.[13] In a report to the school board, Dostie told Hahn, Flanders, and the other members that three hundred students had been expelled for their "obstinateness" in face of the board's demands. "I have informed the disobedient that the requirements were just," he stated, "and therefore, irrevocable, and if they persisted in their rebellion [which they did] they must be expelled from the schools." Thus, Dostie sought to make "treason odious in the public schools." Dostie was also active in the political reformation of the Episcopal Church in New Orleans. As a warden of Christ Church, he was active in the organization of a Unionist-oriented congregation. The Federal authorities took a special interest in this work since the city's churches had been hotbeds of Rebel agitation. "The ecclesiastical institutions of the South were a dangerous power in favor of despotism and rebellion," Dostie's biographer proclaims passionately. "It was necessary to strike the Church from its foundation by the earthquake of reform."

Dostie was indefatigable in his efforts to reform New Orleans. "Among the 'fanatical acts' of Dr. Dostie that evoked the thundering anathemas of the rebel multitude," Reed states, "was his noted performance at the Varieties Theater [a site often used for Rebel demonstrations]."[14] Dostie, in company with B. L. Lynch and some other Unionists, was determined to hold a pro-Union demonstration at the theater. On April 23, 1863, Dostie marched into the building carrying an American flag. The result was a near riot. Rebel sympathizers and Union people in the audience shouted at and threatened each other. Amid cries and general uproar, Dostie demanded that the orchestra play the "Star-Spangled Banner." Instantly, as if on cue, the Unionists in the audience began waving small flags and demanding that the anthem be played. The theater manager then appeared on the stage, complaining that the military authorities had prohibited the playing of "political airs." "That's a lie: We will have it anyhow," the Unionists shouted. At that point, some members of the audience began to climb up onto the stage, and someone pulled a pistol. The theater manager then yielded to the Unionist demands and ordered the band to play the anthem. But even this did not fully satisfy the Unionists. When Vining Bowers, an actor known for his pro-Confederate feelings, appeared on the stage, Dostie's people hissed and called him a "goddamned rebel." Enraged at the insults, the actor challenged one protester to a duel. The disturbance ended when a Yankee major stepped forward with an order from the provost marshal officially commanding the management to have its musicians play "Hail Columbia," "Yankee Doodle," and the "Star-Spangled Banner." The timely appearance of the Union officer indicates that Dostie's demonstration was planned in concert with the military government. Dostie had made his point, but the Rebel-minded elements in New Orleans were livid. They considered Dostie a "fanatic" and a dangerous "agitator."[15]

With the cooperation of Unionists like Dostie, the military authorities hoped, despite the intense opposition in New Orleans, to create a groundswell of support that would eventually lead to the reestablishment of a pro-Union civil government in the state.

The Louisiana Congressional Election of December 1862

Butler initiated the first official phase in the restoration of civil government when he ordered that an election be held on December 12, 1862, for two congressmen to represent the First and Second Congressional Districts (the districts then within the zone of Federal occupation).[16]

Butler's Union Association endorsed Benjamin F. Flanders (for the First District) and E. H. Durell (for the Second District). "The former," Caskey states, "was presented to the voters for his ability as a lawyer, his gentlemanly qualities, and his knowledge of the institutions and interests of Louisiana. The latter had always been a patriotic, public spirited gentleman and 'fully acquainted with' the citizens and their interests."[17] Despite the Union Association's endorsement of Durell, however, Michael Hahn entered the Second District race. Hahn, an ardent Unionist, had strong support within the German-speaking community of New Orleans. Three other "independent" Unionists also entered the race: John E Bouligny (First District), Jacob Baker (Second District), and a conservative Unionist by the name of Greathouse (Second District). The complete returns were never published, but Flanders won an easy victory over Bouligny, and Hahn defeated Durell, Baker, and Greathouse with a slight majority.

George Denison provided this evaluation of Flanders shortly before the election: "Mr. Flanders is the candidate of the Union Association. He did not want to run but it was urged upon him. Politically Mr. F. is an Abolitionist, but not of the blood-thirsty kind. I hope for his election. The whole real Union sentiment is in his favor. If he goes to Washington, he will let a little daylight into the darkened minds of Pro-slavery Democrats."[18] "Mr. Hahn," Denison reported on December 4, 1862, "is elected by a good majority. He was an original and continuous Union man, and is understood to be unconditional in his loyalty. Durell was unfortunately the candidate of the Union Association—unfortunately, for he is not popular and many members voted for Hahn, against whom I know of no objections."[19] Two months after the congressional election in Louisiana, the House of Representatives voted by a large margin to seat Flanders and Hahn, a significant victory for the Free State men.

On February 17, 1863, Hahn delivered his first address before the United States Congress. "I shall be brief in what I have to say," he announced. "I shall deal in facts, not in figures of speech—in blunt, unfinished sentences, not in any attempts at oratorical display." (Hahn's speech was neither brief, free of oratorical display, nor entirely accurate.)

Hahn claimed that the majority of the population of New Orleans, and of south Louisiana, "never voluntarily" aided the rebellion. The First and Second Louisiana Congressional Districts supported Bell or Douglas in 1860. He also claimed that southern Louisiana was not really a part of the mainstream of southern economics or politics: "The northern [part of Louisiana] is the cotton portion of the State where some of the people imagine that 'cotton is king'; but in the first and second congressional districts the culture of sugar and of vegetables is the exclusive occupation of the agriculturists. And those people have always, in every election, and under the most trying circumstances, shown their fidelity to this Government."

Secession, he claimed, was forced upon an unwilling state. This came about as a result of the "wicked acts and doings" of Governor Thomas O. Moore and a clique of aggressive Rebels. Secession, he argued, came as an unrepresentative coup engineered by disloyal state officials: "The Governor and other officers of the State may abandon it, but the people . . . will cling to the Union as they have always done, and will continue to do, until all hope from the loyal portion of this Union has gone, and you refuse absolutely to have us in the Union."

Hahn also described the persecution of the Louisiana loyalists: "It is a notorious fact that the jails of New Orleans were crowded with loyal citizens of Louisiana who refused to approve the treasonable doings and submit to the authority of the rebel government." It was also "a notorious fact," he stated, "that many of our loyal citizens were ruthlessly driven from their home and families and sent to the North." Hahn obviously sought to convince Congress that Louisiana was essentially loyal and that the vast majority of Louisianans opposed strongly the Rebel cause. As proof of this, Hahn pointed to the fact that the population of New Orleans had received Butler's army with open arms, had voluntarily formed Union associations, and had now elected two Union men to sit in the House of Representatives.[20] While "Hahn's chronicle bore little resemblance to accurate history, . . . the House was in a mood to be persuaded that Louisiana was worthy of trust."[21]

In New Orleans and the outlining parishes, those who opposed secession easily converted to the Confederacy once the war began.[22] Those who remained loyal were driven out of political life, forced into silence or exile. They represented, however, a distinct minority, and thus the Unionist movement, and later the Republican Party, in Louisiana rested upon a narrow base. Hahn, who had lived in New Orleans all his adult life and who had an insider's view of state and local politics, must have known this. Obviously, his speech was designed to justify his seat in Congress and not to provide an accurate description of the extent of Union sympathy in Louisiana. Less obviously, Hahn also made no mention of the divisions within the Louisiana Unionist movement itself.

These divisions began to develop quickly. In his history of the early stages of Reconstruction politics in Louisiana, Willie Malvin Caskey provides an interesting analysis of the speeches of the Unionist organizers in New Orleans that reveals the differences of opinion among these Unionist southerners. The speakers, he notes, boldly expressed their undying devotion to the Federal cause, and they condemned the Rebels who had forced many Union men into exile or had compelled other Unionists into the ranks of the Rebel army. In their speeches, the New Orleans Unionists claimed that secession had been forced upon an essentially loyalist Louisiana. "But the spirit of unanimity which the leaders showed in their wholesale condemnation of the secession movement and the prosecution of the war on the part of the Confederacy was not apparent in their discussions of methods of reconstruction and restoration," Caskey observes.[23] These divisions, although they would remain largely dormant until 1864, were evident in 1862.[24]

The Radical Unionists

Disagreement over the methods of reconstruction and restoration led to development of three major factions among the Unionist southerners: radical, moderate, and conservative. The radicals (their leadership included Thomas Jefferson Durant, Benjamin Franklin Flanders, James Graham, Rufus Waples, William R. Crane, and James Ready) championed the rights of laboring men and favored the emancipation of the slaves. This group also advocated the confiscation of Rebel property and the recruiting of blacks for service in the Union army.[25] "Following Butler and Chase in national politics," Fred H. Harrington states, "the group opposed conciliation, favored war to the finish, wanted a full-fledged confiscation program, demanded all-out Negro recruiting, and inclined toward extending suffrage to the colored man."[26]

Thomas Jefferson Durant personified the radical ideals. "The free state cause is gaining rapidly," John Hutchings, a Treasury employee, wrote to Secretary Chase in December 1862. "Meetings are held in some parts of the city most every night. Mr. Durant & I addressed the working men's associations on Thursday evening of last week. There was a large attendance & we took the bold ground that slavery should be entirely abolished. Mr. Durant declared himself to be a *radical abolitionist*."[27] In that same month, Durant wrote to Stanislas Wrotnowski, a Polish immigrant and longtime Louisiana resident, concerning the need to turn public opinion against slavery. Southern antislavery men, he stated, must create "a current of opposition to the principle of slavery." With slavery destroyed, he argued, "we put an end to rebellion and disloyalty." Yet, he had no illusions about the difficulty of their task: "We have a great deal of labor both physical and intellectual to perform, before this happy consummation can be accomplished, but we have been appointed to do the work, and we *must* go through with it."[28]

The Moderate Unionists

The moderate faction (led by Michael Hahn, A. P. Dostie, Benjamin F. Lynch, and others) "supported Lincoln, Seward, and the moderate Republicans in advocacy of caution and conciliation, in reluctance to push Negro rights and in opposition to confiscation." This moderate element, Gerald M. Capers maintains in his study of occupied New Orleans, "opposed political and social equality for Negroes, to which white urban workers [whom the moderates claimed to represent] objected almost as much as small farmers in rural areas."[29]

In an address delivered on November 14, 1863, to the Union Association of New Orleans, Hahn explained his middle-of-the-road position (which he called "Unconditional Unionism") on Reconstruction in general and the restoration to Louisiana of civil government in particular: "I have not yielded in the slightest degree to the busy slanders of those who have unnecessarily and maliciously sought to injure me in this community, on one hand by denouncing me as a 'negro-worshipping abolitionist,' and on the other hand by stigmatizing me as a 'Copperhead.'" He claimed to stand between those two extremes. "I stand fully and squarely on the platform of Abraham Lincoln," Hahn declared. He admitted that he had supported Stephen Douglas in the presidential campaign of 1860, but he now saw "that a better man than Abraham Lincoln could not have been elected."

Hahn then shifted his attention to the divisions within the Unionist forces. He referred to the factions only obliquely, but his intention was clear enough. "I regret that before the rebel army has yet been entirely swept from our State, and while there is still so much necessity for harmony among the friends of the Union," he said, "you should allow your feelings and prejudices on minor questions to lead you so far astray as to resort to all manner of personal and political abuse, bickerings and divisions, calculated to seriously retard the progress of the Union cause."

Slavery, as well, must not be an issue: "My own position is this: I am 'for the Union *with* or *without* slavery, but prefer it *without*.' I am emphatically an unconditional Union man. I will not make it a condition of my Unionism that slavery should be abolished, nor that it shall be maintained. I go for the Union in either case, but prefer it without slavery."

He next spoke on the method by which state government would be restored. Hahn said that he opposed the old pro-slavery, pro-planter state constitution of 1852. He favored calling a constitutional convention (a proposal also favored by the radicals) to rewrite the constitution. A new document, he thought, would destroy the power of the great planters and establish a government that would be "fair and just to the small planters and farmers, the adventurous frontiersmen, the honest mechanics, hardy laborers, the enterprising manufacturers and merchants and the professional men." This was only just, he declared. "Why should a man, because he owns a plantation and slaves, have greater political rights than other men who have no such profitable investments?"

Hahn ended his speech with a discussion of the future of the black race in Louisiana. He encouraged the slaveholders to free their slaves voluntarily. "Let us apply ourselves to the duty of devising some new plan for the prosecution of the agricultural interests," he proposed. Hahn's "new plan" was a system almost identical to the infamous Black Codes soon to be put into force throughout the South. He called for the enactment of "stringent and effective vagrant laws" to force unwilling Negroes to work. "The contracts for hire can be made as to allow the planter to retain in his hands several months' wages until the grinding or picking season is over," Hahn proposed, "and in case the laborer should violate his contract a forfeiture of wages would be the consequence." If a new labor system could not be devised, Hahn proposed that "the negroes be sent to colonies abroad where they will cease to trouble us; and let the plantations be divided into small farms and cultivated by white labor." Even Abraham Lincoln, he reminded the audience, favored the resettlement of blacks outside the country. Hahn also reminded his fellow Unionists that he considered himself "a friend of the colored people" and an advocate of emancipation. But as to civil rights, he was totally opposed to the idea: "I cannot but regret and condemn the course which some of them [blacks] are now pursuing in this city. At a meeting held by them [blacks] . . . resolutions were passed demanding the right to vote with white men." This Hahn could not accept. In the resolution, the blacks had claimed to be "natives of Louisiana," thus implying that they were more entitled to the suffrage than the German and Irish immigrants in the state. Hahn decried this as the "spirit of Know-Nothingism" and defended the naturalized citizens. The Germans, he said, were literate (unlike the blacks) and "as a general thing do not make their crosses, but sign their names, and in beautiful penmanship at that." He conceded that the Irish, because of British oppression, lacked a "book education," but the Irish "vivacity, activity, wit and intelligence, is proverbial."

Hahn concluded his remarks by pleading with Unionists to avoid factionalism and "to discard all personal controversies and irritating discussions calculated to divide Union men." In conclusion, he encouraged his fellow Unionists to avoid "party differences," to avoid "minor issues," and to unite in the cause of unconditional Unionism.[30]

This speech reveals a great deal about Michael Hahn's political persuasion and his ability to sense the direction of the political winds. Amos E. Simpson and Vaughn B. Baker claim that Hahn was "a quintessential nineteenth-century liberal." His "concern for economic freedom and growth, his sincere dedication to the principles of civil liberty, his interest in education, his commitment to rationalism as the basis for action and his dominating nationalism firmly establish him in the Western liberal tradition."[31]

To be sure, Hahn's views had certain things in common with the democratic liberalism of the nineteenth century, but Hahn was ambitious, clever, and adaptable, closer perhaps to the civic-booster tradition than to classical liberalism. He was adept at political in-fighting and followed closely the political currents in Louisiana, as his pre–Civil War political career clearly demonstrates. He became a Douglas Democrat during the secession crisis, and he claimed to be an uncompromising Unionist. Yet, during the brief period of Confederate control in New Orleans, he took the oath of office as a notary public. At the same time, "he purposely and carefully excluded therefrom all that portion requiring fidelity to the Confederate States."[32] The judge who administered the oath was a friend of Hahn's and conveniently overlooked the deletion.

Hahn retained his position without technically taking the Rebel oath. During the Union occupation of New Orleans, he sided with the moderate Unionists; later he became a radical Republican, still later an anti-Grant liberal Republican. He held various state and federal positions from 1862 until his death in 1885, a feat due more to his ability to maneuver than to his idealism. Like many other scalawags, Hahn was a political animal. He enjoyed the rough-and-tumble politics of Louisiana and, perhaps, the material advantages of office holding. Hahn was a go-along-to-get-along politician, more of a realist than an idealist.

In 1866, for example, he would deliver a long speech that directly contradicted his "Unconditional Unionism" speech of 1863. He attacked, in detail, the Louisiana Black Codes and called for black suffrage.[33] In fact, by 1866, not only Hahn but also Dostie and most of the other moderate Unionists had moved into the radical ranks. This political maneuvering in Louisiana had a Byzantine quality. In 1862 and 1863, the radicals and moderates, and even the conservatives, had formed an uneasy coalition. By 1864, the three factions openly opposed each other. In that year, the moderates briefly gained control of the state government. By 1865, however, the moderates were driven out of power and into the arms of the radicals when the returning Rebels and conservatives regained control under Andrew Johnson's scheme of Reconstruction. With the establishment of radical Reconstruction in the state, many of the old moderate and radical Unionists (now Republicans) would be in office again. One had to be clever to survive in such a political arena, more clever than principled. If these men seem too opportunistic or cynical, it should also be noted that there was one idea, or ideal, that remained constant with both moderates and the radicals: devotion to the Union. Men like Hahn and Dostie could adopt one tactic one year and another the next, but there is no reason to doubt their Unionism. Republicanism, in Louisiana at least, was seen by these men to be an extension of their Unionist beliefs. Issues like black suffrage, or a particular mode of Reconstruction, were usually secondary to them at this stage of Reconstruction. Radicals and moderates (Gerald M. Capers refers to them as the "liberal wings" of the Unionist movement)[34] were united in their opposition to the conservatives who seemed, in their view, hardly to be Unionists at all. And until 1864, these wings would present a "united front."[35]

The Conservative Unionists

The conservative faction (led by Christian Roselius, A. P. Field, J. Q. A. Fellows, Thomas Cottman, Jacob Barker, Julian Neville, Bradish Johnson, and E. E. Malhiot) sought "to retain the aristocratic constitution of 1852 intact, hoping for compensated emancipation."[36]

This group, according to Harrington, was "barely Unionist at all." Existing on the edge of the Unionist camp, these conservatives "consisted of Southern sympathizers who swore allegiance to the Lincoln government merely to protect their property. Many of these persons would not vote or otherwise participate in Union politics. Others went into the fray to aid the politicians least likely to destroy the institutions of pre-war Louisiana."[37]

On May 1, 1863, a committee representing the planter interests met at the lush St. Charles Hotel in New Orleans. Hoping to persuade the Lincoln administration to restore the government upon the basis of the old pro-slavery, pro-planter state constitution of 1852, these conservative Unionists appointed three men, E. E. Malhiot, Bradish Johnson, and Thomas Cottman, to go to Washington to appeal directly to the president.[38] When they arrived in the capital, the delegation presented a letter that contended that the act of secession was illegal, and that the constitution of 1852 remained in full force. They also requested that an election for state officers be held.[39] The conservatives' proposal was not unexpected. Michael Hahn, in a letter written on June 6, 1863, had warned Lincoln of their design to effect a quick restoration favorable to the old power elite:

> The Union people of this State (except, of course, office-holders) are all in favor of a reorganization of a loyal State government. The only

> question on which they are divided is as to whether a new Constitution should be made, or the old Constitution of 1852 adhered to. Those in favor of a Convention and a new Constitution are the more radical or free-soil Union men. . . . Others, whose interests are in . . . slavery . . . are strongly opposed . . . and are satisfied with the Constitution of 1852, which unjustly gives the country parishes a very large preponderance over the City in the number of members of the legislature.[40]

Although Lincoln, too, wanted restoration completed as quickly as possible, his firm rejection (dated June 19, 1863) of their request indicates that the president was unwilling to restore civil government without some concessions to the radicals and moderates. "Lincoln, who evidently refused to be embarrassed by the official reception of this committee of Unionists planters," Caskey states, "received its petition . . . and answered in like manner, clearly demonstrating that he was in sympathy with the radical leaders of his party, and with them was taking more advanced ground." Thus, the president replied:

> Since receiving the letter, reliable information has reached me that a respectable portion of the Louisiana people, desire to amend their State constitution, and contemplate holding a convention for that object. This fact alone, as it seems to me, is a sufficient reason why the general government should not give the committal you seek, to the existing State constitution. I may add that, while I do not perceive how such committal could facilitate our military operations in Louisiana, I really apprehend it might be so used as to embarrass them.
>
> As to an election to be held next November, there is abundant time, without any order, or proclamation from me just now. The people of Louisiana shall not lack an opportunity of a fair election for both Federal and State officers, by want of anything within my power to give them. Your Obt. Servt.
>
> A. LINCOLN[41]

Lincoln looked to the radicals and moderates to devise an alternative plan of restoration.

* * *

The Union Association Plan of Restoration

As president of the General Committee of the Union associations, the radical Durant played a leading role in the formulation of a counterplan for the restoration of civil government in Louisiana. (Other radical and moderate Unionists were active in the committee, including James Graham, William Henry Hire, James Ready, Rufus Waples, A. P. Dostie, B. F. Flanders, and Michael Hahn.)[42] On May 23, 1863, Durant and James Graham (secretary of the committee) sent a letter to Brigadier General G. F. Shepley, then military governor of Louisiana. The letter presented a detailed scheme for the establishment of a new state government. This plan called for: (1) a constitutional convention to rewrite the state constitution of 1852 (in the interest of the nonslaveholders); (2) universal suffrage for all loyal white men in the selection of delegates to the convention; (3) an oath of allegiance to the United States to be taken by each voter; and (4) a registration of loyal voters in Louisiana.[43] Shepley responded favorably to the Unionist proposal. He agreed to order a registration of voters and to appoint commissioners to register voters in each parish. "This registration, I shall immediately order to be made of those voters who voluntarily come forward to register themselves," he informed Durant and Graham. "I invite the co-operation and assistance of your committee and of the associations they represent."[44]

The process looked simple enough on paper, but the actual registration quickly bogged down because of the Federal army's inability to clear Louisiana of Rebel troops. "The military stalemate stymied the work of the free state movement, in turn, because," McCrary concludes, "the conquest of Confederate territory was, by definition, the first prerequisite of reconstruction." The problem was compounded when the military reestablished the parish police juries with conservatives filling the positions. And disagreements over the technicalities of the registration between Shepley and Durant also impeded the registration.[45]

General Shepley and General Banks had encouraged Lincoln to believe that the registration process would go smoothly. "Gov. Shepley has informed me that Mr. Durant is now taking a registry [Durant had been appointed attorney general and registrar of voters on June 10, 1863], with a view to the election of a constitutional convention in Louisiana,"

Lincoln wrote to Banks on August 5, 1863. "This, to me, appears proper. If such convention were to ask my views, I could present little else than what I now say to you. I think the thing should be pushed forward."[46]

Lincoln told Banks that he wanted the convention to recognize the Emancipation Proclamation, to provide for the education of young blacks, and to devise "some practical system by which the two races could gradually live themselves out of their old relation to each other."[47] Lincoln desired a simple and flexible restoration in Louisiana, but he was to be sorely disappointed. In November, Lincoln complained to Banks that Reconstruction had not moved an inch further in Louisiana. "Three months ago to-day [November 5] I wrote to you about Louisiana affairs, stating on the word of Gov. Shepley . . . that Mr. Durant was taking a registry of citizens, preparatory to the election of a constitutional convention for that State," Lincoln stated. "I sent a copy of the letter to Mr. Durant; and I now have his letter, written two months after . . . saying he is not taking such registry; and he does not let me know that he personally is expecting to do so. Mr. Flanders . . . is here now, and he says nothing has yet been done. This disappoints me bitterly."[48]

He then commanded Banks to proceed immediately with the registration. "I wish [General Shepley]—these gentlemen [Durant and Flanders] and others co-operating—without waiting for more territory, to go to work and give me a tangible nucleus which the remainder of the State may rally around as fast as it can, and which I can at once recognize and sustain as the true State government." Lincoln, however, reminded Banks that restoration must be based upon loyal men willing to support the Emancipation Proclamation.[49]

The State Election of February 1864

From June to November 1863, little progress was made toward the restoration of civil government in Louisiana, despite Lincoln's request that Shepley and Banks work closely with Durant's Union Association. Now the president demanded action. Banks, with Lincoln's permission, assumed direct control of Reconstruction in Louisiana. Shepley, Durant, and others participating in the registry were relieved of their duties. To speed up the process, Banks decided to hold state elections on February 22, 1864, and then, after the restoration of civil authority, to call a constitutional convention. Thus, the election would be held on the basis of the pro-planter constitution of 1852. Banks, however, did make one concession: the provisions in the constitution upholding slavery would be abolished. But reapportionment (which would favor the nonslaveholder) would be postponed until the convention.

The radical-moderate coalition now began to break apart. The radicals, following Durant's lead, worked against Banks's scheme to reorganize the state. For their part, the moderates were also opposed to the plan, but reluctantly accepted the idea. In a petition dated January 25, 1863, the moderates asked for a convention to be held before the scheduled February election. "But if you, General, should find it more consonant with the public interests to deny this earnest petition," the document stated, "rest assured that these same loyal voters will do their duty as best they may in carrying out the letter and spirit of your proclamation." The petition bore the signatures of James Ready, A. P. Dostie, and William Henry Hire.[50]

Durant summarized his objections in a long letter to Salmon P. Chase on the eve of the election. He claimed that the proposed constitution "was odious to the Friends of Freedom." Banks, Durant further claimed, ignored the constitutional questions and proceeded at the general's own "will and pleasure and that by virtue of it he changes the constitution of 1852 to suit his own view; among other things to enable his soldiers to vote, who by the express terms of that constitution are excluded." Furthermore, Durant charged, "Banks declares that he will order an election of five members of Congress although the state is not divided into Districts and cannot be as there is no Legislature, and Congress has not acted. He declares that his Governor, when elected, shall appoint two U.S. Senators. He announces that he will fix the basis of representation in the convention to form a new constitution at his own will." For a man with Durant's well-developed sense of constitutional procedure, this course was unacceptable. Durant went on to describe Hahn (Banks's candidate for governor) as "a trickster and a trimming politician."[51]

If Durant were uncompromisingly opposed to the Banks-Lincoln scheme, Michael Hahn was more than willing to cooperate. A letter from Hahn to Banks dated October 3, 1863, reveals the close personal and political association between the scalawag and the general:

> After a long trip on the [Mississippi] River, and after spending a few days in St. Louis and New York I arrived here [Washington, D.C.] this morning. While in N.Y. I made two attempts to see Mrs. Banks, but did not find her at home. . . . I left your letter for her . . . I had quite a lengthy interview with the President this morning and have just paid Mr. Chase a visit. The President concurs with us generally in our opinions, and will do all in his power to further our views. He speaks of you in the most friendly spirit and has the utmost confidence in your ability, etc. I saw upon his table a number of photographic views of the interior defenses of Port Hudson, and a map of Louisiana occupied a conspicuous place before him.[52]

The military, Durant charged correctly, was using its authority to promote Hahn's candidacy, and using the *New Orleans Era* to attack B. F. Flanders (the radical candidate for governor) and his supporters in "the most shameful and indecent manner." In Durant's view, the exercise of such power by a military commander was "entirely inconsistent with the principles of our Government." The Lincoln administration, he maintained, "has fallen into the error of trying to hurry on civil reorganization at too rapid a rate. Congress should use more control of the whole matter and fix on an immutable basis the civil and political status of the population of African descent, before any state shall be readmitted into the Union." In conclusion, Durant denied that he and his followers were "fanatics," as the military-backed press had charged, and he warned Chase that, unless Congress acted quickly, the "reactionary . . . men who hate and fear the consequences of this rebellion in the improvement and elevation of the colored man" would take control.[53]

The day after Durant wrote his letter to Chase, the moderates rode to victory on a military bandwagon. In fact, there was little doubt among the politically astute as to who would win the contest. Hahn won 6,183 votes, or 54 percent of the 11,411 votes cast. The conservative candidate, J. Q. A. Fellows, came in second (with 2,996 votes, or 26 percent of the total), and the radical choice, Benjamin Franklin Flanders, ran a weak third (with 2,232 votes, or 20 percent of the total). James Madison Wells, who ran on both the radical and moderate tickets, was elected lieutenant governor. The other victors included Stanislas Wrotnowski (secretary of state), Bartholomew L. Lynch (attorney general), James G. Belden (state treasurer), and A. P. Dostie (state auditor).[54] The active support given to the Hahn faction by the military in addition to the defection of many radicals, and some conservatives, into the moderate camp account for the triumph of the moderate wing in the state campaign of 1864.

Hahn and his followers were ecstatic over their victory. His grand inauguration ceremony on March 4, 1864, was a lavish spectacle. Public and private buildings were hung with gay patriotic bunting, and even the ships and riverboats in the harbor were decorated for the festival. A large circular platform was erected for the dignitaries, and more than fifty thousand chairs were arranged in a semicircle around it. The ceremony began with eight thousand schoolchildren singing "Hail Columbia." Then E. H. Durell administered the oath of office to Hahn. Following Hahn's inaugural address, an orchestra of five hundred musicians played the "Anvil Chorus" from *Il Trovatore,* accompanied by fifty blacksmiths keeping time on their anvils and fifty pieces of Yankee artillery booming in cadence. The featured speaker was General Banks, and the Yankee cannons firing in salute represented the real source of the moderates' strength.[55]

The first phase in Banks's plan of Reconstruction was now complete. The second phase involved the rewriting of the state constitution of 1852. The history of the constitutional convention of 1864 needs no elaboration here. Roger Shugg, in his study *Origins of Class Struggle in Louisiana,* has provided an analysis of the 1864 constitution. He sees it (and Joe Gray Taylor, in his revisionist survey of Reconstruction in Louisiana, concurs) as a victory for white farmers and laborers, who resented the favorable political position of the planters and who wanted and received the establishment of minimum wages and maximum hours for laborers.[56] And, although it outlawed slavery, the constitution was a defeat for the advocates of black suffrage (which most white nonslaveholders opposed, but which Lincoln had urged Hahn to endorse). But the moderates were content. "The Convention thus called, ably and patriotically performed its great work and the people have cheerfully and nobly ratified it," Hahn observed optimistically in October 1864. "Slavery can no more exist, nor can man ever again in Louisiana have or pretend to have property in man."[57]

The period of content, however, would be short-lived. When the voters ratified the constitution of 1864, they also voted into office a new state legislature. In January 1865, the legislature appointed Hahn to fill one of Louisiana's vacant seats in the United States Senate. Hahn eagerly took the position. His acceptance would be the catalyst for a new political crisis in Louisiana.

James Madison Wells and the Conservative Reaction

"It appears to me," George Denison observed in May 1865, "that a crisis has arrived in the political affairs of this State."[58] The resignation of Governor Hahn, which initiated the "crisis," brought into power Lieutenant Governor James Madison Wells. In the state elections of 1864, Wells had appeared on both the radical and moderate Unionist tickets. General N. P. Banks maintained in a letter to Montgomery Blair that Wells "was one of the most violent of the Radicals, and was one of the Flanders party—by which he was nominated for Lieutenant Governor." Also, Banks wrote, "the friends of Mr. Lincoln who nominated Hahn took Wells upon the ticket . . . to pacify the more violent anti-slavery or Chase men."[59]

Although Wells later joined the radical ranks, no evidence exists to support Banks's contention that Wells was a radical at this time. In fact, the two Unionist factions chose Wells for just the opposite reason. As an uncompromising Union man, a plantation owner, a well-known figure in central Louisiana, "and a courtly, aristocratic-looking man," Wells would add stature to the tickets. Wells served essentially as window dressing to provide both sides with "an aura of aristocratic Unionism." Wells remained silent during the campaign, making no statements regarding the central issue of the election, black suffrage.[60]

Both radicals and moderates would regret their support of Wells. He turned out to be, in their eyes, not a steady patriot but a political chameleon. Following his inauguration, Wells quickly ignored the small band of white radicals as he sought to create a balance between the more numerous moderate Unionists and ex-Confederates. The Louisiana radicals found themselves out of office, out of power, and out of sorts.

By June 1865, however, even the moderates' position began to erode, as Wells abandoned his middle course to form a one-sided alliance with the ex-Confederates who, along with their fellow travelers, now made up a majority of the Louisiana electorate.[61] The failure of the Louisiana legislature to disfranchise ex-Rebels, coupled with the numerous pardons granted to the wealthy planters by President Johnson, produced this revival of conservative power.[62] Keenly sensitive to the direction of the political winds, Wells initiated a "policy of conciliation" toward the planters and their allies.[63] This policy consisted of: (1) wholesale dismissal of Unionists and radicals from office and the appointment of ex-Confederates and Rebel sympathizers to state and local positions; (2) removal of the tax base for the support of black schools; and (3) official opposition to black suffrage.[64]

Wells acted out of a sense of political expediency and empathy for the planter class. "The reason for this course and for this condition of things," Denison explained, "is that the Governor belonging entirely to what is known as the planting interest with whom he has been so long connected, and from whom he never has broken away . . . desired to form a party that should support him, and thus would to a great degree strengthen him and consolidate his power."[65]

The "policy of conciliation" sent a shock wave of fear and resentment through the Unionist camps. The radical *New Orleans Tribune* lashed out against Wells and his conservative allies in a bitter, passionate editorial: "We must despair of this generation for this generation had handed [*sic*] the ships and sold human flesh in the market, and they are corrupt. Let them die in peace. But for God and country's sake do not make of them Governors, Lieutenant Governors, Judges, Mayors, Sheriffs . . . and Senators."[66]

N. P. Banks charged that Wells upon becoming governor turned out to be "a Rebel of the boldest type." The new governor displaced prominent Unionist officials "and appointed in nearly every instance rank copperheads and Rebels—in two or three instances men whose names are borne on the Ordinance of Secession, and have steadily sympathized with the Rebellion to this day."[67]

The dismissal of A. P. Dostie caused the loudest outcry from Wells's opponents. An outspoken scalawag, Dostie was a sure target for removal. Wells claimed that Dostie failed to furnish the official bond required of a state auditor. Dostie countered with the argument that the charges against him were false and his removal illegal.[68] Shortly before noon on June 13, 1865, several policemen evicted Dostie from his office. Ever ready to make a speech, Dostie shouted as the police approached, "If I must go, I wish first to say a few words." But before he could finish, two policemen advanced on him and forcibly removed him from the room.[69]

If the radicals and moderates were outraged at the purge, the conservative forces in Louisiana were overjoyed. "Governor Wells is giving us unmistakable evidence of his intention to purify the ballot-box," the conservative leader John A. Rozier wrote, "to rid himself and the country of so many obscure and fifteenth-rate men who have swarmed in the public offices."[70]

The radicals and moderates fumed and fretted as the postwar reaction set in. In their view, ex-Rebels and Copperheads had seized control of Louisiana while the loyal men watched in near helpless desperation. The *Tribune* looked to the "small nucleus of faithful white Union men and the whole mass of colored people" to counter the resurgence of conservative power.[71]

The crisis of the summer of 1865 spurred this core of radical whites (scalawags and carpetbaggers) and their black associates into action. The opposition to the Wells-Confederate administration centered in the "Friends of Universal Suffrage." Organized in early 1865 to promote black suffrage and to secure repeal of the Louisiana black codes, this association became the chief vehicle for radical discontent.[72] The leadership of the movement included several prominent scalawags: B. F. Flanders, Rufus Waples, W. R. Crane, and Thomas Jefferson Durant (the president of the Central Executive Committee of the Friends of Universal Suffrage.)[73] These radicals recognized the critical nature of the situation. Moreover, they saw the issue of black suffrage as vital to their position. Without black votes, the white radicals would remain a powerless minority. The black leadership in New Orleans also realized that the key to political success lay in black suffrage. The *Tribune* reminded its readers that "the colored voters are all loyal, all unionists, all opposed to the reestablishment of slavery." The black voters would unite in a solid bloc, the radical journal stated, and "their votes would weigh, as a single mass, on one scale of the balance."[74] Thomas Jefferson Durant saw black suffrage as "the only way to secure to all the fruits of our victory."[75] The struggle had shifted from the battlefield to the ballot box, and the radicals were prepared to fight it out if it took all summer.

The radicals were under no illusions about the difficulty of their task; the movement to enfranchise the freedmen faced determined opposition. "I think we are going to have great trouble during the next four years, & I see signs of it every day," Denison wrote. This Yankee observer anticipated "continual and bitter antagonisms between the Rebs on the one hand, and the Northern and Union men on the other." Although confident of ultimate victory, Denison predicted "a great struggle in regard to negro suffrage."[76]

In order to mobilize their forces more effectively, the radicals created the Central Executive Committee of the Friends of Universal Suffrage. The formation of this committee on June 16, 1865, marked the transformation of a rather loosely organized pressure group into a tightly structured "instrument for political action."[77]

At the time of the creation of the Executive Committee, Durant announced that the organization stood on the "principle of equality of all men before the law." Also, Durant warned that the ex-Rebels must not be allowed to control the reconstruction of Louisiana. To prevent such a catastrophe, the freedmen must be given the franchise. "When [the ex-Confederates] were concocting treason, and fighting against their country," Durant stated, "it was the black men who gave aid and assistance to the defenders of the Union." Durant looked to "Universal Suffrage" and the "just intervention of Congress" to save the day for the loyal men of Louisiana.[78]

The *Tribune* explained that the Executive Committee members "having charge of the organization of the Universal Suffrage party will have before them matters of the highest importance—the great and arduous duty of putting the political machine of the party in motion." The committee, under Durant's direction, tried to unify the various radical elements in Louisiana by taking control of the finances of the organization, by acting as a committee of correspondence, and by supervising the expansion of the movement into the rural parishes. Through these actions, the radicals hoped to construct a political counterforce to the Wells administration.[79] The next step was the creation of a formal party apparatus.

The Republican Convention of September 1865

Scalawags played the leading role in the founding of the Louisiana Republican Party. Thomas Jefferson Durant, W. R. Crane, Benjamin Franklin

Flanders, Dr. William Henry Hire, Rufus Waples, and Arnaud Commagere were prominent among the southern whites who joined the blacks and carpetbag leaders (there were 111 delegates in all) in the series of meetings that marked the official birth of the party in Louisiana.

At the first evening session, on September 25, 1865, the delegates unanimously selected Durant as president of the convention. Amid great cheering and applause, a committee escorted Durant to the front of Economy Hall. In his keynote address, Durant declared the central theme of the convention to be "universal liberty and universal suffrage." He then entered into a long, detailed explanation of the reasons why the radicals would ignore the November state elections. The contest, Durant pointed out, would have no validity since it would be held under the auspices of the "illegal" constitution of 1864. Durant urged the delegates to look only to the United States Congress for the restoration of civil government in Louisiana.

The next night, W. R. Crane, convention treasurer and spokesman for the committee on resolutions, introduced a series of proposals that, in part, constituted the platform of the embryonic party. The Crane resolutions endorsed the state-suicide theory regarding the status of the conquered states and called for a program of racial justice.

The Crane resolutions declared that the Ordinance of Secession had "disrupted" the relationship between the federal government and the people of Louisiana, rendering them "incapable of exercising the privileges of citizens of the United States." Furthermore, the acts of Congress declaring the people of Louisiana to be in a state of insurrection automatically "unfitted them for the functions of a state in the Union." Declaring it unwise to admit Louisiana immediately to the Union, Crane urged that the state be placed on a probationary status, in a sort of legal limbo, during which time the state would be governed by a "preliminary system of local government . . . to endure so long as may be necessary, to test the fidelity of the people to the United States, and to accustom the inhabitants to exercise in harmony and peace the rights and duties of self-government."

The heart of the Crane resolutions concerned the party's commitment to black rights. Crane protested against the state's Black Codes as a "system of serfdom, or forced labor" designed to turn the clock back on emancipation. The resolutions urged Congress to enfranchise the black man as a reward for his wartime service and as a way of enabling him to protect his newfound liberty through the ballot box. The ninth resolution reaffirmed the delegates' faith in the principles of human rights, as put forth in the Declaration of Independence, and called for the expansion of those principles to include "our loyal fellow-citizens of African descent." The tenth resolution established as the basis of the new party a commitment to "universal suffrage, liberty and the equality of all men before the law." Lastly, the delegates adopted a recommendation calling for the holding of a national Republican convention whose members would be elected "without distinction of race or color."

At the session on Wednesday evening, B. F. Flanders, vice president and chairman of the committee that composed the "Address of the State Convention to the People of Louisiana," read to the assembly the first public statement of the new party. In the "Address," Flanders repeated the basic ideas set down in the Crane resolutions. Flanders stated that the people of Louisiana must accept the fact that slavery was dead, "swept away by the tempest of war," and that "the people of African descent are now free and as free as all other men." Flanders reminded the ex-Rebels that under Andrew Johnson's amnesty program they swore to uphold faithfully "all laws and proclamations which have been made during the existing rebellion, with reference to the emancipation of slaves."

According to Flanders, the people of Louisiana were required to do more than uphold the narrow legal aspects of emancipation. Each voter was "bound in conscience and in honor to treat every man, white or black, as free; and to treat him as he would wish himself to be treated." Flanders reminded the people of Louisiana of the positive contributions of the free black population to the state in the antebellum period. "Whether as a soldier or a citizen," Flanders contended, "the free man of color has invariably shown himself, in all the ennobling qualities of man, the equal of his more favored fellow-citizen, nor has he ever ceased to be a useful member of the State, when treated with justice and equality; and that what those formerly free have been, the newly emancipated class is prepared to be." Flanders then urged the people of Louisiana not to hold the black population responsible for the war or to "continue in the delusion that 'a few fanatics in the North and South' produced the great rebellion." The Civil War, Flanders stated, came about because "the ideal of slavery was incompatible with that of liberty." The war came because "slavery was too arrogant to yield peacefully to its inevitable fate."

Flanders attacked the Louisiana constitution of 1864 and the legality of the existing state government. The Wells administration had no validity as a true state government, he claimed, but existed merely as an adjunct of the Federal military authority in Louisiana.[80] Flanders ended with the recommendation that a territorial delegate be elected "to present the views and feelings of the republicans of Louisiana at Washington."

The major controversy of the convention resulted from Henry Clay Warmoth's proposal that the delegates immediately draft a new constitution and submit it to the voters for approval. Evidently Warmoth's resolution found considerable support among the delegates, for when he concluded his remarks, the auditorium exploded with cheers, clapping, and the sound of stamping feet.

W. R. Crane and Rufus Waples, however, spoke out in opposition to the Warmoth resolution, and the motion was tabled. Waples, the scalawag delegate from New Orleans's Fourth District, attacked the proposal in a long, rambling, convoluted discourse that the legal-minded Durant must have envied. Basing his position on points of international law, constitutional theory, and legal history, Waples sought to persuade the assembly to vote down the resolution. Waples also argued against the proposal on the basis of political expedience. The southern Unionists, he stated, needed the continued protection of the federal government. "If Louisiana is a State," he contended, the Unionists would "inevitably be subjected to taunts, persecutions, denial of free speech, and to all the embarrassments under which they labored at the beginning of the war." Waples pointed out that the Rebel voters greatly outnumbered the loyal voters, and warned the delegates against any precipitous action that might "exchange their protection by the Federal Government for the vain protection" of the ex-Rebels. As for the black population of Louisiana, Waples argued that it was not necessary to write a new constitution in order to invest them with political rights. The black population, exclusive of women and minors, possessed the franchise, he argued, without further legislation since they were now included under the natural rights principle expressed in the Declaration of Independence.

In his speech, Waples expressed a firm commitment to the idea of black suffrage. The "loyal colored population," as he termed them, must be allowed a voice in the formation of a new state government and participation in its subsequent administration. Waples listed ten reasons for investing the freedmen with voting rights: (1) it would "remove the prejudice existing against them"; (2) it would secure "peace and harmony among all classes"; (3) it would "ensure a majority against treason and against slavery"; (4) it would encourage the agricultural population, almost exclusively black, to remain in Louisiana; (5) "it would tend to improve and elevate the blacks, cultivate self-respect and laudable ambition, and thus render them more valuable citizens"; (6) it was obvious that the blacks were "educated to hate slavery, treason and rebellion, and may therefore be safely trusted with a voice upon the great questions growing out of the war"; (7) it was their "inalienable right under our theory of government"; (8) it would remove the charge of inconsistency made by foreign statesmen . . . against our Republic"; (9) "it would increase the whole number of voters, and thus render election frauds and corruptions more difficult"; and (10) it would ensure that loyal men, namely blacks, would participate in elections "and would therefore be valuable to the Federal Government in maintaining its interests here."

Waples ended his discourse with the warning that Louisiana must remain in a territorial status under Federal control until "the whites shall have seen that the colored citizens are sober, industrious and eminently law-abiding; until their present vague hopes of restoring slavery in another form shall have been dissipated." Waples advised that a slow, cautious return to civil authority was necessary to avoid a race war in Louisiana and to prevent the return of Confederate power.

The resolutions proposed by Crane, Flanders, and Waples constituted the platform of the new Republican Party in Louisiana. On national issues, the state leaders adopted the principles laid down in the Baltimore platform of 1864.[81] The national platform that year, for example, called for the "utter and complete" extinction of slavery.[82] The Louisiana Republicans, however, added other, more radical planks. The local party, led by the scalawags, demanded that: (1) the people of Louisiana be considered "incapable of exercising the privileges of citizens of the United States"; (2) the people of Louisiana be declared "enemies of the United States" and also unfit "for the functions of a State in the Union until restored by the action of Congress"; (3) Congress "at the earliest possible moment . . . establish, by act of Congress, a Republican Government in

Louisiana"; (4) the new loyal state government be established not by a military or executive officer, but by the President and Congress"; (5) the Louisiana Black Codes be abolished; (6) the vote be extended to blacks; (7) "a preliminary system of local government . . . be established by Congress, to endure so long as may be necessary, to test the fidelity of the people"; (8) all the principles of the Declaration of Independence be extended to "our loyal fellow-citizens of African descent"; (9) the basis of the Louisiana Republican Party be "universal suffrage, liberty and the equality of all men before the law"; (10) the state organization not nominate candidates for the state elections of 1865; and (11) the national party issue a call for a grand convention "organized on the basis of this Convention, one-half white and the other half colored, to adopt a national platform on the basis of Universal suffrage, and to consider the questions suggested by the foregoing resolutions."[83]

The speeches and resolutions of Durant, Crane, Flanders, Waples, and the other delegates emphasized the justice of recognizing the political rights of the freedmen. They said nothing directly about blacks having social or economic equality with whites. They spoke in terms of political equality and of the necessity of admitting blacks to the political system. The convention record reveals no direct commitment by the scalawags, or the carpetbaggers, to racial justice or economic opportunity beyond voting rights and office holding. What was true in Louisiana was true across the South. As Michael W. Fitzgerald notes of southern white Republican racial attitudes, "few thought racial justice a priority. Rooted as they were in their communities, they were reluctant to flout racial convention more than their politics required." Further, "Scalawags therefore drew an emphatic line between civil equality, which they might support with suitable qualifications, and social equality, which they generally disavowed."[84] Although enfranchising the freedmen was an act of simple justice, the Louisiana scalawags were quite frank in pointing out the political expediency of black suffrage. The white radicals needed black support in their fight against the Wells-conservative alliance. The white Republicans looked to Congress to postpone the reestablishment of civil government until they could forge an alliance of loyal whites and ex-slaves strong enough to counter the resurgence of Confederate power in Louisiana. Because the white Republicans were a distinct minority in Louisiana, the radical leaders looked to the black population to form the bone and gristle of the new party.

Although the role of the black delegates and carpetbaggers like Warmoth was not insignificant, it is clear that it was southern white men who set the tone and defined the issues at the convention. It was southern white men who made all the major speeches and who held most of the important offices and committee chairmanships. (Warmoth, for example, was elected the territorial delegate to Congress only after Durant refused to accept a unanimous nomination.) It was southern white men who took the lead in forming the new black-white radical coalition. Although they were able to create a political party, creating a unified party was more difficult. The local factions appealed for and found conflicting support for their particular positions and ambitions from nation leaders (Abraham Lincoln or Salmon P. Chase, for example). Without a clear or consistent position in Washington on local politics, the Unionist factions developed ominous fault lines that created the constant friction and stress within the movement that eventually helped to fracture and then destroy Republican control in Louisiana.

From 1862 to 1865, politicians such as Durant, Flanders, Hahn, Dostie, Waples, Hiestand, and Hire worked to lay the foundations of a Unionist state. These were the men who collaborated with the Federal occupation forces, led the Unionist movement, and established the Republican Party in the state. Yet it was one thing to create a party on paper, and quite another to lead it to success in the face of internal dissent and in opposition to a sullen, hostile, white population already beginning to mobilize against the Unionists.

5

"WHAT THE HELL IS YOUR HIDE WORTH TODAY?"

THE SCALAWAGS AND THE NEW ORLEANS RIOT OF 1866

> The rebel flag was again unfurled. The men who had bravely resisted it for four years were murdered under its encouragement.
>
> —*Harpers Weekly,* August 18, 1866

In a cartoon entitled *Amphitheatrum Johnsonianum—Massacre of the Innocents at New Orleans, July 30, 1866,* in *Harper's Weekly,* the popular pictorial family magazine, Thomas Nast commented on the political and racial violence in Louisiana. Nast depicted President Andrew Johnson enthroned in a Roman coliseum directing the slaughter of defenseless blacks and whites. The shields of the "gladiators" were embossed with the letters "CSA" (Confederate States of America) and the words "Monroe Police" (a reference to the New Orleans police under the Democratic administration of Mayor John T. Monroe, a former Confederate). One of the black victims was shown waving an American flag.[1] With his masterful gift for caricature, Nast presented the radical interpretation of one of the turning points in Reconstruction history. The radicals saw the riot as the premeditated act of ex-Rebels intent upon destroying the native Republican movement in Louisiana; the Democrats, on the other hand, blamed the radicals for the riot. According to this interpretation, the New Orleans radicals (principally scalawags) purposely instigated violence in New Orleans in the hope that it would bring on Union military intervention and thus save the radicals' deteriorating political position in Louisiana. Seen from the Democratic pro-southern perspective, "the riot was provoked by the incendiary speeches, revolutionary acts, and threatened violence" of the white Republican leaders in New Orleans. In this view, these men (encouraged by the radicals in

Congress) sought to "provoke an attack on the colored population, which was expected to be suppressed by the military before it had seriously endangered the white leaders. . . . This would afford an excuse for [a] congressional investigation resulting in congressional legislation favoring the ultimate design of the conspirators, viz., the destruction of the existing [that is, Democratic] civil government in Louisiana."[2]

Although contemporary observers and historians alike have differed about the causes and details of the riot, there is no doubt that the events of that hot July day in New Orleans profoundly influenced the course of Reconstruction in general, and the fate of the Louisiana scalawags and their enemies in particular. Gilles Vandal's examination of the causes of the riot emphasizes the "confused" and unstable nature of Louisiana politics and "the resistance of the majority of native whites to any government dominated by outsiders and their scalawag allies."[3] He disputes, however, that radicals in particular were in the majority of the movement to rewrite the constitution of 1864 in the interests of black rights. James G. Hollandsworth's account of the riot focuses on the complex causes of the event: political instability, the fight over control of the state government, "deterioration of social restraint in a community demoralized and divided as a result of war," the failure of Federal leadership, the determination to ensure white supremacy by ex-Rebels, and "the emergence of a vocal and well-organized black protest movement." Hollandsworth argues that the story of the riot has "no villains and no heroes, for everyone who participated in the deadly affair had to share the blame."[4] James S. Hogue places the New Orleans riot in the context of five street battles in New Orleans, occurring in 1866, 1872, 1873, 1874, and 1877. He judges that the remote causes of the 1866 riot lay in the violent convergence in New Orleans of two powerful forces: "a large and restless population of Confederate veterans" and the presence of "the largest population of black veterans in the South" encouraged a "nucleus of white Union veterans who stayed in New Orleans after the war." The immediate cause was the prospect of revolutionary change with the enfranchisement of black men, the "recipe for a shocking massacre."[5] Whatever the causes, the riot turned congressional and northern public opinion against the conservative, lenient Reconstruction program of President Johnson, gave weight to demands for harsher policies toward the defeated South, and contributed to the first impeachment of an American president.

The following story is about the role of the Louisiana scalawags in the origins and course of that historic and deadly event and, in part, an explanation for the decline of scalawag leadership in Louisiana.

The Scalawags and Origins of the Riot

The constitutional convention of 1864, convened under the Lincoln-Banks plan of Reconstruction for Louisiana, established a new state government. The state elections of 1865 made it clear that it would be a government of ex-Rebels. By the spring of 1865, the former Confederates controlled both the state legislature and the New Orleans city government. This, plus James Madison Wells's policy of appointing supporters of planting interests to state offices, meant that if Congress recognized the 1864 state constitution and the new conservative regime, then any hope of securing civil rights for blacks would be destroyed, and the radicals in Louisiana would be doomed to political extinction. The only hope for the radicals was to enfranchise the freedmen and disfranchise the former Confederates.[6] The radicals, however, discovered a way by which they hoped to accomplish these twin objectives. An unusual resolution passed by the drafters of the 1864 constitution provided that the president of the convention had the power to reconvene the convention for *any* reason. Although the legality of this resolution was highly questionable, the radicals hoped to use it to convoke a rump convention (packed with radical delegates), rewrite the 1864 constitution to include black suffrage and Rebel disfranchisement, and then have the new radical-oriented document approved by Congress.[7] It was a bold, audacious plan.

Wells was a key figure in the attempted coup. He had been willing to cooperate closely with the conservatives after succeeding to the governorship in 1864, and he had been elected governor in his own right in February 1865, partly with Democratic support. Yet Wells remained at heart an ardent Union man. Thus, he eventually found it impossible to work with former Rebels whose loyalty to the United States was still considered suspect by the Union people in Louisiana. The Democratic-dominated legislature, for example, extended its power so as to almost completely control the state government, and even the governor's own appointees were forced out of office. The legislature filled the vacancies with Confederate sympathizers whom even the planter-oriented Wells could not stomach. By March 1866, the break between Wells and the Democrats was complete.[8] Wells now aligned himself openly with the radicals.

With Wells in the lead, the radicals put their plan into operation.[9] A complication occurred, however, when E. H. Durell, the former president of the convention, refused to cooperate with Wells and use his authority to reconvene the convention. Durell doubted the legality of the scheme. "Some say that the convention having formed a constitution, and that constitution having been submitted to the people, and they having ratified it, and one or two legislatures having been assembled under it, and one or two governors having been elected under it," Durell claimed before the congressional committee members investigating the riot in 1867, "that the resolution adjourning gave no power, under such circumstances, to reassemble it." But Durell also feared that violence would erupt if the new convention met. "In June last I called upon General [Philip] Sheridan [military governor of Texas and Louisiana] and told him I had been very much pressed to call the convention together," Durell stated. "I told him what I understood the convention intended to do. I told him that, from the condition of the public mind, I did not think the convention could be assembled and sessions carried on without a disturbance, and that there would be a riot." According to Durell, Sheridan replied that he would disperse any mob that threatened the delegates, but that he did not have enough troops to protect white and black voters during a ratification election. Durell responded that unless troops protected the black voters, they "would be shot down like dogs."

The Democrats of the city were determined to prevent the convention from meeting. Mayor John T. Monroe, a Democrat and passionate Confederate sympathizer, planned to arrest the members of the convention before they met. Monroe appealed to General Absalom Baird, the acting army commander in New Orleans, to aid him in preventing the assembly. Monroe stated that the proposed assembly was "unlawful" and "calculated to disturb the peace and tranquility," and that it was his duty to prevent it from meeting.

Baird refused to cooperate with Monroe in his effort to forestall the meeting. The general saw the controversy as a purely civil political matter, one that should not involve the military. "If the assemblage in question has the legal right to remodel the State government, it should be protected in so doing; if it has not, then its labors must be looked upon simply as a harmless pleasantry to which no one ought to object," Baird reasoned. The convention controversy, he stated, was a matter for the civil courts to decide. He would ensure law and order, but he would not act in concert with the mayor to prevent the meeting. When Monroe later proposed to arrest the delegates after a grand jury indictment, Baird also refused to cooperate. The general was determined to protect the delegates unless he received orders to the contrary from the president.

Still intent upon preventing the convention, the Democrats appealed directly to Johnson. Lieutenant Governor Albert Voorhies wired the president, asking Johnson what Baird should do if the local authorities acted to prevent the assembly. Johnson sent an evasive and confusing reply: "Sir: The military will be expected to sustain, not obstruct or interfere with, the proceedings of the courts." Voorhies showed Johnson's telegram to Baird. Bewildered by Johnson's stand (or lack of one), Baird sent a telegram to Secretary of War Edwin M. Stanton. When Stanton failed to reply, Baird decided to stick by his decision to protect the delegates. "Stanton favored the convention and consequently approved of Baird's policy," Donald E. Reynolds, an authority on the riot, states. Further, "the secretary, knowing Johnson's opposing views, did not want to risk crossing the President openly by formally endorsing Baird's resolution to protect the convention. His solution to the quandary was simply to do nothing at all." For their part, the conventioneers were under the impression that Baird would protect them from Monroe's police. Baird, however, believed that the convention would convene at 6:00 p.m. It was a fatal error. When the delegates arrived at the institute at noon on July 30, there were no troops present to prevent the ensuing massacre.

Not knowing about the misunderstanding, the radicals proceeded boldly with their plan. On July 7, Wells appointed Rufus K. Howell as president pro tem of the convention (replacing E. H. Durell). Howell then issued a formal call for the convention to reassemble on Monday, July 30.

On the night of Friday, July 27, the radicals held a preliminary political rally in downtown New Orleans. The rally began at 7:00 p.m. at the Mechanics' Institute on Dryades Street. The principal speakers included Ezra Hiestand, Michael Hahn, Rufus Waples, and A. P. Dostie. Hiestand called the meeting to order, and Hahn was elected chairman.

Then a series of resolutions were adopted that applauded Congress for its Reconstruction policies and the Union army and navy for providing security. Further, the assembly declared for "political equality" for black men. They also endorsed President Andrew Johnson's "patriotic declaration" that "treason is a crime, and must be made odious, and that traitors must take a back seat in the work of reconstruction." The final resolution addressed the problem of violence and intimidation and the courage of prominent Unionists: "we commend the course pursued by Judge Howell and Governor Wells, who, regardless of threats, personal violence and unmoved by the ridicule, censure and attempt at intimidation of the rebel press of the city, rise to the heights of the occasion in the performance of acts of duty."[10]

Following the adoption of the resolutions, Hahn addressed the black audience inside the hall. He recalled the old days of slavery when blacks were oppressed by "the slave oligarchy." Under the former system, he reminded them, "colored men could not come together to deliberate over public affairs." He reminded them too of the slave codes that had forbidden black education. As an example, he cited the fate of an elderly black man in New Orleans who was arrested for teaching black children. The teacher had died in prison. But, Hahn continued, the spirit of that martyr had been reborn in the black Republicans of Louisiana.

Now the black man had the upper hand, and "the rebels are trembling in their shoes in consequence." Their fear, he noted, stemmed from the fact that the country was going "to be ruled by loyal men, both white and black." Hahn welcomed the new order, and welcomed, too, the Rebel accusation that he was an abolitionist. "There was a time when the term 'Abolitionist' was considered a shame," he cried, "but I stand before you to-night, raised and educated as I have been in the South, and tell you that I glory in being an Abolitionist and a Radical." He next told his audience that no true Union man could be opposed to black suffrage. Finally, he told the assembled blacks that he "would rather every office in the State was in the hands of colored men than in the hands of unrepentant rebels." The scalawag ended his harangue with a remark that conservative whites must have found particularly galling: "It is to you that the loyal men of the South must look, and when you separate to-night, make up your minds from this day forward you are as good as any white man in the State." The audience responded with great applause.

Rufus Waples then rose and delivered a short legal defense of the plan to reconvene the 1864 constitutional convention. "Congress recognizes the right for the people, in their primitive capacity, in those States destroyed by the rebels, to make their own organic law, and submit it to Congress, and leave it to Congress to decide whether it be consistent with the organic law of the republic." The loyal men of the state endorsed the radical scheme, he noted, and it was ridiculous for the ex-Rebels to talk of injustice being inflicted upon them. If the ex-Confederates did not like the new political order, they could leave the country, Waples stated. The blacks made better citizens than ex-Rebels anyway, he noted, for the mass of blacks had "learned two important lessons—to hate slavery and to abhor treason."

Outside the institute, Hiestand spoke to the black people assembled in the street. "The decree of God has gone forth that there shall be universal freedom and universal suffrage throughout the South," he declared. Dostie closed the outside meeting, and, at his request, the blacks formed a torchlight procession. From the institute, five thousand freedmen marched down Canal Street "to the sound of loyal music . . . making the air resound with cheer upon cheer, for universal suffrage, Congress, and the convention which [was] about to assemble to give them suffrage."[11]

The convention assembled at noon on Monday, July 30, at the Mechanics' Institute. While the convention was getting under way, a parade of about two to three hundred blacks, marching to the tune of a fife and drum, was approaching the hall. When the black demonstrators crossed Canal Street, a white man pushed one of the blacks to the ground. The marcher retaliated, and the attacker pulled a pistol and fired. When the parade reached the institute, the blacks began cheering. At this point, another argument broke out between one of the black men and a white newsboy. One of the marchers apparently fired a shot as the young boy was being led away by a policeman. Then the police fired a volley into the black ranks, and the riot began. The anti-Republican whites included not only policemen, but firemen, ex-Rebel soldiers, and white thugs. Those blacks who could not escape fled into the institute. The mob pursued them and besieged the building.[12]

The report of Albert Hartsuff, an assistant surgeon in the United States Army, provided the grim statistics of the riot. The dead numbered 38, and 146 were wounded. The report of the city coroner detailed the nature of the wounds of the victims. The report mentioned, along with 155 others, Michael Hahn ("incised wound of head"), A. P. Dostie ("gun-shot wound of spine and sword-thrust of stomach"), and William Henry Hire ("pistol wound of hand and contused wound of side, severe").[13] Ten policemen were injured, none seriously, and one white rioter was killed. (This was E. H. Cenas, a medical student who inadvertently stepped in front of a policeman's pistol. "The pistol ball cut the carotid artery.")[14] The police arrested 261 blacks and 4 whites, all radicals.[15]

These are the essential facts concerning the background and course of the riot. Two important questions, however, are open to debate. Did white radicals purposely provoke the conservative whites into attacking? Did white radicals act in collusion with the radical leaders in Congress to incite a confrontation?

A point of dispute among the press of the day was whether the delegates, especially A. P. Dostie, in effect invited violence by making incendiary remarks at the preliminary political rally held on July 27. The conservative press of New Orleans agreed that they had.

The *New Orleans Picayune* argued that the conservative whites had been unnecessarily provoked. "The sensibilities of the people of this city have been very much excited by the revolutionary purposes on the part of Ex-Conventionists of 1864," the newspaper stated. "A meeting of the partisans of these men was held on Friday night, at which the most inflammatory language was employed to incite Negroes to acts of violence. They were told if any white man should interfere with them, 'kill him.' It has been well understood that arms have been distributed among them."[16] Similarly, the *New Orleans Times* claimed that the riot had been brought on by "the incendiary teachings of a pestilent gang of demagogues."[17] The *Times* also claimed that white radicals had manipulated the blacks in the nefarious plot: "A band of poor, deluded negroes, urged on by unprincipled white men, have, unfortunately for themselves, been the principle [*sic*] sufferers. Armed with pistols, clubs and razors, they collected in great numbers around Mechanics' Institute, for the avowed purpose of defending the revolutionary Jacobins who had raised the banner of negro suffrage. . . . Left to themselves, the negroes never would have joined in a treasonable scheme to overthrow the State Government." The article concluded that "the riot was commenced in every instance by negroes, spurred on by white men."[18]

This conservative view of the riot, however, was not limited to New Orleans's Democratic press. E. P. Brooks, New Orleans correspondent for the *New York Times,* was in New Orleans from July 1 until November 1, 1866, and was an eyewitness to the riot.[19] Shortly after arriving in the city, he reported that "there is plenty of immorality here" and "loyalty is at a discount."[20] On the other hand, Brooks apparently was no advocate of black rights. He explained that New Orleans contained "numberless native Americans of 'African scent' which forcibly reminded one of the existences of our free institutions."[21] Moreover, Brooks disapproved of the radical plan to disfranchise the ex-Confederates.[22] And he agreed that the radicals had exceeded the bounds of propriety at the meeting. Although not making specific reference to Dr. Dostie, Brooks reported, "I have heard Sumner, Stevens, and Wendell Phillips speak their political sentiments; but, never before did I hear Radicalism until this meeting [the July 27 rally] as it fell from the lips of Southern Union speakers."[23] The minority (Democratic) report of the congressional riot committee held that "the incendiary speeches, revolutionary acts and threatened violence of the conventionists" that night led directly to and, indeed, were calculated to bring on military intervention, and, ultimately radical rule.[24]

Contemporary Democrats and orthodox historians alike point to the key role played by A. P. Dostie. In the compilation of documents relating to Reconstruction selected and edited by Walter L. Fleming, he includes excerpts from a speech (under the heading "Speeches of a Radical Agitator") made by Dostie before a black audience on the evening of July 27. "I want the Negroes to have the right of suffrage, and we will give them this right to vote." Dostie was reported to have shouted: "There will be another meeting here to-morrow night, and on Monday I want you to come in your power. I want no cowards here. I want only brave men to come, who will stand by us, and we will stand by them. We have three hundred thousand black men with white hearts. Also one hundred thousand good and true Union white men, who will fight for and beside the black race against the hell-hound rebels. We are four hundred thousand to three hundred thousand, and can not only whip but exterminate the other party." If the ex-Confederates dared interfere with the convention, Dostie allegedly threatened, "the streets of New Orleans will run with blood!"[25] The speech was also cited by John Rose Ficklen and Claude G. Bowers in their orthodox histories.[26]

The New Orleans Democratic press and the *New York Times,* however, presented only one side of the story. Richard L. Shelly, a reporter for the *New York Tribune,* also witnessed the July 27 rally and the riot itself. Shelly spent considerable time with Brooks in New Orleans, and the two correspondents wrote and filed their dispatches on the riot at the same time. But unlike Brooks, Shelly "most heartily" sympathized with the objectives of the delegates.[27] As for the July 27 rally, Shelly denied that Dostie and the other radical leaders had created a volatile atmosphere. At the congressional hearings on the riot, he explained that he had stood only a few feet away from Dostie during the rally. According to Shelly, Dostie merely told his audience to defend themselves if they were attacked. Other than that, there was nothing in his speech "calculated to excite animosity or hostile action."[28]

Two other friendly witnesses also observed the rally. John L. Anden, a former secretary to General N. P. Banks and the official shorthand reporter for the convention, testified to the peaceful nature of the July 27 rally: "There was a large meeting, and the speakers addressed the audience favoring Negro suffrage, and telling them that the convention, which would meet on the following Monday, would give the right of suffrage to the colored people. The audience was chiefly composed of colored people. There were no violent proceedings at that meeting. I reported the speeches made in the hall, but those made outside of the building I did not report. The speakers inside made no call for the Negroes to come armed to protect the convention, or anything of the kind. On the contrary, they were advised to be patient and keep quiet, and not urge the matter too strongly."[29] In testimony before the congressional riot committee, Stephen F. Fish, a riot victim and nephew of W. R. Fish, a delegate to the rump convention, also denied that the speakers at the rally incited to violence. "The sentiments uttered at that meeting were radical; that cannot be disputed," he conceded, but no one, including Dostie, Hahn, or Waples, made inflammatory remarks.[30] When asked specifically to describe the character of Dostie's speech that evening, young Fish replied:

> Towards the close of his speech he used this language. I will repeat one sentence almost word for word, and this was the language that looked most towards violence or incendiaries of any that I heard there. They were mostly Negroes there. It was a procession formed of Negroes.

> They had come to the meeting, and Dr. Dostie liked to make a demonstrative speech. He took pleasure in doing so. In his speech he called them brethren and so forth. Near the close of his speech he said: "Now, friends, go home peaceably, quietly; make no noise; disturb no person"; "but," said he, "I learn"—which was true, too—"that there are prowling bands of armed men out to waylay you. As you separate, go home. If you are insulted by any of these bands of men, pay no attention to them; go home right by them without saying a word to them; but if they strike you, kill them." That was the substance of his last sentence, and nearly word for word. That was spoken from the steps of the City Hall, and that was the only language I heard in his speech that encouraged any violence at all, and that was in self-defense.[31]

The Scalawags and the Conspiracy Thesis

No one can know for sure exactly what was said on the night of July 27. Nevertheless, whatever Dostie, Waples, Hahn, and the other radicals said to create the volatile atmosphere, a more serious charge is that the riot resulted from a scheme concocted between white radicals in Louisiana and their leaders in Congress to establish Republican rule in the state.

A *New York Times* editorial of August 1, 1866, espoused the conspiracy thesis. The leading radicals in Congress, the paper charged, wanted the "illegal" convention to meet. Adjournment of the current congressional session could be delayed, and Congress could approve a constitution that enfranchised the blacks and took the vote away from ex-Confederates. Fortunately, the editorial maintained, the good sense of Congress had prevailed, and Congress adjourned on time. However, the *Times* concluded that "the connection between the Radicals in Congress and the Negro suffrage revolutionists in New Orleans does not admit of dispute. To them, jointly, belongs the responsibility of the loss of life that has occurred. . . . The poor Negro is a cats paw [*sic*] in their hands, to be sacrificed if need be, in furtherance of the effort to entrench themselves in power.[32] The Democratic minority report prepared by Benjamin M. Boyer of the congressional committee that investigated the riot came to the same conclusion as the *Times:* "And if there be any members of the federal government who are indirectly responsible for the bloody result," the report read, "they are those members of the present Congress whoever they may be [a veiled reference to Thaddeus Stevens and the other radicals on the Joint Committee on Reconstruction] who encouraged these men by their counsels and promised to them their individual and official support."[33]

John Rose Ficklen (who refers to the event as the "So-called Riot of July 30, 1866") quotes approvingly the minority report's conspiracy thesis in his orthodox history of Louisiana Reconstruction.[34] Claude G. Bowers, in his entertaining, but distorted history of Reconstruction, also adheres to the conspiracy thesis. "Had there been no convention, there would have been no massacre; and there would have been no convention without the encouragement of the Radical leaders in Washington," he concludes.[35] The whole scheme, Bowers reasons, was part of a "mad revolutionary project."[36]

The conspiracy theory rests largely on a rumor to the effect that Benjamin F. Flanders had received a letter from two members of the Joint Committee on Reconstruction encouraging him and the other Louisiana radicals to proceed with the plan to reconvene the 1864 convention. (The theory received more credence when the congressional riot committee failed to call Flanders as a witness.)[37] Although no one testified to seeing the document itself, Eugene Tisdale (a Johnson supporter) claimed that prominent radicals told him about its existence: "I . . . had conversations with [R. King] Cutler and [John] Henderson, who told me that instructions had been received from two members of the Reconstruction committee to assemble the convention at all hazards." When asked to reveal the exact contents of the mysterious letter, Tisdale replied, "It requested them to assemble the convention, and states: 'The great distance you are from us prevents us from telling exactly how to proceed. You will act your own judgment [*sic*]; do the best you can, and trust to consequences.' That was about the way it was read to me."

Each member of the Joint Committee, on the other hand, denied under oath that he had written the letter. Moreover, when Rufus K. Howell had gone to Washington to ascertain the view of Republican congressmen about the advisability of calling the convention, he was disappointed. "I had the impression that there were Congressmen who had suggested this reassembling of the convention, and the submission of their work to

Congress for its acceptance. This I did not find to be the case," he swore before the riot committee.

E. H. Durell, who had refused to recall the convention, also testified to the failure of Washington radicals to support the Louisiana radicals. Despite his doubts regarding the legality of the plan and the danger of a white reaction, Durell implied that he would have recalled the delegates if the radicals in Washington had given him their support. On June 18, 1866, in what was really a plea for their backing, he telegraphed William Pitt Fessenden, Thaddeus Stevens, and George Boutwell asking their advice. Durell provided the committee with a copy of the telegram:

> By resolution of the Louisiana convention of sixty-four ('64,) as president I am authorized to reconvene said convention. If I do so and it amends the constitution of sixty-four, and gives suffrage to the black, and its action is ratified by the people, white and black, will said amended constitution be recognized by our Union friends in Congress as valid; and will the senators and representatives elected there under be admitted by Congress? I am unacquainted with the features of the two (2) enabling bills introduced by you. Shall I call this convention, and when; now or in the fall? If you think it desirable I will come to Washington to confer with you. Please telegraph reply, and write full advices. I am strongly pressed to issue the call, and desire your earliest answer immediately.

The Washington radicals apparently did not answer. "I spoke to Mr. Stevens when I was there [Washington, D.C.] in July last," Durell testified; "I asked him if he received my dispatch. He said he did. I asked him why he had not made me a reply. He said they had nothing to say on the subject, and so said nothing."

Reynolds claims that the congressional radicals had no overriding motive to support the convention recall. "It must be remembered that [the radicals] were at that time locked in a bitter struggle with President Johnson for control of reconstruction," he writes. "While they were in the ascendancy after the passage in June of the Fourteenth Amendment, they had by no means won the battle yet. The amendment still had to be ratified. The New Orleans riot and Johnson's disastrous 'swing around the circle' had not yet occurred to affect Northern public opinion. Victory in the all-important fall congressional elections was in the balance. Therefore, the Radicals were not likely to stake their chances of triumph upon a coup of such dubious legality as that which the Louisiana convention proposed."[38] Joe Gray Taylor, in his extensive revisionist survey of Louisiana Reconstruction, concurs with Reynolds's position.[39]

Although no concrete evidence exists to link the congressional radicals with the recall scheme, as Reynolds points out, "There can be no doubt that the congressional Radicals would have preferred a Louisiana constitution which enfranchised Negroes and disenfranchised ex-Rebels." Undoubtedly, that "Thaddeus Stevens and other Radicals gave some degree of encouragement to the conventionists also is indisputable. But it is highly unlikely that they *conspired* with the Louisiana Radicals or promised congressional support of their work."[40]

The Scalawags Make Their Case

The scalawags who testified before the congressional riot committee, and the military commission that investigated the affair, denied that the radicals had incited violence at the Friday rally or that they had worked in concert with the radicals in Congress. They provided a critical, if not entirely unprejudiced, account in sworn testimony given by Ezra Hiestand, Rufus King Cutler, Rufus Waples, William Henry Hire, James Madison Wells, and Thomas Jefferson Durant, as well as A. P. Dostie's deathbed deposition.

Ezra Hiestand (fifty years old, a resident in Louisiana since 1829, and, in 1866, a judge in the New Orleans Civil and Criminal Department) testified that he attended the Friday evening rally of July 27. Both blacks and whites were in attendance. From a rostrum set out on the street, Michael Hahn, A. P. Dostie, and Hiestand himself rallied the crowd. "There were some intemperate remarks made by some of the speakers denunciatory of the rebels and their cause," Hiestand admitted. "The blacks were also particularly informed that, being citizens of the United States, they had the right to stand upon their rights as freemen, and if attacked that day, the right to defend themselves." Dostie had said something to the effect that "it was time to show the rebels that they were not to enjoy power any longer, and that they ought to be hung," but Hiestand was unsure of the exact words. Hiestand contended that meeting was generally "as orderly as any public meeting usually is; there was no disturbance at all; there was cheering of speakers . . . but no disturbance." When the meeting adjourned, the delegates and their followers formed a procession of between two and three thousand and marched to the New Orleans city hall, "where several speeches were made . . . but nothing was said or done at either place" that could be considered inflammatory: "After the speeches were made at the City Hall the crowd dispersed [about 10:30 p.m.], and so far as I know from the reports of the newspapers of the next day, no disturbance took place during the night."

On Saturday, Hiestand noted the tense and hostile atmosphere in the city: "The next morning in passing along the streets I could hear very denunciatory remarks made against the idea of a convention assembling, and also against the parties who had been at the meeting the previous night. . . . I heard one man, whose name I cannot give, say that it was determined to kill all of them rather than that the convention should meet." Sunday he observed "little knots of men talking excitedly," but the city was at least outwardly calm. On Monday, however, Hiestand saw a large number of men in the streets "wearing a kind of blue badge or ribbon in the buttonhole of their coats." Some had pistols in their belts concealed under their coats. Then, at noon, he heard what he interpreted to be a general signal: "an unusual alarm was run upon the fire-bells; the fire-bells being rung by electric telegraph, an alarm of twelve taps was struck." This was the same signal, Hiestand informed the committee, that the Confederate authorities had used to summon the city militia in case of a Federal attack. Hiestand noticed that the police responded to the call as if the signal had been prearranged: "That portion of them which I saw were going from the stations of the second district towards Canal Street marching two and two, with the bands upon their hats marked with the words 'city police,' and the number of the wearer, so far as I could see, reversed. I stepped up pretty close to where they were passing and could plainly see the bands upon their hats, but could not read them, although under ordinary circumstances they were easily distinguished."

Later in the day, a former business partner of Hiestand informed the scalawag that the police were planning to kill him. "I was notified or requested . . . under no circumstances to go near the State-house, for if

I did so I would certainly be murdered, stating that he had heard some of the policemen and others making inquiry for me, asking 'where is Hiestand? We want to get at that God-damned old son-of-a-bitch.'" On a streetcar that afternoon, Hiestand was approached by a young man who stood squarely before him and shouted, "What the hell is your hide worth today? By God, if you remain in this city until six o'clock to-morrow your hide won't hold shucks." Later, about five o'clock, Hiestand was walking downtown when someone yelled, "There goes one of the scoundrels that ought to be killed." Hiestand did not attend the convention. Under cross-examination by Congressman Samuel Shellabarger, he was evasive: "I left my office about twelve o'clock for the purpose of going to the convention; crossed Canal Street, and went about half a block towards the convention, until I got to St. Charles Street; then, for some reason or other which I cannot explain, I went up St. Charles Street . . . and turned into an alley." It seems obvious that Hiestand changed his mind about attending and hid in the alley for a time to avoid being attacked. Considering the threats leveled against him, Hiestand's strategic retreat was the better part of valor, although he seemed reluctant to admit before the committee that he was afraid.

On July 15, Hiestand and other noted Unionists had been warned to leave the city. "The notices were upon pieces of paper about four inches wide, and addressed in each case to the individual by name." His notice, for example, read, "Judge Ezra Hiestand: Beware! Ten days. Duly notified. Begone!" The anonymous message "was signed with some cabalistic characters, and below were rough representations of a pistol, a bowie-knife, and a dagger."

Rufus King Cutler (forty-one, a radical, and a resident of Louisiana for twenty-two years) also spoke to the black radicals at the July 27 rally. "I firmly believed, and so said," he testified later, "that the time had arrived when we should so change our constitution as to extend negro and colored suffrage, that we should adopt the constitutional amendment, and that it behooved us now to disfranchise rebels. I spoke of President Johnson. I did not speak lightly of the gentlemen, nor kindly." Later, as a delegate to the Monday assembly, Cutler observed directly the terrible events of that July Monday. About 1:00 p.m., he testified, he heard shots being fired outside the hall. "I stepped to the side window and saw policemen firing at colored people on Dryades Street, and ten or twelve negroes throwing brickbats at the policemen," he said. "At about the same time many persons, both white and colored, ran upstairs into the vestibule, in the front part of the hall, exclaiming that the police were firing on the colored people in the street. A moment afterwards shots were fired from the streets through the windows into the hall on the Common Street side." After a brief pause, more shots were fired. The delegates tried to remain orderly, and offered no resistance. But the police continued with the attack. Above the din of firing, he heard someone shout, "We have the conventioneers now—the damned Yankee sons of bitches—and will kill them all, damn them."

Cutler related that the delegates had tried to surrender by waving white handkerchiefs and by sticking an American flag with a white handkerchief on the end through a window. Nothing helped, and the police charged again into the hall. Cutler fled upstairs to the third story. There he remained with several radicals until four policemen discovered and arrested them. As he was being led out, he looked into the main assembly room: "The hall was all bloody and strewn with dead, and the chairs and railings were all broken to pieces, and there were bullet-holes all over the walls. I stayed perhaps a few seconds looking at it; the floor was covered with blood, and in walking downstairs the blood splashed under the soles of my boots."

Rufus Waples (forty-one, and an active radical) attended the Friday evening rally. "It was a political meeting," he informed the committee. "It was very well-tempered in the hall. I was not out of doors, and I cannot speak of the meeting outside. In the hall everything was well-behaved; no disturbance whatever and no unusual excitement." When asked if the speeches that evening were incendiary, Waples replied: "I heard no one . . . advise the negroes to come armed to the convention to defend it, and I did not understand at the time by the speeches, or by any previous conversation, that there would be any difficulty at all on Monday, and I certainly did not anticipate any when I was on my way to the convention at one o'clock on the day of the massacre. I was in conference with the radical Union men . . . and not one of them ever intimated to me that they were going there armed or that they expected any conflict." Waples did testify that the New Orleans police, most of whom were ex-Confederates, were hostile to the radicals. He also knew many prominent ex-Rebels who were quite outspoken in their hostility to the

Union: "I heard them frequently speak of not being ashamed of having engaged in the rebellion. I heard them glory in it. I know they were in the habit of boasting over their victories and laurels won."

William Henry Hire also testified regarding the events of Friday evening, July 27. According to him, "Our friends spoke in the most radical way. I will state to you that I heard Dr. Dostie distinctly say, 'Now, my friends, go peaceably home; go orderly; do not disturb anybody; but if anybody disturbs you, kill him.'" There was that evening, he continued, "a great deal of bold, rash talk by the members of the Republican Party; but I do not think any of us anticipated any serious difficulty, or we would have gone armed." Those present were told to act only if the ex-Rebels attacked them. "I heard some discussion among ourselves that the Southern people had a great deal of braggadocios and it would not do to give way to them." According to Hire, the riot began when a white man fired a shot at one of the black marchers at the corner of Baronne and Canal Streets. A policeman fired a second shot, and "afterwards it became a general melee, and many men were shot." The white mob and the police, Hire maintained, appeared to work in concert. "There was an apparent understanding between those we call confederates and the police."

On his way to the convention on Monday, Hire noticed that groups of "confederates" were assembling on the street corners: "I know many of these men, by name as well as by character, as unmistakably confederates, and I felt some hesitation in passing through them at the corner of Canal and Dryades Streets, but, being perhaps rather rash, I boldly walked through them. I could see that they were armed." Shortly after the meeting began, shots were fired by the police outside the building. The police and the white mob then forced the doors open and fired again. "I want to be particular in that statement, for everybody in that hall would know whether what I am stating is correct or not," Hire claimed. "It appeared to me that they discharged their four or six-shooters as rapidly as possible."

The trapped radicals stood in silent panic for an instant and then drove their tormentors back with chairs and pieces of railings, repeating this action four or five times during the next hour. At last the mob entered the hall. What followed, Hire maintained, were acts of abject brutality. "At one time I saw a colored man kneel down and pray to go out; the only reply the policeman made was the click of a pistol, discharging a shot into his bowels. I saw men shot in this way by policemen several times." But the white delegates were also targets that day. Dostie said to Hire: "They will kill me; they are bound to kill me." A white conventionist by the name of Horton shouted: "Stop firing; we surrender; we make no resistance." At that moment, a policeman shot Horton in the arm. Horton and several other white radicals began waving their handkerchiefs in a pathetic effort to stop the killing. When Hire attempted to leave the hall, he was repeatedly clubbed by a policeman. "At the bottom of the steps, as I came into the street," Hire told the committee, "I was met by five or six parties, each of whom struck me, some with staves and others with pieces of chairs." Then a shot passed through his fingers and someone stabbed him in the chest near the heart. Hire described his torture in vivid detail: "I did not know when I was stabbed. I presume that when I was struck four or five blows I was stabbed at the same time, and that the reason why I was not seriously injured was that in trying to dodge the blow the knife glanced off, and went on the external rib. When I got to the corner of Common and Dryades, a young druggist whom I knew called out, 'Here is Dr. Hire, the great abolitionist'; upon which, a set was made on me from behind. I was driven into the gutter; when the policeman let go of me I fell with my head against the stones in the gutter . . . I was nauseated, sick, and weak from the loss of blood." At about 2:00 p.m., a policeman took Hire to the station house.

James Madison Wells observed the riot in its early stages. That morning Wells was at work in the Mechanics' Institute. "While in my office," he testified, "a number of the members came in and were discussing the probability of a quorum and the possibility of their being arrested for there had been rumor that the sheriff intended to arrest them." About 11:00 a.m., he left his office and went to see General Sheridan, who unknown to Wells was absent from the state. "When I returned," Wells said, "I found that the riot was increasing to a fearful extent, and a friend of mine . . . said, 'This is a terrible riot. I am apprehensive your son is killed, as he is a member of the convention. You had better leave the city and go home.'" Wells fled the hall and returned to his home in Jefferson City, a New Orleans suburb. Shortly afterward his son arrived and told him of the riot. Under questioning, Wells defended his action in recalling the convention. Inexplicably, Boyer, the only Democrat on the congressional investigation committee, declined to cross-examine Wells.

Thomas Jefferson Durant also gave evidence on the tense, anti-Unionist atmosphere in New Orleans during the weekend before the riot and on the events of Monday. In fact, Durant considered the situation so volatile that he refused to take part in the convention. "I was one of those who differed from those of our Union friends who thought the president of the convention . . . had the right to call it together." But Durant stated, "Whether he had the right or not, I thought it unwise, with the feeling existing at that time, inasmuch as it was supposed the convention intended to extend the right of suffrage to blacks. I thought it injudicious and dangerous." Ironically, Durant had been one of the most outspoken advocates of black suffrage in Louisiana.

The first warning that there would be trouble when the delegates assembled came to Durant by way of a French-speaking black man. Durant informed the committee: "He told me that he had occasion to rise very early in the morning, and that he was standing by a fence which separated his property from the street, and that a cab drove by, immediately opposite where he was standing, although concealed from his view by the fence, and some person in it addressed another on the sidewalk. The conversation indicated that there was a plot to attack the black people that day. One was soliciting the other to aid them. Just at this moment some noise or other cause interrupted them, and the cab drove off." Durant advised him to inform General Baird of the conversation. The man replied that he had attempted to see the general, but he could not get access to him. Durant then told him to get in touch with General Sheridan. If necessary, Durant said, he would arrange a meeting. Durant took the Negro's tale seriously, and he felt that it was an accurate reflection of the black community's concern. "The feelings of the black people had, of course, become deeply enlisted in the convention," the scalawag lawyer added, "and it was on that account that these men [the black leaders] came to consult me. I happened to be placed in such relations toward them as to be very usually consulted."

Durant remained in his office the day of the riot. "While I was there, writing at my desk, I heard the first symptoms of tumult—that particular sound which designates a mob," he said. Rushing to a window, Durant observed about thirty policemen marching two by two "with revolvers in their hands." As they approached Carondelet Street, the officers "immediately commenced firing indiscriminately," according to Durant.

"There were several negroes in the neighborhood," he continued, "and they shot and beat such as were there."

Despite the firing, the street filled up with people, and the shots and commotion continued until late afternoon. About 4:00 p.m., Durant, peeking through his window, observed Michael Hahn "in the clutches of several policemen." He provided the committee with this description of Hahn's plight: "He is lame, one foot is shorter than the other, and of course walks with difficulty. He was handled with great violence. His clothing was ragged—torn by violence—his hat was off, and he was bleeding profusely, and covered with blood in a way that led me to suppose he was dying. The mob was shouting around him, and I thought they wanted to kill him."

Durant observed other whites and blacks being attacked. He saw two carts loaded with dead and wounded pass by his window. Although he remained in his office, Durant became concerned that he, too, would be attacked. An informant, whose name Durant refused to divulge, warned him that he was marked by the conservatives for vengeance. Frightened by the violence and threats, Durant arranged for a closed carriage to meet him in an alley behind his office. He then ran to his house, gathered some clothing, and made his way to a friend's plantation near Carrollton. There he boarded a steamer. He fled all the way to Washington, D.C., never to return to New Orleans.[41]

A. P. Dostie provided his own eyewitness account of the New Orleans riot in a deathbed deposition. The document is preserved among the papers of the military commission that investigated the affair from August 10 to September 5, 1866. During the hearing, the board of inquiry, accompanied by a shorthand reporter, went to the Hôtel-Dieu (a private hospital operated by the Sisters of Charity). The commissioners asked Dostie to describe the disturbance at the Mechanics' Institute. Dostie testified that he went there with "the most peaceful intentions." Only twenty-seven delegates answered the roll call. "Undoubtedly," he stated, "in consequence of the fears of the members." A recess was called in order to round up the missing delegates. At that point, Dostie said, the police moved toward the institute, breaking windows and firing into the building. He swore that to his knowledge the members of the convention were unarmed, and thus helpless before the attack. In Dostie's view, the firing was part of a plot to destroy the radicals: "I saw that there was a deliberate massacre planned of our party; that those who were to be massacred in the most diabolical manner were Hahn, W. R. Fish [a carpetbagger], Shaw [unidentified in the testimony but probably Alfred Shaw], myself, and such men, and sure enough it proved so." The delegates tried to barricade the door with chairs, hoping that the military would soon come to their rescue. "It was too late for that," Dostie continued, "they got complete possession of us. I wanted to be taken prisoner with Governor Hahn for the purpose of protecting him, for he was lame, and they refused that and dragged me away." Dostie begged the policeman to protect him, to arrest him if necessary and take him to jail. When they came out of the building, however, the policeman turned the dentist over to two other officers: "I went along some distance and a policeman just drew his pistol, and I do not know what his name was. A dozen rushed at me. I was stabbed and shot. . . . In the attack on me, I was told there was a man dressed in white who jumped upon me and stabbed me in the back." Other whites, he claimed, stabbed him with pen knives. Dostie then fell to the ground and pretended to be dead. "They took me finally and put me in a wagon. I kept my eyes closed," he stated. At the conclusion of his deposition, Dostie described one of his tormentors: "He had dark eyes, black eye-brows, black side whiskers, a mustache not large, and black hair. His teeth were broken. . . . He shot me behind the spinal column. . . . He was a man above the medium size."[42]

Others collaborated Dostie's story. In testimony before the congressional committee in December 1866, J. B. Jourdain (a thirty-four-year-old black witness) stated: "I saw the crowd, after he was shot, get hold of him by the legs and start off running with him. He was lying on the banquette. After he was brought out by the policeman and shot, he was left lying on the banquette till these men got hold of him. Then they commenced hurrahing. They took him by the legs and dragged him from where they surrounded him. They were a parcel of firemen and young men that had white handkerchiefs about their necks."[43] William Hanksworth (a twenty-nine-year-old civil engineer and New Orleans resident since 1852) also provided an eyewitness account of the attack on Dostie: "I saw a crowd about the Institute dragging something with them. I did not know what it was. I was told it was Dr. Dostie. . . . The crowd was hurrahing and shouting . . . I saw a cart brought down and something thrown into it. I was told it was Dr. Dostie. I saw boys not more than ten or twelve years old running around Canal Street with revolvers cocked in their hands and raising a row."[44] Dostie died six days after the attack. The conservative *New Orleans Times* offered this suggestion for the proper disposal of the radical's remains:

> What to do with him? This is a practical age in which we live, and we must turn everything to account. There are a great many suffering negroes in the South, in spite of the Freedmen's Bureau, and the number of plantations demanding the hoe. Let Dostie's skin be forthwith stripped and sold to Barnum—the proceeds to go to the Freedmen's Bureau and negro newspapers, to be used by them for the benefit of negroes who have no taste for work. Dostie's body will make good soap. Let him be boiled down, preparatory to being distributed in bars to Yankee "school marms." Delicious will be the kisses by those angular females from ebony cheeks, late lathered with sweet scented Dostie.[45]

No doubt the newspaper's humor was not lost upon the New Orleans police department. The Democratic *New Orleans Daily Picayune* echoed the sentiments, if not the tastelessness of the *Times,* in its report of Dostie's demise: "Thus ends the worldly career of a manimaniac [*sic*] upon a subject [black rights], who, in his heated infatuation has caused much strife and bloodshed. We draw the veil upon the past."[46]

The testimony of the scalawags cannot be taken at face value. But when combined with the other evidence in the records of the congressional committee which investigated the riot, the records of the military commission, and the articles published in the *New York Times* and the *New York Tribune,* as well as other sources, a more comprehensive picture takes shape.

The evidence indicates that the political rally held on the evening of July 27 did in fact create a volatile situation. Even if A. P. Dostie did not make the violent speech that the conservatives attributed to him, other sources reveal that the radical orations that night were certain, if not calculated, to incite violence. In a city seething with pro-Confederate feeling and racial hatred, a small group of white men—scalawags—stood before a black audience and described a brave new world where black men were as good as white men, a world where black men voted and held public office. And the ex-Rebels could love it or leave it. No real evidence exists to show that the scalawags schemed to create violence and thereby bring on military and congressional rule, but the white critics were right at least in this: the speeches made on the Friday before the riot could hardly have failed to bring on a violent confrontation.

This, of course, does not justify the action of the police and their white allies. Members of the press offered strong evidence that the attack was premeditated. On September 2, 1866, the *New Orleans Tribune,* a radical newspaper, published a letter from O. F. Breaux. He reported overhearing two men discussing a plan to "run the Convention into a pool of blood." One of the men went on to say "that there was a plot on foot to intimidate by assassinations the people of color."[47]

While the *Tribune* report is suspect because of the paper's radical political orientation, the accounts of New York correspondents support the thesis of a premeditated attack. Even Brooks reported to the *New York Times:* "It is asked, was the riot preconcerted? It plainly was! There was no regularly organized premeditated attack at any one point or time, but there was a general understanding among all of the young bloods about town that a riot would occur. I heard for days before the occurrence just such talk in the hotels and restaurants, and on the streets."[48] In a similar vein, Shelly explained at the riot hearings "that there was a conspiracy upon the part of a great many to forcibly disperse that convention, and prevent the facts from being made known at the north."[49]

The correspondents for the *Times* and the *Tribune* likewise agreed that the New Orleans police led the attack on the members of the convention, that it was, in effect, a police riot. Brooks filed a report based partly on unnamed sources, but mostly on direct observation. He reported that after the procession of blacks entered the Mechanics' Institute, police entered the building. While the police claimed that they were merely trying to arrest black rioters, one of the police mounted a platform inside the building and drew a pistol. The conventioneers, a few of whom were armed, drove out the police, who then encountered a large group of blacks. A struggle ensued. Police reinforcements arrived and, aided by a white mob, attacked the institute, "firing pistols at any one they could see inside the building." A gun battle took place between the police and those inside the institute. After the men inside the institute ran out of ammunition, they tried to escape, but were "either arrested or shot down." Brooks did not think that any blacks got away from the building alive.

Although the police "behaved well toward the white prisoners, comparatively speaking," a policeman shot Dr. Dostie in the back and "after he fell, a crowd jumped on him and cut him horribly with knives."[50]

The police, according to Brooks's report, did not stop at shooting down the conventioneers and their black supporters. They obtained some wagons to carry off the dead. At the bottom of one wagon were two wounded men. "A policeman mounted the cart and shoving his revolver down between the bodies on top, killed the poor fellows, with one shot for each."[51]

At the hearings on the disorders, Shelly testified that after the riot he met the chief of police at Moreau's restaurant. The chief admitted nervously that "outrages had been committed by his force." Although he told Shelly that he planned to have these men punished, they never were.[52]

The conservative press of New Orleans presented the police in a far more favorable light. The *New Orleans Times* explained lamely that the police had done their best to prevent the mob from attacking those who were trying to escape from the institute. "Only when a person attempted to escape was he fired at." Even the *Times,* however, admitted that there was "testimony of some firing at prisoners by policemen that was both wanton and, as it appeared, unnecessary."[53] Similarly, the New Orleans grand jury concluded that, while the police "behaved with humanity" and "used no unnecessary violence," there were "a few exceptions."[54]

Whether they intended it or not, the scalawags and their conservative enemies created a situation that would completely alter the political order in Louisiana. The New Orleans Riot of July 30, 1866, was a major factor in the coming of radical Reconstruction not only in Louisiana, but throughout the South. The New Orleans disturbance, coupled with the riot in Memphis in May 1866, the rejection of the Fourteenth Amendment by the Johnson state legislatures, and the passage of the Black Codes, turned northern public opinion against Johnson's plan of Reconstruction and paved the way for more radical measures. Although the riot marked the advent of radical Reconstruction, it also marked the high tide of scalawag influence in Louisiana. It was, as George Rable argues, an organized act of terrorism aimed at the destruction of the radicals.[55] A. P. Dostie, the most outspoken Louisiana radical, was dead, and Thomas Jefferson Durant, a scalawag with a keen eye for constitutional issues, had fled the state. Though the atmosphere in New Orleans remained vicious following the riot for both white and black Republicans, some scalawags remained in Louisiana and in the Republican Party, but in a diminished role. Now the carpetbaggers and their black allies came forward to assume leadership of the Republican movement in Louisiana.

6

THE SCALAWAGS AND THE CARPETBAG PRINCE

> All of us were soon caught up to our eyes in politics, made so by conditions which none of us could control.
>
> —HENRY CLAY WARMOTH, *War, Politics, and Reconstruction: Stormy Days in Louisiana*

The Scalawags and the Coming of Radical Reconstruction

In August and September 1866, Andrew Johnson made his controversial "swing around the circle," a speaking tour in defense of his Reconstruction policies in opposition to the radical Republicans. Johnson's behavior during the "swing" was undignified, and the tour turned out to be a political blunder of the worst sort.[1] On September 8, Johnson delivered an address from the balcony of the Southern Hotel in St. Louis, Missouri. It was a dismal performance, but typical of his series of disastrous speeches. According to the *Missouri Democrat* (actually a Republican newspaper), Johnson said, in part: "Perhaps if you had a word or two on the subject of New Orleans, you might understand more about it than you do. If you will take up the riot at New Orleans, and trace it back to the radical Congress . . . you will find that the riot at New Orleans was substantially planned. . . . You will also find that the convention did assemble in violation of the law . . . and every man engaged in that rebellion—in that convention . . . I say that he was a traitor to the Constitution of the United States (cheers), and hence you will find that another rebellion was conceived, having its origin in the radical Congress." Not content with attacking the "radical Congress," the president went on to pour invective upon individual senators and representatives: "I have been maligned, I have been called Judas—Judas

Iscariot, and all that. *Judas, Judas Iscariot, Judas!* There was a Judas once, one of the twelve apostles. Oh! Yes, and these twelve apostles had a Christ. . . . If I have played the Judas, who has been my Christ that I have played the Judas with? Was it Thad Stevens? Was it Wendell Phillips? Was it Charles Sumner? . . . Are these the men that sit up and compare themselves with the Savior of men, and everybody that differs with them in opinion and try to stay and arrest their diabolical and nefarious policy, is to be denounced as a Judas?"[2] The speech, far from winning support for Johnson, helped turn the tide of northern public opinion against his policies. Considering the outrageous events in New Orleans, people in the North were appalled at his behavior.[3] Johnson was, in effect, delivering the eulogy at his own political funeral.

While Johnson was on the tour, scalawag Michael Hahn was making his own swing through the North. In an address delivered in Des Moines, Iowa, in early September 1866, Hahn attacked the president, his Reconstruction program, and his ex-Rebel supporters in Louisiana. In addition, Hahn made a strong plea for black suffrage. Andrew Johnson, Hahn stated, was directly responsible for the resurgence of Confederate power in Louisiana. At the end of the war, the Rebels had flocked back to the state and, with Johnson's pardons in their hands, seized control of the state government. "Johnson's policy emboldened them; and pardons were issued to them by the bushel." These ex-Rebels, Hahn went on, "received favors from Johnson while loyal and deserving men were ostracized and made to take back seats." Johnson had been at one time a strong Union man and an advocate of a harsh Reconstruction policy, but now the president "has forgot his old view of reconstruction which he advanced while he lived in Tennessee, or while running for Vice-President." "It was a grand theme for him at one time to denounce traitors," Hahn stated sarcastically, "but now this second Moses, found among the bulrushes of Tennessee, had changed his character and abandoned those who had found and taken him up." When James Madison Wells became governor of Louisiana, he had traveled to Washington, where he consulted privately with the president. Wells returned "a great friend of Johnson, a supporter of his policy, and he immediately made favorable endorsements on all applications for pardons, appointed rebels to office, and encouraged them in every way to enter the service of the State, and treated them with most extraordinary kindness." Wells, himself an ardent Union man, had been brought under Johnson's "evil influence." Armed with Johnson's pardons and supported by Wells, the Rebels "turned out of office all loyal men, and elected men on account of their persistent and conspicuous services in the rebel cause," Hahn continued. When they took control of the state legislature, the Confederates rebuilt the Mississippi River levees with public funds. Previously, the levees, which existed for the benefit of the rich planters, had been constructed with private monies. Yet ex-Rebels refused to pay taxes for the support of black schools. Union men had faithfully paid such taxes. The Rebel legislature also had the audacity to invite Mrs. Jefferson Davis to visit the state assembly and receive her with "great demonstration."

Hahn observed that many tributes had been paid to Andrew Johnson's "fearless and consistent loyalty." But in Louisiana there had lived a man "infinitely his superior in patriotic fervor and devotion to his country." That man was A. P. Dostie. And only "one month ago, in the city of New Orleans, he was brutally murdered by the minions of" Andrew Johnson. Hahn assured his Iowa audience that Dostie's death would be avenged.

Hahn then returned to the question of Reconstruction policy. The ex-Rebels must be disfranchised, he insisted. They cannot be trusted with the reins of power. Although they claimed to be loyal and "reconstructed," they remained in their hearts "unmitigated and unrepentant." The only way to prevent the ex-Rebels from returning to power was to give the vote to black men: "What the loyal men of the South desire as a remedy for all these evils . . . is impartial [that is, Negro] suffrage." Black suffrage was necessary to strengthen the position of the southern Unionists as well as fulfill a debt that the country owed to the black veterans of the Civil War. There could never be peace in the South, Hahn warned his audience, until black men voted. The new black voters, Hahn contended, opposed their old masters and supported the white Unionists: "They are not well educated," he said, "but they know their friends."

To those who insisted that blacks were not qualified by intelligence or education to participate in the political system, Hahn countered with the argument that, although uneducated, the southern Negroes were as well prepared to vote as white immigrants who came to America: "Of him [the immigrant] intellectual or educational qualification is not required. Then why demand it of the colored man?" Besides, the black man was far better qualified to vote than the wealthy white Rebels who now held the franchise. "The negro has intelligence enough to serve his country and hate treason," Hahn said. Hahn ended with an appeal to the audience to support the adoption of the Fourteenth Amendment: "Let me say to you, it is a debt you owe to us as Union men at the South, and to yourselves, if you wish to have peace."[4]

Hahn's bitter, passionate attack on Johnson did provide a reasonably accurate assessment of the political situation in Louisiana. Johnson's policy in the state was a disaster. The ex-Confederates had, in collaboration with Wells, dominated the state government to the detriment of southern Unionists. He was correct, too, in his judgment that southern Unionists needed black votes to counter the pro-Confederate reactionaries in Louisiana. It is interesting to note, however, that not once in the speech did Hahn mention the Republican Party by name. He interpreted the contest in Louisiana solely in terms of loyalty versus disloyalty. Although the Republican Party had been formally established in Louisiana for over a year, Hahn referred to its supporters as "unionists." Hahn's speech thus provides evidence of the appeal that the Republican Party had in Louisiana to former wartime Unionists. Hahn, and most other southern loyalists, saw the Republican Party as an extension of their Unionism. The ex-Rebels were despised not because they were Democrats, but because they were still at heart Confederates. Finally, the speech, so confident in tone, also reveals that Hahn sensed that the tide of public opinion was now running against Johnson and his ex-Confederate supporters.

Hahn was not the only Louisiana scalawag to attack Johnson's plan of Reconstruction; there was a dismal chorus of complaint. Between December 1866 and February 1867, Unionists appeared before the committee appointed by Congress to investigate the New Orleans Riot to express their anger toward the ex-Rebels and fear of their resurgence. Among those who testified were eleven of Hahn's fellows: James K. Belden, W. Jasper Blackburn, Rufus King Cutler, R. F. Daunoy, Thomas Jefferson Durant, Ezra Hiestand, William Henry Hire, Rufus K. Howell, B. L. Lynch, James Madison Wells, and Rufus Waples. Their testimony echoed the views expressed by Hahn in the Des Moines speech regarding the condition of southern loyalists, the need for military protection, and the absolute necessity of black suffrage and Rebel disfranchisement.

The scalawags testified that the southern Unionists in Louisiana were vilified and persecuted:[5]

> A degree of bitterness exists now on the part of the rebel population of Louisiana against the loyal population which is scarcely to be described. —James K. Belden
>
> In the city of New Orleans many societies have been formed by the rebels, such as the society among merchants not to employ a clerk in their business except he be of rebel sentiments. —Rufus King Cutler
>
> They scoff and scorn those of their neighbors who do hold social intercourse with (as they call them) Yankees. —Rufus King Cutler
>
> I was physician to the Screwman's Benevolent Association before the war; one of these men . . . went to Mayor Monroe for employment, stating he had a wife and six children to support. The Mayor said, "So you were the first man to join the Yankees, and you said you liked the old flag. I have no place for you." —William Henry Hire
>
> The feeling of enmity against the government and against southern loyalists is, in my opinion, more intense than it has been the last twelve months, and, if possible, more intense than it was during the war. —Rufus K. Howell
>
> I know young men who have been driven from their places of business. I know how it affects my business. It affects me very much, individually. I am a member of the bar, and it affects me very seriously. —B. L. Lynch

Rebel bitterness toward southern Unionists and resistance to Reconstruction was so great that military occupation was an absolute necessity, they testified:

> Without military support, I would not remain there [Louisiana], gentlemen, an hour—not one hour; and I think when I speak for myself I speak for all who would be able to get away. —James K. Belden
>
> My impression is that it would be unsafe, if those whose duty it is to preserve order were not aided by the military forces of the United States. —Thomas Jefferson Durant

* * *

Along with military protection, the scalawags recommended black suffrage and ex-Rebel disfranchisement:

> We have from thirty to thirty-five thousand Negro and colored voters in [Louisiana], and about twenty-eight to thirty thousand white voters. We could have all the Negro and colored men to vote with the Union men, and that, with the disfranchisement of the leading rebels, would give the ascendancy to the Unionists, and I think they could sustain themselves. I think that with a sufficient military force to enforce these provisions, we could establish a government . . . and we could sustain it after its establishment. —Rufus King Cutler
>
> The right of suffrage should then be conferred upon all the people of the State, white and black, and upon such disloyal people as is thought might be trusted. As to what proportion that should be, I do not know. I think we should avoid having too large a proportion of dissatisfied men among us. —Rufus Waples
>
> I am in favor of excluding the leaders who went into the rebellion, but not the soldiers who were forced into the confederate army. —R. F. Daunoy
>
> I believe the extension of universal suffrage to the black race, and the disenfranchisement of those who aided and abetted the rebellion . . . would place the loyal people of the south in a majority. —James Madison Wells

Thomas Jefferson Durant, writing from Washington, D.C., summed up the Unionist position. "In my opinion," he stated," a territorial government should be established in Louisiana . . . supported by military force, and that it should be based on equal suffrage of all citizens without distinction of color; that it should be held in that subjection until it was clear that the citizens of the State were fit to carry on a State government . . . however long it might take."

Since the committee report was not published until after the radical victories in the congressional elections of 1866, the effect of this testimony on public opinion was limited. Nevertheless, the statements of the witnesses, along with testimony taken by the Joint Committee of Fifteen on Reconstruction (January and May 1866) and statements taken by the congressional committee on the Memphis race riot of 1866 (May 22 to

June 6, 1866),[6] presented a picture of the southern states that served to undermine congressional support for Andrew Johnson. Hans Trefousse writes: "The testimony showed that in the minds of many there was some question about the security of Union men in the former Confederacy. It also raised the problem of the treatment of the freedmen, the intransigency of the ex-Confederates, the difficulties encountered in carrying out Johnson's plan, and the almost universal resistance to Negro suffrage. Finally, the witnesses brought to the attention of observers the existence of violence in the region to be reconstructed." This evidence, and earlier newspaper reports of outrages, had a great impact, Trefousse concludes: "It is not surprising that Congress became convinced that more stringent measures were needed to protect both black and white Republicans in the South and safeguard the gains of the Civil War. Radical Reconstruction involving black suffrage and military rule was the result."[7]

Congress began the process of radical Reconstruction with the passage of the Reconstruction Act of March 2, 1867. This act divided the former Rebel states into five military districts, each governed by a military officer. (Louisiana and Texas comprised the Fifth District.) The military commanders had two essential duties: to protect lives and property and to supervise the election of delegates to a new state constitutional convention. Participation in the election of delegates and in the ratification elections was open to "male citizens . . . twenty-one years old and upward, of whatever race, color, or previous condition, who have been resident in [the state] for one year previous to the day of such election, except such as may be disfranchised for participation in the rebellion." The first Reconstruction Act also required that the new state constitution provide for black suffrage. Three other acts, passed in 1867 and 1868, strengthened congressional control in the South.[8]

General Philip Sheridan, an ardent Republican, commanded the Fifth Military District. Sheridan initiated the restoration process in Louisiana with the removal of state and local office holders, including Governor James Madison Wells, on June 3, 1867. Although Wells had now allied himself with the radicals, Sheridan resented his earlier collaboration with the conservatives. When the general and the governor clashed over state patronage appointments, Sheridan removed Wells from office and replaced him with Benjamin Franklin Flanders.[9] In a letter to Secretary of War Edwin M. Stanton, Sheridan justified his action: "I say now . . . that Governor Wells is a political trickster and a dishonest man. I have seen him . . . when I first came to this command, turn out all the Union men who had supported the government and put in their stead Rebel soldiers, some of whom had not yet doffed their gray uniform. I have seen him again during the July riot of 1866, skulk away . . . instead of coming out as a manly representative of the state and join those who were preserving the peace. I have watched him since, and his conduct has been as sinuous as the mark left in dust by the movement of a snake."

Sheridan's other removals included such prominent conservatives as Attorney General Andrew S. Herron, Mayor John T. Monroe, and the entire board of aldermen of New Orleans. His new appointments included several blacks. In fact, the general enforced the radical program with such enthusiasm that Johnson relieved Sheridan of his command in September 1867. On June 17, 1867, Sheridan issued an order for an election to be held on September 26 and 28 for delegates to the constitutional convention. According to the official count, 127,639 men were registered to vote in the election. Of this total, 44,732 voters, or 35 percent of the total, were white, and 82,907 voters, or 65 percent of the total, were black. The registration was carried out by registrars appointed by Sheridan. The general, however, found it difficult to find Unionists able or willing to serve as registrars. "Few of those appointed were distinguished enough before or after 1867 to be identifiable, but many, probably most, were not residents of the parishes where they functioned. Probably the majority were Union soldiers who had settled in Louisiana at the end of the war," Joe Gray Taylor writes. "None of them was black." The use of Union veterans (carpetbaggers) as registrars, of course, ensured that the registration process was firmly in radical hands. "Probably . . . the registrars discouraged native white registration," Taylor notes. Taylor also lists racism and apathy as reasons for the low turnout of native white voters. Hence, the vast majority of those registered were black, and they voted overwhelmingly for holding the convention. The constitutional convention met at the Mechanics' Institute from November 23, 1867, until March 9, 1868. The conservative *New Orleans Times* reflected the supercilious attitude of most white Louisianans when it referred to the radical congregation as the "Bones and Banjo Convention."[10]

The Scalawags and the "Bones and Banjo" Constitutional Convention of 1867–1868

The southern white Republicans took part in the Louisiana convention proceedings (the "Bones and Banjo Convention" to its enemies),[11] are here identified by name and parish:

L. W. Baker (Bossier)
John Barrett (Union)
Simeon Belden (Orleans—Second District)
W. Jasper Blackburn (Claiborne)
William Cooley (Pointe Coupee)
William R. Crane (Orleans—First District)
Thomas Crawford (Calwell)
George Dearing (Rapides)
Andrew Demarest (St. Mary's)
Charles Depasseau (Orleans)
Joseph Deslonde (St. John the Baptist)
John Drinkard (St. Landry)
Charles Duplessis (Orleans)
Edward Fielding Edwards (Avoyelles)
Thomas Harrison (Morehouse)
W. H. Hiestand (Natchitoches)
Simeon Jones (Orleans)
James B. Lewis (Sabine)
John T. Ludeling (Caldwell and Ouachita)
Frederique "Fred" Marie (Terrebonne)
Benjamin McLearn (Caddo)
James Mushaway (Orleans)
Nathan Schwab (Jefferson)
Charles Smith (Orleans, First District)
Gelderoy Snider (DeSoto)
James G. Taliaferro (Catahoula)
Napoleon Underwood (St. James)
John Vandergriff (St. Martin)
Michel Vidal (St. Landry)
Rufus Waples (Orleans, Second District)

The delegates selected Taliaferro, at that time an associate justice of the state supreme court, to be president of the convention.[12]

An analysis of ten selected roll call votes reveals that the scalawag delegates frequently crossed ideological lines when voting on measures designed to aid the freedmen, to restrict the political and economic activities of the ex-Rebels, or to strengthen the political and economic position of the pro-Reconstruction forces. Belden, Blackburn, Ludeling, Taliaferro, Underwood, and Vidal voted against an equal division of convention offices among black delegates and white delegates. Among the scalawags, only Crane, Smith, Waples, and Wickliffe (who introduced the measure) were recorded in favor of the pro-black measure. It was eventually tabled. Blackburn and Harper registered in favor of a racially segregated public school system. Belden, Crane, Taliaferro, Vidal, and Wickliffe, however, voted in favor of integration. The measure passed 62 to 12. Crane, Harper, Ludeling, and Wickliffe voted against requiring "licensed establishments of a public character" to serve both races. Belden and Vidal favored the proposal. The delegates acted in favor of integration with 58 in support and 16 opposed. Belden, Crane, Harper, Underwood, and Vidal voted in favor of requiring public officials to take an oath affirming their belief in the equality of all men. But Blackburn, Ludeling, and Waples opposed the measure. It passed 40 to 23. When a motion was made to insert the equality oath into the new constitution on January 28, 1868, Belden, Harper, Underwood, and Wickliffe were among the 49 delegates in support, and Blackburn, Crane, Ludeling, and Waples joined the 19 who opposed the proposal. Rufus Waples favored a proposal designed to disfranchise Louisiana's illiterate voters after 1872, while Belden, Crane, Harper, Smith, Underwood, Vidal, and Wickliffe voted against it. The measure failed 56 votes to 8. On restricting the voting rights of ex-Rebels, Blackburn, Harper, Vidal, Waples, and Wickliffe were in support. But Belden, Crane, and Smith opposed it despite its obvious benefit to the Republican movement. It passed 44 to 29.

No scalawags were recorded in opposition to a constitutional article requiring that land sold under court orders be marketed in small plots. Crane, Smith, Vidal, Waples, and Wickliffe were recorded in support of the measure designed obviously to aid small landowners that passed 42 to 11. Finally, Wickliffe and Smith supported a second article limiting the amount of land that could be purchased by individuals at sheriffs' sales. Crane and Waples stood with the majority (39 to 16) in opposition. Although the recorded votes indicate that the scalawags were not bound in a firm radical alliance during the convention, the final vote for the adoption of the radical-oriented constitution shows clearly that the scalawag delegates favored the radical document. Belden, Blackburn, Crane, Underwood, Vidal, Waples, and Wickliffe supported the adoption of the "Bones and Banjo" constitution. Ludeling, Smith, and Taliaferro either abstained or were absent during the final vote.[13] In the final count, the scalawag delegates, despite individual objections to certain articles, supported what Joe Gray Taylor calls "probably the most radical of any of the constitutions which resulted from the Reconstruction Acts."[14]

Issues like the integration of the public schools or Rebel disfranchisement were not the only subjects of concern at the convention. While the delegates debated these issues, an intense, internal power struggle was going on among the radicals themselves for control of the Republican movement in Louisiana. The contest involved two factions: one composed mostly of carpetbaggers and led by Henry Clay Warmoth, and the other the "pure radicals," led by Louis Charles Roudanez, an "octoroon" (a person of one-eighth black ancestry) and publisher of the *New Orleans Tribune*).[15] The origin of the struggle dates back to April 1867. At that time, the carpetbaggers (most of whom were former Union army officers) began to organize "Ben Butler Clubs." The Roudanez faction feared that the carpetbaggers would use the clubs to take over the state Republican Party. Although the Warmoth faction included many blacks who regarded the carpetbag ascendancy as the wave of the future, the "pure Radicals" feared that the clubs were part of a design to assume power at the expense of the freedmen and the southern Unionists. The Roudanez faction also believed that the carpetbaggers' commitment to civil rights was shallow and that their advocacy of black suffrage was simply "a device to catapult themselves into political power." The "pure radicals" had, moreover, a personal resentment of carpetbaggers, "many of whom had taken little or no part in the Radical movement of the past two years, but who now jockeyed for prominent roles in the reconstruction of the state."

At the Republican Party state convention in June 1867, the two factions had clashed over control of the important Republican state central committee. Using the convention's committee on reorganization, the

Warmoth faction successfully placed forty-six of their supporters (many of whom were recent arrivals in Louisiana and some who were not even official members of the party) on the seventy-nine-member State Central Committee. The "pure radical" *Tribune* accused one of Warmoth's scalawag allies, Michel Vidal, of precipitating the coup. Vidal denied the charge, claiming that he, as the secretary of the Committee on Reorganization, had simply recorded the names of the new members of the Central Committee. He did not know, he insisted, whether they were "those of Blue noses of New Brunswick, or Black Republicans living in the upper districts of New Orleans." Roudanez was unconvinced. Vidal was not the only scalawag to side with the carpetbag faction. In April 1867, a rival radical newspaper, the *New Orleans Republican,* began publication. The editor and manager was Bavarian-born scalawag Michael Hahn. The newspaper championed the carpetbag faction and became the main rival to Roudanez's *Tribune.*

The chief villain in the struggle to dominate the radical movement, in Roudanez's eyes, was not Vidal or Hahn, but the young carpetbagger Henry Clay Warmoth. According to Roudanez, Warmoth had masterminded the takeover of the State Central Committee. The radical journal also attacked three other carpetbaggers who, it claimed, were trying to seize the reins of power from the "pure radicals," that is, those who had worked for and led the party since its founding. The *Tribune* named them as being Joseph Hale Sypher (an ex-Union army officer), Lionel Sheldon (a close associate of Warmoth's and also a former Federal army officer), and Thomas W. Conway (a northern Methodist minister and a former Federal army chaplain from New York), who headed the Freedmen's Bureau in Louisiana.

Thus, the warring factions continued to fight when the radical-dominated constitutional convention assembled in November 1867. Convention president James G. Taliaferro and delegates William R. Crane, Charles Smith, and Rufus Waples led the pure radicals at the convention. The issues were control of state printing, qualifications for office holding, and the creation of a state board of registrars. The first test came when the Warmothites proposed that the *New Orleans Republican* be selected to print the official proceedings of the convention. The Roudanez faction immediately countered with a motion that the *Tribune* be favored with the patronage. The Warmoth faction lost by a narrow margin (46 to 45). Although defeated, their near victory foreboded the future successes of the carpetbag faction.

The debate over the qualifications for office holding also aroused the two factions. The Committee of the Executive proposed that the age requirement for governor be lowered from thirty-five to twenty-five. It was no coincidence that the leader of the carpetbaggers, Henry Clay Warmoth, was twenty-five years old. Thomas Isabelle, a black delegate and Roudanez ally, attempted to have the minimum age for governor set at twenty-eight. But this time the carpetbag faction scored a major victory: by a vote of 69 to 11, the convention adopted a provision that did away completely with the age requirement, requiring only that the governor be a qualified voter and a resident of the state for at least two years.

Near the close of the convention, a third major confrontation occurred, this one over the creation of a seven-member board of registrars to oversee voter registration and the state elections. Obviously both sides saw the board as a device to count their friends in and their enemies out. The Roudanez faction (including Crane, Smith, and Waples) and some conservative delegates, realizing that the Warmothites would control the board, opposed the measure. However, the article passed by a vote of 36 to 18. Waples then attempted to adjourn the convention *sine die* to prevent the convention from filling the board positions. But his motion failed, and the convention filled the positions with Warmoth backers.

Thus, the factional squabbles that later plagued the carpetbag government were evident even before the beginning of radical control. While the radicals fought among themselves, most white Louisianians stood expectantly on the sidelines.

Although the new Louisiana constitution was ratified by 57.6 percent of the registered voters, the election returns revealed little white support for the radical document. The discovery of a rare military document ("Tabular Statement of the vote for and against the Constitution . . .")[16] made possible a reasonably accurate estimate of the number of scalawags in Louisiana at the onset of radical Reconstruction.[17] The value of the report lies also in the fact that the document provides the votes for and against ratification by race in each parish (excluding Orleans and DeSoto).

The report reveals that a total of 114,891 registered voters took part in the election. Unfortunately for this study, the votes in Orleans and

DeSoto Parishes (30,844) were not recorded by race. But of the remaining 78,291 ballots, 49,759 black votes and 28,532 white votes were recorded. Of the total black votes, 88.2 percent were cast in favor of ratification. But only 5 percent of the white votes were recorded in favor of the radical document.[18]

In the central pine-hills region (Caldwell, Catahoula, Natchitoches, and Winn Parishes) of the state, only 296 persons, or 17.1 percent, of the white voters, voted for the constitution. The voters in this region of piney woods and hills, subsistence farms, and poor whites overwhelmingly opposed the new constitution (1,435 out of 1,731 white voters, or 83.9 percent).

The returns from the oak uplands region, known as the north Louisiana hills (Bienville, Claiborne, Jackson, Sabine, and Union Parishes), showed that 95.5 percent of the white voters, mostly yeomen slaveholders, cast their ballots against ratification. This area contained large numbers of migrants from Alabama, Mississippi, Georgia, North and South Carolina, Virginia, Kentucky, and Tennessee who engaged in cotton and subsistence farming. Only 4.5 percent (174 out of 3,891) of these hill-country yeomen were willing to support the radical constitution.

The north Louisiana planter parishes of Bossier, Caddo, Concordia, East and West Carroll, Madison, Morehouse, Ouachita, Rapides, and Tensas also demonstrated little radical support. Of the 3,910 white voters in this planter-dominated, alluvial-valley region, only 149, or 3.8 percent, favored ratification. In 1860, this area contained the highest proportion of slaves of all the voter-type regions. In Bossier Parish, for example, the slaves accounted for 70.4 percent of the population in 1860. Of the 1,325 black voters in 1868, 987 (74.5 percent) voted in favor of ratification, while only 2 (.47 percent) out of the 424 white voters in this rural parish cast their ballots for ratification.

In Franklin Parish, located in the Macon Ridge area, the whites voted overwhelmingly against the new constitution. This planter-controlled parish contained a sizable number of family farms, but here, too, only a small minority of the voters (15.8 percent) was willing to cooperate with the blacks in the election.

In the Florida Parishes (the planter-dominated, Anglo-Saxon, Protestant, northeast cotton parishes of East Baton Rouge, East and West Feliciana, Livingston, St. Helena, and St. Tammany), the Republican cause also generated little support among the whites. Only 3 percent of the 4,452 white voters favored the "Bones and Banjo" document.

The plantation was the hub of the political, economic, and social life of the south Louisiana parishes of Ascension, Iberville, Pointe Coupee, St. Charles, St. James, St. John the Baptist, St. Mary, and West Baton Rouge. Here 3,186 whites cast ballots, and of that number, only 236, or 7.4 percent, favored ratification.

Located in the lush south Louisiana bayou country, the parishes of Assumption, Avoyelles, Lafourche, Plaquemines, St. Bernard, St. Martin, and Terrebonne contained both sugarcane planters and Acadian "peasant proprietors." Again, the whites in landslide proportions rejected the radical constitution. Out of 5,328 white ballots, only 231, or 4.3 percent, were marked in favor of the Republicans. In St. Martin Parish, for example, only 14 of 1,288 whites sided with the radicals.

In only three parishes did more than 20 percent of the white voters support the Republicans. In Concordia, Caldwell, and Winn Parishes, the support was 21.8, 33.5, and 22.3 percent, respectively. Two of these, Winn and Caldwell, were white farmer parishes, while Concordia was situated in the planter region of north Louisiana. In these three parishes, only 211 voters supported the radicals. In the forty-six parishes for which the registrars kept separate black and white tallies, only in Winn did the number favoring the constitution exceed one hundred. Here 113 whites out of 506 voted Republican.

The urban areas of Jefferson and Orleans Parishes contained 20 percent of the state's population. New Orleans was the focus and chief center of political activity in the Reconstruction era. A total of 30,707 black and white votes were cast in these two parishes alone. In Orleans, where the votes were not separated by race, the constitution narrowly passed with 50.8 percent of the vote. In Jefferson Parish, only 75 of 1,653 whites, or 4.5 percent, voted for ratification.

Finally, the returns for the parishes of southwest Louisiana (Calcasieu, St. Landry, Vermillion, and Lafayette) reveal that an infinitesimal number (2.35 percent) supported the Republicans. In this prairie region of family-size farms, the white voters, as in all the other voter-type areas, firmly and decisively rejected the new radical constitution.

Although the "Tabular Statement" cannot provide a definite answer to the question of the level of southern white support for the Republican

Party with precision (it is impossible to tell, for example, if the whites who voted in favor of ratification were carpetbaggers or scalawags), the document does, nevertheless, permit some cautious conclusions. First, the black votes were decisive in passing the constitution. Second, the vote reveals that no black–poor white alliance existed in Louisiana, at least in this critical election. Third, the rural parishes gave no significant support to the Louisiana Republicans. Discounting the urban parishes of Orleans and Jefferson, only 5.1 percent of the whites favored ratification, and, of course, some of these were carpetbaggers. "If every white man outside of New Orleans who voted for ratification became an active and zealous member of the Republican Party," Joe Gray Taylor surmises, "there still would be only fifteen hundred white Republicans in the country parishes." Taylor also contends that "it can be assumed from the vote on ratification that at this time [1868] there were probably fewer than a thousand so-called scalawags in Louisiana outside of New Orleans."[19] The fourth indication is that even in the urban setting of Orleans and Jefferson (the chief centers of political activity), white support for the Republicans was slight. In Jefferson, only 75, or 4.5 percent, of the white voters favored the Republican program. And in Orleans, the constitution passed by only 1.6 percent of the vote (14,763 to 14,291). Undoubtedly, the negative votes were white votes.

The Scalawags and the Louisiana State Elections of April 1868

While the 1868 convention was still in progress, the Louisiana Republicans held a state nominating convention in preparation for the upcoming April state elections. Six prominent radicals emerged as potential gubernatorial candidates: Francis E. Dumas (a free man of color), George M. Wickliffe, W. Jasper Blackburn, James G. Taliaferro, P. B. S. Pinchback (a black political leader and future governor of Louisiana), and the young carpetbagger Henry Clay Warmoth. Pinchback pulled out of the race, explaining that the political climate was not yet right for a black governor. Dumas, however, remained in the contest. On the first ballot, Dumas received 41 votes but failed to gain a majority. Warmoth ran a close second with 37 votes. None of the other candidates showed any strength: Wickliffe received 4 votes, Taliaferro 3, and Blackburn 3. On the next ballot, Warmoth won a narrow victory (45 to 43) over his black opponent.[20] Under pressure from Roudanez, Dumas refused the nomination for the lieutenant governorship, offered to him as a consolation prize. Oscar J. Dunn, another black Republican, agreed to run on the ticket with Warmoth. The other radical candidates included Wickliffe (state auditor), Simeon Belden (attorney general), and Thomas Conway (superintendent of education).[21]

Roudanez's pure radical faction, however, would not support the Warmoth ticket. These "bolters," as the Warmoth Republicans referred to them, decided to field their own slate of candidates. They nominated Taliaferro for governor and Dumas for lieutenant governor. Angered at Roudanez and Taliaferro's defection, the Warmoth-dominated Republican State Central Committee removed the state printing rights from the *Tribune* and awarded them to Hahn's *New Orleans Republican*. Deprived of the profit incurred from state patronage, the *Tribune* went out of business in April 1868. The committee then went even further and expelled several well-known pure radicals, including Charles Smith and William Crane, from the party ranks. Lacking the support of the regular party apparatus, the bolters had little hope of victory, even with the aid of the Democrats who now allied with the Roudanez-Taliaferro splinter group. The Democrats saw Taliaferro as the lesser of two evils, and, too weak to run their own ticket, they formed an alliance with the radical bolters. There was a certain irony in this since the Roudanez-Taliaferro group "was considerably more 'Radical' than the party led by Warmoth."[22] Apparently, the Democrats resented the carpetbagger more than the scalawag. Warmoth, the *Daily Picayune* informed its conservative readers, "is an adventurer, who held a quasi-military title during the war, but was best known here as a provost judge, who filled his carpet bag with fines wrung from the poor people whom his spies and informers brought before his inquisitorial tribunal." Taliaferro, on the other hand, was "an old citizen, who embraced the Union side when secession was triumphant in [Louisiana], and stood his ground throughout the war, and . . . never took a dollar which did not belong to him."[23] A second editorial also emphasized Taliaferro's honesty and southern origins. Taliaferro, the journal stated, "is an old citizen, born South, and a resident of the state for thirty-years—altogether identified with it; was an honest and consistent Union man from the beginning to the end of the war, and therefore, not a mere changeling, hunting office; is a man of character and intelligence—a gentleman in his associations and habits."[24] Such Democratic support had little impact upon the election. The Warmoth ticket won in a landslide of black votes. Warmoth himself carried the state with 65,270 votes, or 63 percent, to Taliaferro's 38,118 votes, or 37 percent. The radical Republicans also seized a majority of the seats in the state legislature.[25]

The state elections of 1868 marked an important turning point in Louisiana Reconstruction. The Roudanez-Taliaferro faction was not only defeated, but destroyed as a viable political force in the state. "Hardly a single figure among the Roudanez-Taliaferro faction remained in the political life of the state," F. Wayne Binning remarks.[26] Taliaferro, for instance, never held another elective office. Although appointed to the state supreme court by Warmoth, he was effectively in political limbo after 1868.

The Scalawags and Factional Politics during the Carpetbag Years

As James Alex Baggett notes, as a result of congressional Reconstruction two new political factions appeared in Louisiana: the "pure radical" (freedmen of color) and the carpetbaggers (led by Henry Clay Warmoth). "Thereafter, the carpetbaggers controlled the party and few significant scalawags entered, although some continued to acquire important state posts."[27] Warmoth is one of the most interesting players in the story of Louisiana Reconstruction. Here he sums up his political military and political career in his lively 1930 memoir, *War, Politics and Reconstruction: Stormy Days in Louisiana:* "Having fought all these battles incident to public life, openly and squarely, in the most spirited State in the Union and through a most turbulent era, and having experienced about all the triumphs and defeats incident to such a life, and having not a drop of any other than southern blood in my veins, I think I may say, at eighty-seven years of age, that I was never a 'Louisiana Carperbagger,' though I might, in common parlance, be termed a 'scallawag.'"[28] Warmoth was no "scalawag." In fact, Richard Current, in his definitive study of "those terrible carpetbaggers," begins his history with a "Cast of Characters in order of their appearance." Warmoth is first on the list: "Once an Illinois farm boy, he arrived in Louisiana as a Union officer, became governor of the state at twenty-five, remained to prosper as a sugar planter, and lived on into the time of Huey Long, who viewed him as something of a model."[29]

Joe Gray Taylor concurs and adds a note on Warmoth's image in the Louisiana tradition: "Warmoth continues to fascinate students of Louisiana history. Perhaps that is because this young lawyer, union soldier, carpetbagger, and radical Republican almost perfectly represented the type of politicians Louisianans admire." The kind of politician "who took his cut with skill, aplomb, a smile, and a wink."[30] Perhaps Warmoth considered that his long life in Louisiana made him a postwar adopted son of the South—with a wink. There is no doubt that Warmoth was a carpetbagger. He was, in fact, "the prince of carpetbaggers."[31]

Despite the decline of scalawag leadership in Louisiana, several prominent scalawags and other less well-known southern white Republicans remained active in politics during the carpetbag years. Scalawags served as federal, state, parish, and municipal office holders (both appointed and elected) and as Republican state party officials. The Republican ranks included, after 1868, for example, the following scalawags:

- Simeon Belden (elected state attorney general on the Warmoth ticket, 1868)
- W. Jasper Blackburn (U.S. congressman, Fortieth Congress, 1868–69; delegate to the Louisiana State Teachers Convention, 1872; state senator, 1874–78);
- M. F. Bonzano (special agent in charge of the United States branch mint in New Orleans and superintendent of federal lighthouse construction, 1870–71; chairman of the Republican electoral college of Louisiana, 1872; federal surveyor-general for the port of New Orleans, 1873–74; superintendent of the United States branch mint in New Orleans, 1874–75; assayer-in-charge of the United States assay office in New Orleans, 1874–78; coiner, United States branch mint in New Orleans, 1868)
- J. Ernest Breda (appointed state district attorney, 1873; elected Natchitoches parish judge, November 1874; elected state district judge, November 1876)

- Mortimer Carr (Speaker of the State House of Representatives, 1870–71)
- George W. Carter (appointed Cameron parish judge by Warmoth in 1870; elected Speaker of the State House of Representatives, 1871; editor of the *New Orleans National Republican,* 1871)
- Valentine Chase (judge of St. Mary Parish, 1868)
- Armand Commagere (Internal Revenue collector for the Eighth Division of Louisiana, 1890)
- Thomas Green Davidson (state representative, Livingston Parish, 1870–74)
- Richard C. Downes (elected Madison Parish judge, 1868)
- Louis Dupleix (appointed registrar, United States Land Office at Natchitoches, by President Grant, 1872)
- E. H. Durell (United States district judge, 1863–74)
- A. W. Faulkner (member from Caldwell Parish, State House of Representatives, 1870; delegate to the Republican state convention, 1870)
- Benjamin Franklin Flanders (military governor of Louisiana, 1867 and 1868; mayor of New Orleans, 1870–72; assistant treasurer of the United States at New Orleans, 1873–82)
- James Graham (state auditor, 1872)
- Michael Hahn (editor, *New Orleans Republican,* 1867–71; member of the state legislature, 1872–76)
- Andrew Hero (notary public, 1866–70; appointed city notary, 1870)
- Ezra Hiestand (appointed assistant New Orleans city attorney, 1868)
- William Henry Hire (New Orleans city physician for the Second and Third Districts, 1868; secretary and treasurer of Charity Hospital, 1870–73)
- Rufus K. Howell (associate justice of the Louisiana Supreme Court, April 3, 1865–January 9, 1877)
- Oscar Jeffrion (president of the Pointe Coupee Parish Republican Executive Committee, 1868–1878; elected parish sheriff in 1872; member of the Republican electoral college for Louisiana, 1876)
- Charles Leaumont (judge of the Fifth District State Court for the Parish of Orleans, ca. 1868–72)
- James Longstreet (surveyor of customs for the port of New Orleans, 1869–72; adjutant general of the State of Louisiana, 1870–72; major general of the Louisiana state militia,1872–75; member of the State Returning Board, 1872–74; member of the federal levee commission of engineers, 1873–76)

- John Theodore Ludeling (chief justice of the Louisiana Supreme Court, November 1, 1868–January 9, 1877)
- George W. Mader (United States Customs inspector, 1870)
- William G. Phillips (elected Rapides Parish judge, 1870)
- E. L. Pierson (appointed Natchitoches Parish judge by William Pitt Kellogg)
- J. R. G. Pitkin (state registrar of bankruptcy for the Fourth District, 1868; United States marshal, 1876; secretary of the Republican state central committee, 1876)
- John Ray (state senator, 1868–72; registrar of the state land office, 1873–77)
- Robert Ray (Ouachita Parish judge, 1868–1870; judge of the Fourteenth State Judicial District, 1870–77)
- James Ready (assessor in the United States Internal Revenue Department, First Collection District of Louisiana, 1868)
- Charles Smith (Custom House employee, 1870)
- Eugene Staes (elected judge of the Second Recorder's Court for the Parish of Orleans by the city council of New Orleans, 1870; judge of the Second Municipal Court of New Orleans, 1872–76)
- James Govan Taliaferro (associate justice of the Louisiana Supreme Court, July 1, 1866–November 3, 1876)
- James Veazie (New Orleans city attorney, 1871–72)
- Michel Vidal (United States congressman, Fortieth Congress, 1868–69; appointed United States commissioner to Peru, 1869–70; United States consul at Tripoli, 1870–76)
- Rufus Waples (assistant city attorney of New Orleans for special cases, 1870–72; director of New Orleans public schools; trustee of Straight University)
- James Madison Wells (delegate to the Liberal Republican national convention, 1872; member of the State Returning Board, 1874 and 1876)
- George M. Wickliffe (state auditor of public accounts, 1868–70).[32]

Although it is not the purpose here to recount the full story of the pull and tug of Louisiana politics during the carpetbag era,[33] it is necessary to define and highlight the role played by the scalawags. James Baggett notes that there were more scalawags than carpetbaggers at the constitutional convention of 1868, but "in the legislatures that followed, scalawag numbers were small." In the state elections of 1868, Democrats carried the larger towns and the "piney woods" parishes. And black districts elected black candidates. The few leftovers went to the scalawags.[34] As noted, the southern white Republicans in Louisiana served in a variety of federal, state, parish, and party offices. Because of this, the scalawags were chest-deep in the swamp of Louisiana politics. The following stories of George Wickliffe, George W. Carter, Thomas Green Davidson, and James Longstreet during this period illustrate the part played by southern white Republicans in the sordid and self-destructive domestic wars of the Louisiana Republican Party.

Wickliffe's Challenge

George W. Wickliffe was elected state auditor on the Warmoth ticket in 1868. Reported to be the editor of an "anti-abolition journal" before the Civil War, this dentist from Clinton, Louisiana,[35] was one of the most ardent and controversial white radical Republicans in the state. Despite their initial alliance, Warmoth and Wickliffe became embroiled in a bitter political fight. In March 1869, a grand jury, apparently at Warmoth's instigation, handed down fourteen indictments against the state auditor, including charges of extortion and the issuance of illegal warrants. Warmoth then ordered the Metropolitan Police, a state agency directly under the governor's control, to arrest Wickliffe, and take possession of the auditor's office and official records.[36] Warmoth then appointed T. L. Delassis, a black, as acting auditor.[37]

Warmoth's motives for attacking Wickliffe are not entirely clear. He may, of course, have been genuinely concerned about corruption in the state auditor's office (considering the high tolerance of corruption in Louisiana, though, this seems unlikely). Or, perhaps, in the governor's eyes, Wickliffe had crossed the fine line between taking advantage of opportunities and outright stealing—the line that distinguished what George Washington Plunkett of Tammany Hall called honest and dishonest graft—becoming too public an embarrassment to the new Republican administration. Wickliffe, for his part, attributed Warmoth's action to the governor's desire to remove a political rival from power. Warmoth, according to Wickliffe, was a "desperate villain," engaged in a "bold game" of political intrigue.[38] Wickliffe did not intend to give up without a struggle.

Wickliffe denied that Warmoth had the authority to remove him from office. The ousted auditor then boldly set up a new office directly across the street from the Mechanics' Institute, and announced that the auditor's department was reopened for business. Wickliffe obtained an injunction from the Seventh District State Court prohibiting Delassie from performing the auditor's duties. Warmoth countered with an injunction of his own, signed by Judge Charles Leaumont, a scalawag, of the Fifth District State Court, forbidding Wickliffe from performing his official duties.[39]

Wickliffe, however, was not content to let the courts decide the issue. In a letter to State Senator John S. Harris, the scalawag auditor asked Harris to supply incriminating evidence that could be used to undermine Warmoth politically. Wickliffe was especially interested in Warmoth's army record. (The governor, a former officer in the Union army, had been dishonorably discharged during the Civil War, but he was later restored to his command.)[40] "If you have not gotten hold of those records of his dismissal," Wickliffe urges, "I wish you would . . . effect to get them. You can get information from President Grant and also Gen'l Sheridan on this point. I want his record in this matter very much."[41]

Although Wickliffe would eventually lose his political war with Warmoth, he did score an initial victory when a sympathetic jury refused to convict him on the first two charges in the grand jury bills. The presiding judge then dismissed the case, stating that the jury was so prejudiced in the auditor's favor that there existed no possibility of conviction. Attorney General Belden then dismissed the remaining twelve charges on the grounds that an elected official could not be tried by a jury until after his impeachment and removal from office.[42]

Temporarily checked by the jury's failure to convict Wickliffe, and by Belden's ruling, Warmoth allowed the auditor to regain possession of the state records relating to the public accounts. But when Wickliffe attempted to move back into his office in the Mechanics' Institute, Warmoth had the police dump the auditor's records and office equipment on the sidewalk outside the building. The governor, on January 5, 1870, then issued a special message to the Louisiana House of Representatives asking the legislature to begin impeachment proceedings against Wickliffe. The message read, in part:

> It becomes my duty to communicate to your honorable body grave charges against George M. Wickliffe, Auditor of Public Accounts. His offenses against the constitution and laws of the State have seriously embarrassed the government and rendered it difficult to pay the interest on the State bonds. He has been guilty of numerous acts, involving extortion against individuals and against the charitable institutions of the State, also involving fraud against the commonwealth and collusion with evil disposed persons to defraud the same. He has extorted sums of money from the creditors of the State as a condition precedent to the issuance to them of the certificates of indebtedness of warrants to which they were entitled by law.[43]

Warmoth provided various examples of Wickliffe's malfeasance and then concluded with a hypocritical statement that must have brought smiles to the faces of the members of the state legislature. He was particularly mortified at the auditor's conduct, Warmoth said, because Wickliffe was a fellow Republican. "No party," Warmoth remarked, "is worthy [of] the confidence of the people, or can retain the same who will permit such conduct to pass uncensored and unpunished." The legislature responded to Warmoth's impeachment message by appointing a committee to investigate the charges. The House voted overwhelmingly to impeach Wickliffe (72 to 2). The twenty-eight articles of impeachment included charges of soliciting and receiving kickbacks on state printing warrants —he refused, for example, to honor a claim from the *Attakapas Register* unless the editor paid him three hundred dollars—and incompetence in managing the auditor's office. Wickliffe's attorney did not deny that his client took bribes; rather, he denied that the charges leveled against his client were crimes under state law. During the course of the trial, Wickliffe, realizing that his cause was lost, attempted to resign and thus escape conviction and future disqualification from office. The auditor's move was declared invalid, however, and the senate proceeded to convict him by a unanimous vote.[44] While the trial was still in progress, a second grand jury handed down a new series of indictments involving forged state warrants. Out of office and facing these new charges, Wickliffe fled the state and disappeared from history. The complete extent of Wickliffe's wrongdoing is unknown, but one estimate puts the amount of money he stole at between $200,000 and $700,000,[45] an amazing amount for the times. Although Warmoth succeeded in destroying Wickliffe, this did not eliminate the opposition to the young carpetbagger from within the party.

Carter's Betrayal

Scalawag George W. Carter also emerged as a leading anti-Warmoth partisan.[46] Like Wickliffe, Carter was at first a Warmoth ally. "He was," Warmoth wrote in his memoirs, "a man of exceptional education and polish, and was gifted with a remarkable ability to state and illustrate a proposition. He was a fine speaker, and I was attracted to him at once, and showed him various social courtesies. Later I appointed him to a lucrative office under the State administration." Warmoth, however, had underestimated Carter's feral cunning.

Carter aligned himself with Warmoth in 1870 as the Republican Party began to organize for the state elections of that year. According to Warmoth, Carter "said that he thought he would like to be a member of the new state legislature and asked me to use my influence to secure his nomination for a seat in the House of Representatives." Warmoth was unable to secure a nomination for Carter, but he did arrange to appoint him judge of Cameron Parish. Warmoth explained: "The Legislature during its session had passed an act to create the Parish of Cameron, taking a part of the large Parish of Calcasieu. I had not yet signed the bill and had the right, under the Constitution, to hold it up until the first day of the next session of the Legislature. I did not regard the territory composing this proposed Parish as having sufficient population to warrant its organization into a Parish. But I was so anxious to get my friend to help me carry on the government, that I conceived the idea of signing the bill and communicated my views to Colonel Carter, who entered into the spirit of the move at once." Warmoth signed the bill on March 16, 1870, and then appointed Carter parish judge with an annual salary of two thousand dollars. He also provided Carter with blank commissions with which to fill the positions of sheriff, justice of the peace, police jurors, registrars of voters, and constables. "The reader will not be surprised," Warmoth wrote, "that with all of this power Colonel Carter was able to fulfill his ambition and my wishes by being elected a member of the Louisiana House of Representatives from Cameron Parish. He was unanimously elected." When the new legislature assembled in January 1871, Mortimer Carr, a scalawag, was elected Speaker of the House with Warmoth's support. Shortly after his election, however, a faction composed of anti-Warmoth Republicans and Democrats forced Carr to resign and in his place elected Carter.[47]

The new Speaker began immediately to reorganize the House committee assignments in favor of the anti-Warmoth faction.[48] Carter, in fact, became the chief spokesman of the anti-Warmoth Republicans in the House of Representatives. "On November 6, 1871," Warmoth wrote, "the . . . Custom House faction established a newspaper called *The National Republican* to lead the war upon me and my friends. It was edited by Speaker George W. Carter, and it certainly was a lively sheet."[49]

As an additional reward for his aid, the new Speaker received a lucrative position in the United States Custom House.[50] In his memoirs, Warmoth claimed that Carter's defection to the opposition was motivated by sheer greed. When the new legislature convened, Warmoth stated, "it became known that Speaker Carter was at the head of a ring, composed of Democrats and Negro and white Republicans, which proposed to control all legislation which could stand a liberal 'blackmail.'" Warmoth, however, did not break openly with Carter until the latter became involved in a public scandal.[51] Carter refused to approve a railroad construction bill until the Chattanooga Railroad Company agreed to retain him as an attorney at a fee of ten thousand dollars.[52] According to Warmoth, the revelation of the railroad scandal forced him to break with Carter. "The fact became a public scandal and the result," Warmoth wrote, "was a break between Speaker Carter and me, after a very plain interview in which the matters were fully and frankly discussed." Warmoth continued his bitter assessment: "I discovered that this mild-mannered, able, and accomplished man was absolutely demoralized; that he was dishonest, faithless, and in a position to do great harm. He had surrounded himself with a number of the most desperate men in New Orleans. . . . He developed a fondness for drink, and his bar-room tirades and threats against me and my friends were being constantly reported to me."[53] The real reason for the break between Carter and Warmoth was not Carter's corruption, but rather his defection to the growing anti-Warmoth element within the Republican Party and the prospects of being on the winning side of the contest for control of the party and patronage. This coalition included the black Lieutenant Governor Oscar J. Dunn; the members of the Republican State Central Committee, including United States Marshal Stephen B. Packard, a carpetbagger, and J. R. G. Pitkin, a scalawag; United States Collector of Customs James F. Casey, a carpetbagger, and his employees; and Postmaster C. R. Lowell and the postal employees in New Orleans.[54]

The reasons for the formation of the coalition were varied. Some members, like Carter, were greedy for power and the spoils of office. Others were concerned about the governor's appointment of Democrats to office. For their part, Dunn and his allies (both black and white) believed that Warmoth was cool toward black rights. Their suspicions were confirmed when Warmoth refused to support state civil rights bills in 1868 and 1870. By the spring of 1871, the opposition to Warmoth within his own party had grown enormously. The anti-Warmoth forces were now formidable and bold.

Warmoth, however, was not without resources of his own. He controlled the Metropolitan Police, the state militia (commanded by James Longstreet), and the state's voter registration and election processes. He also had the support of almost all of the Republican parish office holders.[55] Understandably, it was opposition to this influence that cemented the anti-Warmoth coalition. As Joe Gray Taylor puts it, Warmoth's "virtual dictatorship . . . stimulated the jealousy and enmity of his political friends who resented his almost unlimited powers."[56]

Thus, the Republican organization in Louisiana was a party at war with itself. The first major battle occurred when the anti-Warmoth forces attempted to seize complete control of the party apparatus in Louisiana and drive Warmoth and his partisans from the party ranks. The test of strength occurred when the Republicans assembled for the state party convention in 1871. Packard arranged for the meeting to be held on August 8 at the Custom House. He also informed the local military commander that he expected trouble from "thugs and bruisers." To preserve order, the United States Army provided a company of soldiers and two Gatling guns. Packard also appointed forty deputy marshals to help "prevent violence." When Warmoth and his followers arrived at the building, they faced a small army determined to bar them from the proceedings. Warmoth and 118 supporters (including scalawags Napoleon

Underwood, A. W. Faulkner, and W. Jasper Blackburn) then gathered at Turner Hall. While the Warmoth Republicans convened at Turner Hall, his rivals held their "Gatling Gun Convention" at the federal building.[57]

The Turner Hall Convention was the scene of much excitement as the Warmoth delegates and approximately four thousand supporters filled the auditorium on August 9. The highlight of the first evening was a long, bitter, often sarcastic attack by the governor, recorded in the proceedings of the state party convention, on his political enemies, including Packard, Casey, Lowell, Carter, and Pitkin. Warmoth claimed that Carter was a Democrat disguised in Republican clothing. According to the governor, Carter told the *New Orleans Times* "that [Carter] was not a Republican that he never had been a Republican . . . was now a Democrat, and that he was only pretending to be a Republican that he might divide the party, and give the State back to the white people, to whom it belonged." Warmoth also accused Speaker Carter, an ex-Confederate, of still harboring anti-Union and anti-Negro sentiments. The governor then inserted a bit of low comedy, referring to Carter as a "man who was the pet and pride of the Methodist Episcopal Church South; a man who preached Christ . . . from the State of Virginia way down to the Rio Grande—a man who was the peculiar pride of the Methodist Church, especially of the female members." The hall, it is recorded, erupted with laughter and cheers. Encouraged by the audience response, Warmoth continued the attack: "He says I have done some big things in this state—that I have made a big fortune; that I have created for the State of Louisiana a big debt, and I forget what other big things he charged me with." Warmoth wondered, in fact, how Carter knew that he had made a fortune while governor: "How did George W. Carter become familiar with my bank account? Who of this audience can tell me how much money I had when I went into office, and how much money I have now? How did this apostate angel get his information?" Again, the hall roared with laughter.

Warmoth then pointed out that Carter, after one session of the legislature, had bought an expensive home in New Orleans, and had spent "in one night seventeen hundred dollars in a gambling house." For his part, Warmoth challenged Carter to present evidence to the legislature that while governor, he had taken bribes or prostituted his office for personal profit. Warmoth then proceeded to draw a parallel between Carter and

Wickliffe: "While George W. Carter was at the head of the Texas Legion—while this light of the Methodist Episcopal Church South was waging a war in which, he himself says, he killed nobody—this other gentleman [Wickliffe] was on the banks of the Mississippi River cutting the throats of Union men who were non-combatants, and burning all the cotton he could lay his hands upon. This was the patriotic service that George W. Wickliffe was rendering the Confederacy." The governor ended his attack upon Carter by calling the Speaker of the House "a drunkard . . . a gambler . . . and a political bummer." Carter was not the only opponent to feel the sting of Warmoth's tirade; J. R. G. Pitkin was also included in the attack: "I will not tell you of Pitkin—that soft-mouthed poetical linguist . . . who is so fond of letters that it takes nearly the whole alphabet to make his name: 'J.-R.-G. Pitkin.' I won't tell you how he joined the confederate army, deserted from its ranks, joined the Union army, became frightened, and by the dexterous use of a piece of soap under his tongue, threw himself into fits and frothed himself into a discharge. Nor of the eloquent exposition he made of the McClellan Democracy in 1864, denouncing the war for the Union as unconstitutional and wrong, and ought to cease [*sic*]."[58]

While Warmoth entertained the Turner Hall delegates with his denunciations of the anti-Warmoth crowd, Carter was busy attacking Warmoth before the Republicans at the Custom House. Warmoth, Carter charged, "received bribes, stole the public money, and was the greatest living practical liar."[59]

The Turner Hall delegates and those attending the "Gatling Gun Convention" both claimed to represent the true Republican Party in Louisiana. Accordingly, each faction named its own Republican state committee and, as the rivals adjourned, each planned to drive their opponents from power.[60] Since neither side was willing to compromise, let alone give in entirely, the result was that politics in Louisiana remained in a state of constant dissonance. Again, Warmoth and Carter were the principal antagonists. The contest this time centered on control of the state legislature. The Carterites, with Democratic support, planned to take over the legislature and then impeach the governor.

The sudden death of Lieutenant Governor O. J. Dunn in November 1871 favored Warmoth's position. If Warmoth could secure the election of one of his supporters to fill the vacancy, the impeachment move would be aborted. But Warmoth had to act quickly, for Dunn's death left Carter, as Speaker of the House, the next in line for the succession. The governor discovered a simple yet clever answer to this problem. He called the senate into session to elect a new lieutenant governor, but he did not call the House (where impeachment charges would be introduced) into session. Warmoth's allies in the senate successfully, though narrowly, elected P. B. S. Pinchback (the future black governor of Louisiana) to fill the vacancy. Warmoth had won the first skirmish, but the battle was far from over. Throughout January 1872, the two factions engaged in an intense and sometimes violent struggle. Soon after the legislature convened, the anti-Warmoth forces succeeded in getting the legislature to pass a resolution expressing confidence in Carter.

On the third day of the new legislative session, Carter left the Speaker's chair in an effort to defend himself against charges of corruption and, at the same time, to denounce Warmoth. As soon as Carter resumed his seat, a motion was made to declare the Speaker's chair vacant. Carter, however, ruled the motion out of order.[61]

In the midst of the confusion and uproar, Mortimer Carr and a band of anti-Carter Republicans advanced toward the Speaker in an attempt to oust him physically. Carter apparently anticipated this, and, at a prearranged signal, approximately twelve armed bodyguards emerged from behind the dais. At this point, the House adjourned. Carter had met the challenge, but it was obvious to all that his grip on the legislature was loosening.[62]

In order to strengthen his position, Carter counterattacked during the next session of the legislature with charges of fraud against Carr and E. W. Dewees, the two main Warmoth lieutenants. While this motion was still pending, the pro-Warmoth Republicans again tried to unseat the Speaker, but, once again, Carter fought off the challenge. The charges against Carr and Dewees, however, were indefinitely postponed. The contest was far from over. The Carterites struck again. This time they planned to oust enough Warmoth Republicans through parliamentary maneuvering and, if necessary, by sheer brute force, to give the anti-Warmoth forces a majority in the legislature. On January 4, Carter and his allies prevented seven Warmoth legislators from taking their seats and admitted six Carter supporters in their place. The legislature also gave Carter the power to prevent the Metropolitan Police from entering the hall. To back up Carter, the Speaker was authorized to appoint as many sergeants-at-arms as necessary to "preserve order."[63]

Meanwhile, Packard ordered the arrest of Warmoth and twenty-two state senators and representatives "on charges of violating the laws of Louisiana and the United States."[64] At that point, the remaining Warmoth legislators walked out of Mechanics' Institute, leaving the Carter-dominated assembly without a quorum.

Clever and tough, Warmoth was, of course, fully capable of some political chicanery himself. After being released on bail, Warmoth issued a proclamation calling a special session of the legislature on the grounds that a conspiracy was afoot "to overthrow the government by unlawful and revolutionary means."[65] The governor, however, purposely failed to notify the Carterite faction of the extra session. Warmoth failed to get a quorum of the senate, but he was able to assemble enough of his supporters to achieve a quorum of the House. The Speaker's chair was declared vacant, and O. H. Brewster, a carpetbagger from Illinois, was elected to the position. The Warmoth legislature then reseated the members expelled by the Carterites. To ensure that the Mechanics' Institute remained under his control, the governor ordered the Metropolitan Police and a force of state militiamen to guard the state house against an assault by the Carter Republicans.[66]

When Carter learned of Warmoth's coup, he immediately ordered his followers to convene at the "Gem Saloon" on Royal Street. Carter claimed that this body represented the "legal House of Representatives." Warmoth, on the other hand, called the Gem Saloon legislature "revolutionary, unconstitutional, and illegal." Carter ignored Warmoth and, to achieve a quorum, ordered the arrest of those not attending his Gem Saloon meetings. Tempers were hot, and one Warmoth supporter was shot and killed resisting arrest. Although Carter and three of his supporters were arrested and charged with the killing, the charges were later dropped.[67]

Warmoth decided now to use force to destroy Carter. On January 7, a large body of Metropolitan Police (with Longstreet in command) seized the Gem Saloon and expelled the Carterite legislature. The Speaker retreated to the office of Marshal Packard, and later moved (with twenty followers) to the rooms of the New Orleans Cosmopolitan Club. Rallying his forces, Carter attempted three times to seize Mechanics' Institute. Each time, however, Federal troops intervened to preserve order, and Carter's takeover failed.[68] But Carter was unwilling to give in. He planned one last, desperate effort. On January 20, Carter issued a proclamation in which he recounted the history of his contest with the governor. In the conclusion, Carter appealed to all citizens (black as well as white) to arm themselves and assemble under his command:

> The question before our people is no longer a simple one of reform, the graver issue is presented by the revolutionary and treasonable acts of the Governor, and that is, whether they will quietly permit him to subvert the State Government and destroy the independence of the Legislative Department thereof, by the most violent and revolutionary acts. The premises considered, we earnestly invite the citizens, irrespective of race or party, to organize and arm themselves . . . and report in force in the neighborhood of 307 Canal Street, where they will be provided with necessary commissions and sworn in as Assistant Sergeants-at-Arms. . . . I want a force so potent in numbers, and so representative of the community, as will preclude bloodshed and insure abstinence on the part of the Executive from further interference with the General Assembly.[69]

On January 22, Carter and several thousand "assistant sergeants-at-arms" marched on the Mechanics' Institute. Once again Federal troops, under orders from Washington to remain neutral but to allow no armed conflict in the city, blocked his way. Carter's position was now hopeless. His supporters, tired of the constant turmoil and realizing that Warmoth could not be overthrown, began drifting over to the statehouse to make their peace with the governor. Soon Carter was a general without an army. His support evaporated quickly, and Warmoth carried the day. Carter's supporters were admitted to the Mechanics' Institute on the condition that they recognize the Warmoth legislature as the legal state assembly and also recognize Brewster as Speaker of the House.[70]

Carter's career ended in a burlesque: the last that was heard of scalawag George W. Carter was a report in the *Daily Picayune,* dated February 20, 1872, stating that Carter and Algernon Sydney Bager, a young carpetbagger and commander of Warmoth's Metropolitan Police, had crossed over to Bay St. Louis, Mississippi, and there fought a duel with rifles at sixty paces. Both missed.[71] But the protagonists and their friends were immediately reconciled over a "sumptuous lunch of crackers, cheese, and whisky."[72] After that, Carter, like Wickliffe, disappeared.

Thomas Green Davidson: Democrats, Money, and Patronage

Warmoth's victory over Carter was due in large measure to Thomas Green Davidson. Although he remained in name a Democrat throughout the Reconstruction period, Davidson allied with the Republicans during the administrations of Warmoth, P. B. S. Pinchback, and William Pitt Kellogg. He would even run on the Republican ticket. In 1868, like most other Louisiana Democrats, Davidson had supported the Taliaferro ticket. "I wish you to know that every old line Democrat that could register, voted for you," Davidson informed Taliaferro, "and those that could not got their friends to do it. I done [*sic*] what I never expected to do again, I went to every man . . . that [I] had any influence with and got him to vote for you." During the state elections in 1870, Davidson allied himself with the Warmoth radicals. His name, in fact, appeared on the Livingston Parish Republican ticket. Davidson worked hard for the party and his own election. He was, apparently, so eager for a Republican victory that he proposed buying black votes. "There are about ninety African votes in the lower part of St. Helena and on the Amite River in Livingston Parish that can be encouraged with a little money," he wrote to A. W. Walker during the campaign, "I think that [with] two hundred and fifty dollars I can get every one of these for the ticket." Walker replied that the money was not available, but he was confident that Davidson could carry the parish.

Davidson's alliance with the Republicans did not sit well with his neighbors and most fellow Democrats. "Tom Green Davidson demoralized as far as he could the old line Democrats," a critic wrote in November 1870. "The money and patronage of the dominant party and our confidence in the whites, who failed to do their duty, conspired to disappoint us. . . . My God! How can a Southern man become so destitute of principle as to endorse Republicanism by voting with these Devils?" Because of his association with Warmoth and his Republican friends, Davidson "became the most hated person in the Florida Parishes." But despite the antagonism of the hard-line conservatives, Davidson remained a leader among the Louisiana Democrats. At least one Democratic journal felt that Davidson's alliance with Warmoth, although distasteful, nevertheless provided the Democratic Party with "a measure of influence on the course of legislation." Davidson's power and influence rested on his close friendship with Warmoth, his virtual monopoly of patronage in the Florida Parishes, and his chairmanship of the powerful House Judiciary Committee, where all proposed legislation was subject to his review. Warmoth found Davidson's support invaluable during his struggle with the Carter–Custom House Republicans. Indeed, Davidson's support made it possible for Warmoth to maintain a majority in the state assembly. Later, as Warmoth's power and influence declined, Davidson shifted his support to the anti-Warmoth Republicans. Although he did not run for reelection in 1874 (he was then sixty-nine years old), Davidson remained a power in Livingston Parish and reentered politics in 1880.[73]

Longstreet's Southern Strategy

Early in 1867, the *New Orleans Times* asked eighteen prominent citizens to give their views regarding Reconstruction and military rule in the South.[74] James Longstreet responded with a plea for moderation, cooperation, and acceptance. He counseled his fellow southerners to make the best of a bad situation. The South, he reminded the *Times* readers, had lost the war, and, like good soldiers fairly defeated, they should accept the victor's just terms.[75] In a second letter, dated April 6, 1867, Longstreet spoke again with the "bluntness of a soldier" and urged ex-Rebels to realize that the Confederacy was dead and that the South was powerless. The only way to effect a quick, if not painless, restoration of civil rule, he stated, was to accept the conqueror's surrender terms. If some, including himself, had lost their political rights, it was, after all, the price one paid for a failed rebellion.[76]

William L. Richter, in the latest assessment of Longstreet's military and postwar careers, notes that at first Longstreet's position, made public in March 1867, made sense to many ex-Confederates: southerners must accept the logic of defeat (secession as a doctrine was dead, the

Confederacy was dead, and slavery as an institution was dead) and make the best of it. Longstreet went further in a letter published in the *New Orleans Republican* in June 1867 to John M. Parker, a New Orleans Republican and brother-in-law of General Ben "Spoons" Butler, the hated Yankee general who had commanded the Union occupation forces in the Department of the Gulf in 1861–62. Here Longstreet came out in support of the Republicans. "The war was made upon Republican issues and it seems to me fair and just that the settlement should be made accordingly," Longstreet reasoned.[77] When he showed a draft of the letter to his uncle, Augustus Baldwin, he was emphatic: "It will ruin you, son, if you publish it." The letter proved a stunning miscalculation, and a "deafening scream of protest" resulted. Longstreet tried to put a spin on his remarks, but it was too late.[78] Nevertheless, his motive was restoration without Reconstruction. And his late conversion to Unionism reflected a combination of pragmatism and self-interest. Here is Longstreet's rationalization for joining the Republicans in his own words in a remarkable private letter, uncovered by historian William Piston, dated July 4, 1867:

> My politics is to save the little that is left to us, and to go to work to improve the little as best we may. I believe that the course that some politicians have pursued, tends to increase our humiliation and distress, and leads us to greater trouble, until we shall have confiscation & expatriation. Since the negro had been given the privilege of voting, it is all important that we should exercise such influence over that vote, as to being injurious to us, & we can only do that as Republicans. As there is no principle at issue now that should keep us from the Republican party, it seems to me that our duty to ourselves & to all our friends requires that our party South should seek an alliance with the Republican party. . . .
>
> Congress requires reconstruction upon the Republican basis. If the whites won't do this, the thing will be done by blacks, and we shall be set aside, if not expatriated. It seems plain clear to me that we should do the work ourselves, & have it white instead of black & have our best men in public office.
>
> No one has worked more than I, and lost more. I think the time has come for peace & I am not willing to lose more blood or means in

procuring it. If there are any in the country inclined to fight this question, I hope not to be included in that number.[79]

What seemed "plain clear" to Longstreet was not clear at all to unreconstructed whites.

White conservatives were unconvinced of his loyalty to the South; white Republicans were largely accepting, but, as Richter notes, they were unsure of his loyalty to their cause. Perhaps, Richter reasons, some Republicans were pleased to see him left swinging in the wind lest he and others ex-Rebels like him take over the party from true Union men. Louisiana freedmen, for their part, were clearly unconvinced of his conversion to Republicanism. The black *New Orleans Tribune* was biting in its commentary on Longstreet's political conversion: "Look out new, enfranchised citizens. . . .We have by this time so many kinds of Republicans that General Longstreet is already nominated as your leader, and Jeff Davis himself will soon claim to be your best friend." The newspaper stated that it should not be open to former Rebels who intended to use the radical movement to soften the peace terms in the interest of the ex-Rebels: "A Rebel seeking the relief of his comrades is just another friend of the oligarchy, trying to save the oligarchy from its doom."[80]

If at first there was little criticism of Longstreet's views, resistance to Reconstruction hardened among former Rebels, and the general's position found few adherents among white southerners. When Longstreet expanded on his ideas in a letter reprinted in the *New Orleans Republican* on June 5 and 6, 1867, he faced a barrage of criticism. Longstreet argued that the war had decided some things permanently. The Confederacy was dead, and the ideas that supported it were dead too. He told fellow southerners "to abandon ideas that are obsolete and conform to the requirements of law."[81] The *Daily Picayune* stated that his argument was "too puerile and illogical to have effect on the course of any person."[82] Longstreet would benefit financially from his association with the Republicans, but his reputation among the unreconstructed was virtually destroyed. He was an apostate in their eyes. "They will crucify you," his former comrade John Bell Hood told him.[83] He was right, and any reconciliation was a long time coming.

In response to a critical editorial in the *New Orleans Times,* Longstreet defended his views again. His letter, he stated, "was expressive of a desire to relieve my 'late confederates in arms' of the unnatural condition in which they have been placed by the progress of revolution." Political resistance, the general continued, was futile: "I am well satisfied that order cannot be organized out of confusion as long as the conflicting interests of two parties [Republican and Democratic] are to be served. The war was made upon Republican issues, and it seems to me fair and just that the settlement should be made accordingly. . . . If I understand the object of politics, it is to relieve the distress of the people and to provide for their future comfort." Longstreet insisted that he was not a politician: "I should not presume to interfere with politics. . . . But these are unusual times, and call for practical advice."[84] But to white southerners, a people more often attracted to the romance than the reality of political issues, Longstreet's "practical advice" was unacceptable.

Governor Warmoth saw Longstreet differently. In welcoming Longstreet into the Republican movement and appointing him commander of the new state militia, he saw a chance to attract ex-Rebel white support. It would work this way: Warmoth would undermine the white conservative opposition by recruiting white conservatives.[85] There was still another motive to appoint Longstreet. Grant had removed Warmoth from command during the war. Now, as a friend of President Grant, Longstreet might also ensure the president's support for Warmoth's regime. The plan met with success. Longstreet reported in 1871 that "one half of our force is composed of officers and soldiers who were in the military service of the Southern states during the late civil war." Brigadier General Frank J. Pargoud, for example, was a former Confederate cavalry colonel from the city of Monroe in Ouachita Parish who commanded the Second Division of the state militia. Napoleon Underwood was appointed colonel of the Fourth Regiment (East Baton Rouge, Lafourche, and Plaquemines Parishes), a unit that, in fact, may never have actually been brought into active service.

In his analysis of the state militia, Hogue contends that its ranks and leadership contained a significant number of experienced ex-Rebel veterans with "exemplary" war records. However, "few of these southern white men could properly be termed 'scalawags,'" he states, "though some militia officers, like Longstreet himself, did hold patronage positions under the Republicans and joined the Republican Party." In any case, many resigned after 1872, disgusted with "Republican in-fighting."

Despite Warmoth's ability to attract ex-Confederates, its usefulness to Warmoth was limited primarily to New Orleans, the seat of government. But the militia had little effect in the country parishes and was largely unable to protect polling places and individual supporters. Further, it took political talent to keep the alliance together—a stretch even for the able Warmoth. Under William Pitt Kellogg's inept leadership, the state militia collapsed under the White League attack in 1874. Certainly, Longstreet tried his best. He served Warmoth faithfully until he resigned in frustration in 1875.

Richter contends that Longstreet was a sincere moderate who sought a middle course in a period "of rapid, uncertain and unwelcome transition."[86] If he was trying to preserve the power of the prewar establishment, however, and only tepid in his support of black rights (he argued that if the experiment in black voting proved a mistake, Congress could reverse its position), black Republicans and true radicals were right in being suspicious of his conversion. Nevertheless, white southerners in New Orleans shunned him as a political and social leper, and, as a result, his business of cotton merchandising and insurance (the Great Southern and Western Fire, Marine and Accident Insurance Company of New Orleans) failed.[87]

On March 11, 1869, President Grant, who had recommended Longstreet's pardon, nominated him for a plum position, surveyor of customs in New Orleans. At the end of the month, an anxious Longstreet wrote to Grant about "the continuous delay" of his case. He was concerned that there was opposition to him taking such a politically influential position in the state. There was danger the senate would adjourn before he received the appointment. In the event that happened, Longstreet asked to be made a commissioner for the settlement of claims between U.S. citizens and Mexico, a job that had no local political implications.[88] Apparently any good patronage position would do. He need not have worried; the nomination was approved.

Grant had simple political reasons as well for appointing Longstreet to the post. "There does not seem to have been anything accidental or impulsive about this act," Donald Bridgman Sanger and Thomas Robson Hay state in their biography of Longstreet. "Rather, all signs indicate that it was deliberately planned. Under the circumstances, Longstreet could stay in New Orleans only if he had both position and income; by appointing Longstreet surveyor, Grant was placing both a friend and a political ally and supporter in an important spot." In return, Longstreet served the Republican cause during the carpetbag era. The carpetbaggers were, in fact, his "principal associates, to whom he looked for support and preferment." Throughout this period, they argue, "his activity was entirely political, as he supported first Warmoth and then Kellogg as the head of the party and state political machine."[89] Longstreet, at the head of the state militia and Warmoth's police, prevented the Carter forces from wrenching power away from the governor in January 1872. When Warmoth's control over Louisiana politics began to weaken, however, Longstreet defected to the Kellogg wing of the party. As a member of the State Returning Board, in November 1872, Longstreet supported Kellogg, the Custom House candidate, for governor, and helped count out John McEnery, the Warmoth-backed candidate.[90] Longstreet's service did not go unrewarded. Shortly after the election, he received an appointment to the State Levee Commission for a four-year term at six thousand dollars per year.[91] Throughout the remainder of "carpetbag rule," Longstreet supported the Republicans.

The Reconstruction political experiences of scalawags like Wickliffe, Carter, Davidson (a scalawag by any other name), and Longstreet illustrate the role played by southern white Republicans in the factional struggles of the Louisiana Republican movement. They illustrate, too, the sordid and corrupt nature of politics during the carpetbag era. Traditional-minded historians like John Rose Ficklen and Ella Lonn were correct: the radical regimes in Louisiana were riddled with corruption. As journalist Edward King observed of Louisiana politics in 1873: "The commonwealth is . . . convulsed to its center. Meanwhile professional politicians and lobbyists constantly arrange new plans for the pacification of difficulties, for compromises never to be won; the state goes onward to ruin which seems likely to be permanent."[92] But, after all, this was the Gilded Age, and the Wickliffes and Carters were perhaps no worse than their counterparts in Tammany Hall. And, as Joe Gray Taylor points out, "Louisiana government has never been simon-pure, and the Republican years were not much worse than those to follow."[93] Corruption and political in-fighting were endemic to Louisiana politics, but they do not entirely explain the failure of Reconstruction in the state; white terrorism also played a role. As a result, there were few native white Republicans during the Reconstruction years in Louisiana—perhaps no more than two hundred "politically active" scalawags.[94] The low number reflects the failure of white Republicans to extend their base and the impact of terrorism. Riddled with factionalism and without effective federal protection, southern white Republicans could not, over time, resist the enemy's determination to "bulldoze" the scalawags.

7

"DOOM FOR THE TRAITOR"

BULLDOZING THE SCALAWAGS

> The conspiracy was carried out by armed bodies of men, known by the name given them by themselves, as bull-dozers.
>
> —"History of Former Elections in Louisiana," 1880

I am safe to say," scalawag Thomas Hudnall testified in October 1868 before a congressional committee investigating violence in the South and the use of the United States Army, "that there is not a single white man whose sympathies are with the Republican Party who can be able to live in the parish of Morehouse."[1] Hudnall knew from personal experience the dangers that awaited white men who joined the radical movement in that rural, hill-country area. He reported that, in August 1868, Tom Daily, a local Republican, was murdered on the highway near Girod Station: "I am reliably informed that the body of Daily was terribly mangled; he had received nearly forty loads of shot, and that no one dared to remove it for a whole day, and it remained there until his . . . brother came with a man by the name of Doltrey, who helped to put it in a coffin. . . . I saw the coffin which Doltrey and Daily's brother were carrying on a wagon to the ridge to have it buried. Blood matter was leaking from the coffin and under the wagon." Sometime after the burial, a gang of thirty horsemen went to Doltrey's house about midnight. "Some of them dismounted, broke in the house, searched for Doltrey, loudly cursing him, saying," Hudnall testified, "that he was a damned black son of a bitch, living with negroes and voting for them." Doltrey escaped and came to Hudnall. "I advised him," Hudnall stated, "to leave the country; he did so. I believe that he is either at New Orleans or St. Louis."

Soon after Daily's murder and Doltrey's hasty departure, Hudnall himself received a visit from the local Ku Klux Klan. On the night of August 19, 1868, Hudnall claimed, a party of mounted men, armed and with their faces blackened, rode up to his brother-in-law's house, where he was spending the night. When they called out Hudnall's name, his sister Mrs. C. R. Balfour went to the door and asked them why they had come at night and in disguise to see her brother. Their leader, a man named Haddock answered: "Madam, we do not come to hurt anybody; we only wish to see Mr. Hudnall and have a private chat with him." Unconvinced, the sister asked, "Have you gentlemen come here to murder my poor old brother [Hudnall was then fifty-one years old]?" "No," Haddock repeated, "but we must have a private chat with him." Meanwhile, Hudnall had been hiding in an upstairs bedroom. His sister then went to him and begged him to speak to Haddock. Reluctantly, Hudnall went to the front door and asked Haddock what he wanted. Again, he repeated, "Come out, we want to have a private chat with you." Hudnall prudently refused.

At that point, the riders edged their horses closer to the porch. Impatient and angry, Haddock shouted that unless Hudnall came out they would drag him out. Again, Hudnall refused. "Attention, K.K.'s . . . be ready to hold some of these horses," Haddock ordered as he dismounted. The sister, now joined by her husband, begged the Klansmen to leave. "They paid no attention to these entreaties," Hudnall stated, "and we heard then the click of the pistols' triggers they were cocking." Mr. Balfour asked what crime Hudnall had committed. "They said," Hudnall reported, "that I had refused to join the democrat party after having voted the radical ticket. Haddock added that I had voted the damned negro ticket." Realizing that it was useless to argue with the gang, Hudnall retreated from the doorway and seized a double-barreled shotgun; his sister drew a knife from her blouse. She then dared Haddock to try and take her brother from the house. "I am the wife of C. R. Balfour," she stated with grim determination, "this house is all mine . . . it is now nearly day; if you are to take my brother and you too [addressing Haddock], I want you to come foremost, you bully . . . as I am now ready to die by my brother's side." Apparently taken aback by the woman's boldness, the Klansmen, who were now standing on the porch, stepped back and held a conference. Haddock then came forward and addressed

Mrs. Balfour: "You may take it to yourself that you saved your brother's life; we will now give him five days to leave this country." Hudnall left Morehouse Parish the next morning and did not stop until he reached the comparative safety of New Orleans.

Hudnall's encounter with the Morehouse Klan was typical of the experience of many Louisiana Republicans purged from public life: Louisianians, and their black and carpetbag associates, willing to vote Republican or hold public office. Such assaults and intimidation would eventually reduce the Republican Party in the rural parishes to a state of political paralysis.

Scalawag Josiah Fisk also testified to the perils facing southern white Republicans in rural Louisiana. In an affidavit dated October 22, 1868, Fisk, a New Orleans lawyer, stated that he traveled to St. Mary Parish to advise the Republican sheriff, Colonel Henry H. Pope (a native of New York and former Union army officer), on certain legal matters.[2] Pope warned Fisk in advance that "the people had become hostile, and had resolved that no republican should hold office or have a house in the parish." Pope also advised Fisk not to bring his family or let anyone know that he was acquainted with the sheriff until he had found a room to rent. Otherwise, he would be unable to secure lodging. Nevertheless, the word about Fisk's politics preceded his visit. When he arrived in Franklin, one landlord informed him that he only rented to Democrats. "I ask you plainly are you a democrat or a republican?" the landlord inquired. Fisk replied that he was a Republican. "Then you cannot have my house at any price," the owner stated firmly. Fisk later approached a widow who rented rooms to travelers. "But if he was a republican," Fisk reported her as saying, "she would not dare to let him have the house for fear the democrats would either kill her or burn her house." After Fisk eventually found accommodations, securing a place to sleep proved to be his least pressing problem. "He was informed," according to his affidavit," that the democrats were pledged to kill or drive away every republican officer in the parish, and, at the request of Colonel Pope, he never but once appeared in the streets with him, and on that occasion they had to separate on account of the crowd gathering, hooting, and yelling, "Here comes Pope, the carpet-bagger, and his scalawag lawyer."" Later, on the evening of October 17, a black man warned Fisk that a group of Democrats planned to murder him. "These men belonged to the Seymour Knights [a paramilitary political club]," Fisk testified. "They put on their uniforms and commenced to parade the streets." Fisk watched them for a time through his window, and when they marched away, he left town in the opposite direction. Fisk escaped by crossing Bayou Teche, wading through the swamp to Grand Lake, and then paddling a skiff to Brashear City. He waited through the night outside the town. The next morning someone warned him that the local Democrats had stationed pickets on the outskirts of the town. Fisk remained in hiding until a detachment of Federal troops arrived. On his way back to New Orleans, however, Fisk encountered one of the Democrats who had been waiting for him near a bridge outside of Brashear City. "You old scalawag," the man yelled, "I will get you yet." At that point, the man pulled a pistol and exclaimed, "I will give you hell now." But Fisk spurred his horse and was out of range when the man fired.

When he arrived safely in New Orleans, Fisk learned of the murder of Pope and parish judge Valentine Chase. Pope and Chase were attacked at a local inn. "Colonel Pope and Judge Chase were together, on the gallery in front of Pope's room," Fisk stated; "the murderers came along under the gallery softly until they reached the stairs, up which they rushed and fired several balls into Colonel Pope before he had a chance to rise, when Colonel Pope jumped for his room, into which he fell dead. Judge Chase struggled with them on the gallery and stairs, they stabbing and shooting all the time; finally he fell dead near the banks of the bayou." Chase was "an old citizen of the Parish and a Union man." Warmoth recalled in his memoirs, and "connected with some of the best people of the Parish." Tragically, "his only offense was that he was a Union man and had been elected to the office of Parish Judge by the Republicans."[3]

Although the expression would not be commonly used in Louisiana until the close of Reconstruction, Daily, Doltrey, Hudnall, Pope, Chase, and Fisk had been "bulldozed." To bulldoze was to use terrorism, violence, and intimidation for political ends, to coerce Republicans, black and white. The object was to remove them from office or prevent them from voting the Republican ticket. It was a brutal and effective strategy. The evidence is overwhelming that throughout the Reconstruction era Republicans in Louisiana were subjected to intimidation and physical attack.[4] The focus of the attacks on the Republicans occurred in two general areas: in New Orleans (the seat of state government) and in the rural parishes. The New Orleans "street battles" of 1866, 1873, 1874, and 1877, and the failure to control the countryside were fatal to Republican control.[5] The ebb and flow of counter-Reconstruction violence was keyed to political objectives associated with elections or other political events or goals: the reconvening of the constitutional convention in 1866, the passage of the Fourteenth Amendment, state elections, and control of local office, as in the Colfax Massacre case of 1874.

In the country parishes, the insurgency demoralized the Republicans: "In this place [Minden, Louisiana] yesterday the election was held, and conducted without violence owing, I presume, to the fact that no opposition was offered," scalawag John L. Lewis stated. "The white Republicans as well as the freedman were afraid to vote as they really desired—having had intimidations before the election that they should suffer if they did not vote the Democratic ticket. There were but two Republican tickets voted at this box—I voted one openly. . . . I had been told that no 'Radical' ticket should be voted."[6]

Lewis also complained bitterly that the local authorities were doing nothing to protect Claiborne Parish Republicans. "In Homer, a white man was tied, stripped, and whipped, day before yesterday," Lewis wrote to Governor Warmoth on July 10, 1868, "not a word said or anything done to bring the guilty to punishment. The same night Hon. W. Jasper Blackburn's printing office . . . was broken open, type, press, and everything broken, scattered, and destroyed. I address you as our governor, and ask you to give us officers not in fear of or sympathy with the miserable and cowardly clans that have committed these outrages."[7]

One white Republican reported that in Shreveport only twelve whites dared to support the radical ticket. "All we lacked was numbers in our force. . . . All the white citizens were a unit against us but were not satisfied at having overwhelming numbers and fighting us fairly on the political issues but resorted to all possible kinds of frauds—threats and violence." The result was that "no man of our party could go into the country to hold a political meeting without running the risk of being bushwhacked and assassinated." "This is not a *healthy* locality for *Radical politicians,*" this man wrote with studied understatement. He added: "Do not publish any part of this we have about as much as we want to do to dodge the *bullets* of the *Thugs* in this place now without stirring them up with a sharp pole."[8]

Radical E. B. Goodwin summed up the effect of terrorist violence and intimidation in Lafayette Parish in 1868: "I regret to say that in this Parish true, earnest working Republicans, 'are like angels . . . few and far between.'"[9]

The situation in Grant Parish was typical. "Let me tell you frankly," Elcey Breda wrote to her thirty-two-year-old husband Ernest on April 11 1873, "that I would . . . rather see you poor as a church mouse than in the position you have, for you have made yourself enemies and your friends have abandoned you, . . . [G]ive up all these political ideas, leave the Radicals. I do not say for this [*sic*] that you must turn liberal, no, remain quiet and Ernest you will see that your friends will return to you, and for me Ernest I will love you more and more each day."[10] Elcey had good reason to be frightened. Two days later, on Easter Sunday, April 13, 1873, more than sixty black men and two white supporters were killed in a fight over control of the parish government. The contest involved approximately one hundred poorly armed blacks and their few white allies and about two hundred white men armed with a cannon and repeating rifles. Scalawag Ernest Breda was at that time the state prosecutor for the Ninth Judicial District. Grant Parish was within his authority. Scalawag Edward H. Durell was the U.S. district judge. Breda was determined to bring at least 140 of the perpetrators to justice. Justice proved impossible: On July 25, when Breda attempted to continue with the prosecutions in Colfax, he was confronted by sixty men armed with guns and knives. They were determined, they shouted, to kill more "Negroes and radicals" to stop the proceedings. A shot was fired, and Breda escaped and fled Colfax after dark. Breda was appalled at the inability of Kellogg and the Federal authorities to control the insurgency in his parish despite his willingness to prosecute those whites responsible for the massacre. He was appalled that Federal troops posted only thirty miles southeast in Pineville did not act to suppress the insurrection: He recalled with bitter anger that the army in Louisiana apparently existed only to amuse and befriend "the sportsmen who kill Negroes in Colfax."[11]

On November 14, 1873, Breda wrote to his wife, mentioning that he had encountered some of his neighbors on the riverboat *Royal George* near Grand Ecore. "Suddath and Murphy are the only two who spoke to me . . . [while] Russell, Charles and others acted as if they did not know me, and I did the same thing to them, the poor low flung trash, I wonder if they expect to make anything by that, enough of the contemptible *things* for they are not worth mentioning."[12] As northern journalist Edward King observed in 1873: "there is, of course . . . both ostracism and hostility for such as take sides for the [radical] government."[13]

Bulldozing became bolder as the conservatives grew in confidence. Although they were never tightly organized, the Ku Klux Klan, the Knights of the White Camellia, and other gangs harassed Louisiana Republicans from the beginning of radical Reconstruction. Even more effective was the White League, a loosely structured, paramilitary, and anti-radical organization that appeared in 1874. Organized into trained units, armed with surplus army rifles and navy revolvers, and recruited, in part, from battle-seasoned Confederate veterans, the White League forces in New Orleans posed a serious threat to the Republican administration of carpetbag governor William Pitt Kellogg.

In September 1874, the White League rose up in open rebellion in the streets of New Orleans. The conservatives had smuggled arms into the city by railroad and steamboat. Metropolitan Policemen had, in fact, seized seventy-two rifles on September 8. But the flow of weapons continued unabated. On September 12, the steamboat *Mississippi* docked with a large cargo of weapons. When it became known that the police intended to confiscate the arms, the White League officers ordered their followers to assemble for a mass rally at the corner of St. Charles and Canal Streets.[14] The result was the "Battle of Liberty Place," September 14, 1874.

When Longstreet, commander of the state militia, learned that the White League intended to prevent the police from seizing the weapons, he mobilized his forces. Longstreet's command consisted of 500 Metropolitan Police, 100 other policemen, and 3,000 black militiamen. In addition, he had one Gatling gun and a battery of artillery.[15]

Longstreet's troops advanced to Canal Street. The Gatling gun and artillery units then opened fire. According to Longstreet's report, the insurgent line, numbering about 8,400 men, began to waver until one of the Metropolitan captains suddenly withdrew his company from its position in the Republican line and defected to the enemy. "This movement," Longstreet reported, "together with the accurate fire of sharpshooters from windows and roof tops in all directions had a very demoralizing influence upon the other infantry company, which fell back under severe fire and left the artillery exposed and unprotected."[16] The commander of the Metropolitan Police, A. S. Badger, later testified that the White Leaguers were positioned behind cotton bales and that these protected them from the Republican artillery and machine-gun fire. With the White League marksmen picking off the exposed gun crews, the Metropolitans and the black militia began to retire in confusion. The retreat turned into a rout. Some of Longstreet's men fled back to the Custom House, confident that the enemy would not attack a federal building, and others reassembled at Jackson Square. Longstreet's men were forced, however, to abandon the Mechanics' Institute (the official statehouse) to the enemy.[17] The defeat must have been particularly humiliating for James Longstreet. One of Robert E. Lee's finest officers found himself at the head of an unreliable little army defeated by a force of ex-Rebels. And to add injury to humiliation, Longstreet was wounded and captured by the enemy, according to one account.[18]

Two days after the encounter, General W. H. Emory, the Federal commander at Jefferson Barracks, arrived and restored Kellogg to power.[19] That the Kellogg regime did not collapse immediately in the fall of 1874 was due to the continued presence of Federal troops. Although the rural parishes remained largely unpoliced, in New Orleans at least the radicals still retained control of the state government. But it was obvious that without the continued support of Washington, the carpetbag government in Louisiana would fall like a ripe pear into the hands of the White League and its sympathizers. The conservative troops remained organized and now drilled openly in New Orleans, waiting for the departure of the Union soldiers.[20]

The radical defeat in New Orleans further weakened the party structure in the rural areas.[21] Now the conservatives became even more aggressive. "I must say," a Republican wrote to Stephen B. Packard from Bienville Parish, "that I never have seen the republicans in this parish so completely run off the track as the White Leaguers has [*sic*] them now. I doubt very much our standing any hand in the coming election; they have made two or three of our most prominent republicans leave the parish. The white and colored republicans are so intimidated, or have been, that they are not registering."[22] In a confidential letter dated October 1874, the president and the secretary of the Vermillion Parish Republican Executive Committee appealed to Stephen B. Packard to dispatch Union soldiers to the Cajun town of Abbeville. "The immediate presence here of a body of Federal troops," they stated, "would give confidence not only to the colored men, but many white creoles, who are republicans at heart—men who during the war hid themselves in the sea-marsh rather than serve in the confederate army, and today are well aware that their only salvation is with the republican party."[23]

That same month, Richard Talbot, a Napoleonville Republican and secretary of the Assumption Parish Executive Committee, asked Packard to send twenty-five United States cavalrymen to bolster the radical cause in this area. "On election-day every colored man in the parish would come to the polls and vote the straight ticket," he claimed, "while a large number of 'poor whites' who have fed on the rations sent from the North, and are even now unwilling to register or to vote, would be strengthened in their resolution to remain at home, or else come forward and vote the republican ticket."[24] But it all depended upon the presence of Union troopers. Such was the fragile base of Republicanism in these two rural parishes.

Violence and intimidation were not the only weapons employed by the conservative whites. Social ostracism accompanied terrorism. Conservative whites refused white radicals a place in the community life, striving, often successfully, to freeze them out of white society. When Ouachita Parish scalawag John Ray voted for an equal rights bill in the state assembly in 1868, for instance, the *New Orleans Daily Picayune* lashed out in a particularly vicious editorial headlined, in all capital letters, "Doom for the Traitor":

> Men and women of Louisiana, in whose veins courses the pure blood of the race which has always ruled that of Africa, what must you think of the conduct of this degenerate white man? This man who has a white wife and children, who has been the associate of white men and women, received into their homes, feasted at their boards, sheltered under their roofs, who does not come to us from Vermont, Massachusetts, or Michigan, with their perverted theories, against God's eternal decree of separation of the white and black races. . . . [Ray] had the shameless hardihood to vote that hereafter the negro, reeking with fetid odors, hideous in face, brutal in manner, rude in speech, shall be the social equal of the proud and sensitive whites of Louisiana.

Now, the newspaper warned, white women and children "are to find negro men, and women, and children at the hotels, theatres, and on the railroad trains, received on equal footing with themselves, crowding them at tables, or in steamboat cabins, and compelling them to inhale their sickening stench or listen to their vulgar talk." The editorial concluded with a demand that Ray be ostracized from white society: "Let him go forth, and return to his outraged white neighbors to receive his social doom. If the 'slow and moving finger of scorn' be not henceforth his lot among white people, a great social criminal will escape merited punishment."[25]

Appeals for white Louisianians to coerce their white radical neighbors had multiplied with the founding of the White League. "We infinitely prefer the negro to the carpetbagger and renegade [scalawag]," the *Alexandria Caucasian,* a White League journal, editorialized in April 1874, "and if we must make a choice between the ignorance of the one and the rascality of the other, give us, by all means ignorance, and instruct it into some sort of semblance of knowledge and reason. Give us his Satanic Majesty and all the imps of hell in preference to the sneaking, whining, sleek-haired, cowardly, impecunious, lying, deceitful, and thievish carpetbagger, and his town companion, the miscegenation-loving, would-be negro and no less corrupt scalawag."[26]

In 1874, the *Natchitoches Vindicator* warned the Louisiana scalawags that the time had come for them to leave the radical movement or be excluded forever from white society: "We advise our native white fellow citizens of Louisiana, who have arrayed themselves against their white brothers, to retrace their steps while there is still time left to do so." But it was not enough for the scalawags simply to desert the Republicans; they must also actively aid the conservative forces. "When a war of races is imminent—and we tell them that it is imminent—they should be found but on one side battling with the Caucasian race; words of sympathy will not do. The people will be satisfied with nothing short of acts, plain and unmistakable. They have yet time to redeem themselves." The scalawag, the journal stated, had no alternative but to join the white ranks. The conservatives were determined to win, and the struggle would be "quick, sharp, and decisive." Finally, the editorial addressed its conservative readers: "Let us never cease to make war upon them, both in their official and private capacities; discountenance any person who meets them as gentlemen on the street. Shut your doors and your hearts to them; let them be outcasts to every feeling of mercy you may have, so that living they may only encumber the earth, and dying descend to hell covered with the curses of every virtuous man in Louisiana."[27]

The White Leaguers of St. Mary Parish for their part pledged themselves to ostracize all white Republicans. "We regard it the sacred and political duty of every member of this Club to discountenance and socially proscribe all white men who united themselves with the radical party." Conservative whites were encouraged to compile

> a black list or book of remembrance, in every parish, wherein should be inscribed the names of those white men, who, in this emergency prove recreant to the duties and instincts of race and cast their lot with the African. The infamous record should be as conspicuous, for all time to come as the pictures of notorious criminals in the rogues' galleries of large cities. These men must not be forgotten. Let their names be written in the Black List . . . that they and all who descend from their loins to the fourth generation may be Pariahs, forever cast out from all association with the Caucasian race. Let all who adhere to the Negro party . . . be reckoned as Negroes and treated as such.[28]

The White League Club of Sandy Creek, Louisiana, vowed to "consider it beneath our moral and social dignity to associate with any white man who refuses to enroll his name among those who have openly declared themselves to be white men with principles favoring a white man's government." For a white man, even remaining neutral had its dangers: The members of the Baton Rouge chapter organized a committee to report "the names of all white men, who through indifference to the future welfare of the white race of Louisiana have failed to register [to vote]; and that a list of those names be kept for publication after the election, together with the names of all white men who voted the radical ticket."[29]

Violence, intimidation, blacklisting and social ostracism were fatal to a Republican movement already weakened by internal fighting. Many of the radicals lived under the most intense pressure, fearful of a night visit by the White League or some equally dangerous gang of conservative terrorists.

Still clinging to patronage, scalawag Ernest Breda remained active in the party despite the violence and ostracism. But he was cautious—watching for danger. His correspondence indicates that he was whistling past the graveyard. Following the Louisiana state elections of November 1874, he visited with party leaders in New Orleans:

> I have made many acquaintances and have met with my usual good fortune, that is becoming a favorite of all whom I meet and converse with and have received the expressions of heartfelt congradulations [*sic*] from the highest officials of the state on my successes and the ability shown while District Attorney, and expressions of assurance as to my future career in the Judiciary. It is true we are beset by enemies and surrounded by dangerous elements, but it gladdens and strengthens our hearts to meet men in sympathy of feelings and of like opinions who have the fortitude to think as freemen, and the courage to battle for their rights. [E. L.] Pierson [a fellow scalawag] and I were the heroes of North Western Louisiana.

He concluded with a promise to return home soon, but, he cautioned, "so not let any stranger know this and I will turn up *all right* when you least expect it."[30] The bulldozers forced Breda to flee Natchitoches in 1876. The *Vindicator* noted his flight with considerable glee. "Quite an amusing spectacle was presented to our people Tuesday last, and the mirth of the affair has its point well made," the White League organ stated. "As soon as the troops departed . . . Breda and other hitherto 'bold and outspoken Republicans,' took flight with them." The radical "Hegira," the paper reasoned, marked "the return of order and prosperity" to Louisiana.[31]

In 1878, Breda, now in hiding in Shreveport, wrote to his wife. "Let no stranger know of our moves," he warned, "let them find out for themselves. After we will be in New Orleans then it is all right."[32] It was not all right. The day of the carpetbagger, scalawag, and the vision of a new political and racial order in a reconstructed Louisiana was over.

The Republicans did not exaggerate when they charged that in Louisiana there was a "conspiracy to suppress by force and violence, the Republican vote. That the means used for that end were night-riding, patrollings, whippings, shootings, hangings, mutilations, assassinations, murder and massacre."[33] Violent actions reflected precisely the conservative agenda seeking to control elections and intimidate scalawags, carpetbags, and blacks. Bulldozing accompanied the revival of Democratic participation in politics. This terrorism was encouraged by ineffectual and inconsistent federal intervention. The dual strategy of controlling the ballot box and bulldozing the Republicans buried Louisiana Reconstruction.

8

AFTER THE DELUGE

THE SCALAWAGS AND THE WANING OF LOUISIANA REPUBLICANISM

> The clock is always ticking. Reconstructions are races between change and reaction; they cannot last long before they seem to be another form of oppression. Reconstructions must make their changes quickly or they are not likely to make them at all.
>
> —EDWARD L. AYERS, "The First Occupation: What the Reconstruction Period after the Civil War Can Teach Us about Iraq"

The Louisiana scalawags did not suddenly disappear from the political scene after 1866. But the day of the scalawag was over, and the window of opportunity was now closed for an early and lasting reconstruction of civil government led by native white southern Unionists. By the end of Reconstruction in Natchitoches Parish, for example, only ten white men could still be identified as Republicans.[1] A few remained in politics, reconciled in one way or another to their former enemies and no longer a threat. Some abandoned radicalism. Some went over to the Democrats. And some retreated from the hurly-burly of Louisiana politics and left the state in frustration. But if any scalawags persisted in their old ways, the bulldozers were still on hand to remind them of the meaning of "Redemption."

Among those who continued to hold elective office was Michael Hahn. Although he remained a Republican in name, Hahn withdrew from the radical camp after 1871 and worked closely with the Liberal Republicans and Democrats. This, in part, explains his survival as an office holder after 1877. Hahn also continued to edit the *New Orleans Republican* until 1871. He then moved to his sugar plantation in St. Charles Parish, where he founded the village of Hahnville. He became a school director of the parish in 1872 and in that same year served as president of the Louisiana State educational convention. Hahn was also elected to the state legislature for three successive terms in 1872, 1874, and 1876. While a member of the state assembly, he was chairman of the Judiciary Committee and served briefly as Speaker of the House. In August 1876, he was appointed registrar of voters. Hahn was, apparently, one of the few elected officials who was able to avoid the controversy surrounding the election that year. In 1878, President Hayes appointed Hahn superintendent of the United States Mint at New Orleans, a position he held until January 1879. In November 1879, Hahn won election as a state district judge (his jurisdiction comprised the parishes of Jefferson, St. Charles, and St. John).

In 1880, Hahn founded the *New Orleans Ledger,* a partisan newspaper aimed at promoting the local and national party candidates. Four years later he was reelected district judge, apparently without opposition. In October 1884, Hahn was elected as a Republican to Congress from Louisiana's Second District, one of the state's strongest Democratic areas. Hahn died suddenly of a massive stroke at Willard's Hotel in Washington on March 15, 1886. He was fifty-six years old,[2] still prosperous, still in office, still a Republican.

Thomas Green Davidson did not seek reelection to the state assembly in 1874. From that time until 1880, his political activities were restricted to local affairs in Livingston Parish. In 1880, however, Davidson, then seventy-five years old, ran successfully for the Louisiana House of Representatives. "It appeared," E. Russ Williams writes, "that [his constituents] chose to remember him for the service of his earlier career and to overlook the confusion of the dark days of war and reconstruction." Three years later, on September 1, 1883, Davidson died while still in office at Springfield, Louisiana.[3]

Chauncey Kellogg, a lawyer and a persistent Republican, tried to rebuild the party in Louisiana in the late 1870s and 1880s. One Louisianian, Ambrose Snow, asked United States Senator Frank Hiscock (Republican, New York) to assist Kellogg in securing a position with the United States Mint in New Orleans. "There being no republican Senator from Louisiana and only one republican congressman [Michael Hahn]," Snow wrote, "it seems to Mr. Kellogg's friends that it will not be out of place for republicans from other states who know of his high character and fitness to make recommendations as may aid the President in making good appointments."[4]

Theodore Fontelieu of New Iberia continued to work for the Republican Party as late as 1889. "He is a native born Republican," G. R. M. Neuman wrote from Abbeville that year, "true to the core and deserves consideration at the hands of the party." (Fontelieu had recently applied for a position with the United States Mint at New Orleans.) "He was shot [at] several times . . . on the stand while making a speech in 1884. . . . This outrage on him was repeated in 86 and in the spring and fall of 88. He was elected Dist. Judge in 79–84 and 88 and counted out each time."[5]

Oscar Jeffrion continued to lead the Pointe Coupee Republicans after 1876. In 1878, in fact, he claimed that the Republican Party was still alive in his parish but in danger. He wrote to President Hayes in December 1878: "I will take occasion to state that at every election—even the late [state] contest of 1878—my Party has achieved a victory in my Parish and always by large majorities. While the Rep Party has become disorganized and mismanaged in nearly every Republican Parish[,] the Parish of Point Coupee has again been true to her past record as is evidenced by the victory again this year. Although violence and intimidation were practiced[,] this *Parish* has been classed as one of the '*bulldozed*.' These results ought to command the attention of your Excellency."[6]

In 1872, Eugene Staes became judge of the Second Municipal Court of New Orleans, an "office he held up to the downfall of the Republican party" in Louisiana. Staes, however, remained an active Republican, and in 1888 he ran unsuccessfully for the state senate from the Second Senatorial District. "Although defeated," A. A. Braver, president of New Orleans's Ninth Ward Republican club, wrote to President Benjamin Harrison in recommending Staes for a position with the United States Mint in New Orleans in 1899, "he ran ahead of the republican ticket by several hundred votes." And, Braver added, Staes "was one of the few Louisianians who have not abandoned the Republican Party and principles at the downfall and gone over to the Democratic Party." He also informed the president that Henry Clay Warmoth, J. R. G. Pitkin, P. B. S. Pinchback, and Andrew Hero endorsed Staes's application.[7]

"Major [Andrew] Hero is a sugar planter and a notary public, and has been voting the Republican ticket for the last twenty years, openly, boldly, and fearlessly," one of Hero's supporters wrote in 1889.[8] Hero, an ex-Confederate, remained an active Republican in New Orleans as an unsuccessful candidate for lieutenant governor and for a seat in the United States Congress in the 1880s.[9] Various letters recommending Hero for a position with the United States Mint in New Orleans, written in 1889, emphasized the need to reward such old-line white Republicans as Hero for their years of service to the party. A Texas Republican, W. B. Merchant, argued, for example, that not only would a patronage position benefit Hero, but his appointment would also be a step toward the rebuilding of the Republican Party in the South: "While I have no confidence in the pretenses of the Southern Democrats . . . giving colored people any fair chance in political matters I am of the opinion that a *white* Republican party can be built up in Louisiana that will at some future time be able to demand and force a free ballot and fair count." This Republican looked to Hero and men like him to "organize a strong party of both white and colored Republicans in the Commonwealth of Louisiana" (emphasis added).[10]

Thus, one important reason for the continued, though diminished, presence of the Republican Party in Louisiana was its influence over federal patronage in New Orleans, especially the United States Custom House on Canal Street and the United States Mint on Esplanade Street.[11] James Madison Wells was fortunate in securing a federal appointment. He had served on the State Returning Board in 1874 and 1876. During the 1874 canvass, Wells and the other Republican board members threw out enough disputed returns (that is, Democratic votes) to ensure a radical majority in the state assembly.[12] The Democrats, of course, responded with a great howl of discontent since they considered the board's proceedings a fraud. There were, in fact, at least two attempted assassinations of Wells in 1874 as a result of the decision.[13]

Wells's service to the party did not go unrewarded. In May 1875, he received an appointment as surveyor of customs for the port of New Orleans. The position was not very lucrative, but it did enable him to begin to recoup his finances, which had declined since the war, even allowing him to send his daughters to boarding school in Virginia.[14]

The election of 1876 brought Wells back into the public eye. Once again the Republicans and the Democrats were locked in a bitter dispute; once again the Republican-dominated board proceeded to count its friends in and its Democratic enemies out; and once again, the Democrats fumed with outrage. At the conclusion of its deliberations, the board announced that Republican Stephen B. Packard had been elected governor and Rutherford B. Hayes had carried the state.[15]

During the congressional investigations of the Returning Board following the disputed election, Wells defended himself against a variety of allegations, including charges that he had personally falsified the returns from Vernon Parish and that he had solicited bribes totaling $1 million. The evidence and testimony were so contradictory that the truth regarding Wells's role in the election will probably never be entirely clear. As one student of Wells's political career states: "The tremendous mass of testimony taken by Congressional committees, Senate committees, and that uncovered by newspapers was successful in showing that the Louisiana Returning Board did change the results of the election as delivered to them by election supervisors. The testimony did not show, however, that the Board had changed the results illegally. The tremendous power, granted by its creating act, was wielded by Wells [as the president of the board] and his companions according to their consciences. They firmly believed that their actions were justified. Wells himself never admitted that his decisions were wrong."[16]

In June 1877, however, an Orleans Parish grand jury indicted Wells and the other board members for perjury, forgery, and altering the returns of several parishes.[17] Wells appealed to President Hayes and Secretary of the Treasury John Sherman to save him, but there was little the Washington Republicans could do since the indictments were a purely state matter. Wells at one point even hid in the Custom House to avoid arrest. He contemplated fleeing the state, but in February 1878, he surrendered to a local sheriff and returned to New Orleans. Incarcerated briefly in the parish jail, Wells secured his release on ten thousand dollars bail. Although one member of the board was convicted and sentenced to two years at hard labor, the state Supreme Court later overturned the verdict. In Wells's case, which had not yet come to trial, all charges were dismissed.[18]

Safe now from future prosecution, Wells continued working at the Custom House until he retired in 1880 to his plantation at Lecompte in Rapides Parish. After his retirement, he withdrew completely from public life. He died on February 28, 1899, at the age of ninety-one.[19]

Louis Dupleix was one of the few rural Republican office holders to survive the Democratic takeover in 1877. Appointed registrar of the United States Land Office at Natchitoches by President Grant in 1872, he continued in that position during the administrations of Presidents Hayes, Garfield, and Arthur. Out of office during Cleveland's tenure, Dupleix was reappointed to the land office position by Benjamin Harrison in May 1900.[20]

From 1873 until 1882, Benjamin Franklin Flanders served as United States treasurer at New Orleans. In 1888, he was the unsuccessful Republican candidate for state treasurer. Despite his failure to return to active politics, the postwar years seem to have been good to Flanders. On March 13, 1896, he died on his country estate, Ben Alva, near Youngsville, Lafayette Parish.[21]

Maximilian Ferdinand Bonzano was coiner of the United States Mint during Hahn's brief tenure as superintendent. He later worked as melter and refiner for the mint until his retirement in 1883. That same year, he received the "token" Republican nomination for state treasurer, but he was easily defeated by a Democrat, E. A. Burke. Bonzano's career in government service was not unprofitable. In 1878, he purchased a mansion outside of New Orleans. The Hermitage, as he called it, had been the headquarters of Andrew Jackson during the Battle of New Orleans. It also received local fame for having been the temporary residence of the Marquis de Lafayette during his visit to New Orleans in 1825. Bonzano equipped the mansion with a chemical laboratory and an extensive scientific and classical library. The building included "the latest inventions of the day [1892], the phonograph, the type-writer, the self registering thermometer, telegraphic connections with the city and other marvels of comfort and ingenuity."[22]

The Republicans rewarded Philip Hickey Morgan's persistent party loyalty through federal patronage: He was appointed U.S. district attorney in Louisiana by President Grant and served from 1869 until 1873. He then sat on the Louisiana Supreme Court (1873–76) through appointment by Governor P. B. S. Pinchback. Morgan later served as a diplomat during the administrations of Rutherford B. Hayes, James A. Garfield, and Chester A. Arthur as an envoy to Egypt (1876–80) and Mexico (1880–85). He did not return to Louisiana but practiced law in New York City from 1885 until his death in 1900.[23]

Robert Ray served as judge of the Fourth Judicial District of Louisiana until the Democratic takeover in 1877. He then returned to his law practice. Ray, however, did not desert the party. In 1888, he ran for attorney general of Louisiana but failed to win the election. Later, as a reward for his continued loyalty to the party, Benjamin Harrison appointed him postmaster at Monroe, Louisiana. Ray died in October 1899 at the age of sixty-nine.[24]

John Ray did not return to Ouachita Parish following the collapse of the radical regime. Two months before the 1876 presidential election, scalawag B. H. "Benny" Dinkgrave, the former sheriff and tax collector, and leading Ouachita Republican, was assassinated in broad daylight in Monroe, the parish seat. Dinkgrave was a Confederate veteran and outspoken Republican who became a special target of the Redeemers in the lead-up to the election. The Republicans understood that the murder was "calculated to . . . spread a terrible fear and feeling of insecurity." For Ray, the message clear enough, he did not return to Ouachita Parish: "I am satisfied that there was a feeling too much nugatory to attempt to control votes there by any argument whatever," he testified later before a congressional committee, "and besides some of my friends . . . advise me that if I filled these appointments [Ray had been scheduled to stump the parish for the Republican ticket in 1876] I might subject myself to personal violence."[25] Dinkgrave and Ray, like many of their fellow Republicans, black as well as white, had been "bulldozed." Ray retreated to New Orleans, where it was safer. He served as legal counsel to the Returning Board during the disputed electoral count of 1876, and as a reward for his service to the party, John Sherman, then secretary of the Treasury, appointed Ray special prosecuting attorney for the "Whiskey Ring" cases in Louisiana in 1878.[26] His other legal activities involved cases dealing with Louisiana's claims to certain Gulf Coast swamplands and the claims of French citizens in New Orleans for damages arising out of the Federal occupation of the city during the Civil War.[27] During his last years, Ray built up a thriving legal practice in New Orleans. He died on March 4, 1888.[28]

Thomas Jefferson Durant fled Louisiana following the New Orleans Riot of 1866 and settled in Washington, D.C. Although he never returned to the state, he continued to correspond with Louisiana's Republican leaders, especially Benjamin Franklin Flanders and Henry Clay Warmoth: "The statesmanship of Mr. Lincoln was to let things drift, . . . no plans, and let events carry him forward; for the Executive this may have been wise; but our Congress has for two sessions been doing the same thing," and "Mr. Johnson is steering the ship right towards the rocks," he wrote to Flanders in 1867. Durant wanted Congress to take the initiative and establish a firm policy toward the South. His letters dealt with a variety of subjects, including congressional Reconstruction policy,[29] the Louisiana constitutional convention of 1867–68,[30] and the congressional hearings on the New Orleans Riot of 1866. Flanders supplied Wells with certain documents discovered in the city comptroller's office relative to the riot. "They show," Durant stated, "the callous inhumanity as well as the blood-thirsty clutches of the men . . . Wells and Johnson handed the loyal people over to."[31] He was also involved with federal patronage and Republican factional politics. He recommended, for example, that Blanc F. Joubert, a freedman, be appointed to a position in the New Orleans Custom House: "Justice as well as sound policy demands that in the appointment to office under the United States Government the newly enfranchised citizens should be adequately represented."[32] Durant was fearful that divisions within the radical party would lead to a conservative resurgence. He urged Warmoth in March 1868 to make peace with the Roudanez faction and find some middle ground for agreement. A split in the Republican ranks, he reasoned, "can only be avoided by compromise which when as in the present case principles are identical, implies nothing dishonorable and I hope nothing impossible."[33] Durant remained a popular figure with many Louisiana Republicans. In December 1867, for example, the *New Orleans Tribune* had advocated the nomination of Durant for governor,[34] and in 1868, James Graham supported Durant for one of Louisiana's seats in the United States Senate.[35] Yet Durant showed no interest in returning to Louisiana, and he remained in Washington tending to his busy and lucrative legal practice. Durant appeared as counsel in approximately 154 cases before the United States Supreme Court and the United States Court of Claims. The majority of these cases dealt with Louisiana affairs.[36] He appeared, in fact, as an associate counsel before the Supreme Court in the landmark Slaughter-House Cases.[37] But Durant played a relatively minor role in this litigation, and his briefs had little or no effect on the court's final decision.[38]

Durant, however, did play a major role in another important Supreme Court case, *Walker v. Sauvinet* (1876). In the instance, Durant and his legal partner, C. W. Horner, defended the right of a bartender, Walker, to refuse service to a black man, Charles S. Sauvinet. In their brief, Durant and Horner argued that the Louisiana statutes of 1869 and 1871, which enforced the radical constitutional provision that all persons, regardless of race, have equal rights upon any public conveyance and in all places of business of a public nature, were unconstitutional. "These acts," they argued, "have in direct intention to compel all persons engaged in business to sell their commodities whenever called upon to do, and whether willing or not. Such compulsion is an abridgment of the right of a citizen, who has the natural right to sell or keep his commodities as best suits his own purposes; and this compulsion is a violation of the XIVth Amendment to the constitution."[39] In a split decision, the Court ruled against Durant's client, basing its decision not on his right to discriminate, but rather on a technical matter involving his right to a trial by jury.[40] Ironically, Sauvinet's lawyer was J. Q. A. Fellows, an old-line conservative. Durant, on the other hand, had been one of the most outspoken advocates of black rights in Louisiana.

In 1881, Durant received an appointment as counsel for the United States before the Spanish and American Claims Commission. "The sad-faced and thin-featured New Orleans Unionist," as the *Boston Daily Advertiser* described Durant, died one year later on February 3, 1882.[41]

Once removed from Louisiana politics, Durant became something of an elder statesman, and his name came up from time to time in regard to a Supreme Court seat. Hans L. Trefousse provides this neat summary of Durant's career: "A narrow constitutionalist, Durant was a distinguished member of his profession. His effectiveness in reconstructing Louisiana was hampered by his quarrels with Banks, A. P. Dostie, and the Lincoln administration."[42]

W. Jasper Blackburn also left Louisiana at the close of Reconstruction and returned to his native Arkansas. During the 1880s and 1890s, Blackburn published two newspapers, the *Little Rock Republican* and *Blackburn's Free South*.[43] Although he remained an active supporter of the Republican Party, Blackburn complained that white Republicans in the South were ignored by Washington. "It was well known," he editorialized in 1899, "that a Republican negro of the South is always in far more favor with the National Republican Government, and with the leading organized influences here at home, than a native white Republican. And as a striking illustration of which, a dead negro was recently appointed to a federal office here in Little Rock for which a 'live' native white Republican was not noticed any more than a 'yellow dog!'"[44] Blackburn's bitter outburst was perhaps motivated by his own inability to secure federal patronage. In June 1889, two months previous to the publication of the editorial, Cyrus Bussey, the assistant secretary of the Treasury, responded to a request from Blackburn for a position with the Bureau of Internal Revenue. "If I was not overwhelmed with requests for office from almost every man I have ever known [he declared] I might exercise some influence but am rendered powerless in consequence of the great number that have asked me for my interest in their behalf." But, Bussey added, "I would be very glad to say any word in your favor knowing as I do the grand stand you took in the dark days of the War in behalf of the Union."[45] Blackburn continued publishing the *Free South* until 1892. He died on November 10, 1899, and was buried in Mount Holly Cemetery in Little Rock.[46]

James Longstreet hoped to remain in New Orleans following the collapse of the Kellogg regime: "It seems more than probably that the Federal offices here will change very soon," he wrote to an old friend close to the Hayes administration. "I beg therefore you will intercede in my behalf. I would like the appointment of Collector of Customs for this Port." The appointment of white southern Republicans to federal positions, Longstreet reasoned, would "soon enable us to Southernize the party and regain its lost morale and strength here."[47] "Southernize" the Republican Party? Those days were long gone. And Longstreet, no doubt, was as much interested in his own financial future as he was in the future of southern Republicanism. In any case, he did not secure the position, and he settled in Gainesville, Georgia, in April 1877.[48] The general did not give up hope that the Republicans in Washington would remember him. He wanted, in fact, to be the United States marshal for Georgia. "Although but recently returned to Georgia I and my family have been more closely identified with Georgia and Georgia interests than any other state," he wrote to President Hayes in 1877. "I grew up in the State, but, from a short time prior to my going to West Point, for my military education, to the return to the State, about eighteen months ago, I have not been located any great length of time in any State. My record as a faithful officer of government is on file at Washington. I refer you to the endorsement of friends who have urged me to this step for political views in this connection."[49] Longstreet was not forgotten by his party. From 1880 to 1881, he served as United States minister to Turkey; from 1881 to 1894 he was United States marshal for the State of Georgia; and from 1897 until his death on January 2, 1904, he was a United States railroad commissioner. His last years were also devoted to writing his memoir, *From Manassas to Appomattox* (1896), and articles on the Civil War.[50] "When there were no real wars to fight," Glen LaFantasie judges, "when all the real battles were finished, Longstreet wandered about in life rather aimlessly, searching for himself and for his rightful place in the world."[51]

At the time of Longstreet's death at age eighty-three, the Lost Cause devotees were divided as how to react. The Savannah chapter of the United Daughters of the Confederacy voted not to send flowers; Confederate veterans in North Carolina decided not to send condolences.[52] There were, nevertheless, reconciliations of a sort for the old "scalawag." His funeral on January 6, 1904, was attended by the ladies of the General James Longstreet Chapter of the United Daughters of the Confederacy.[53] A Rebel veteran approached the casket and offered a part of his uniform and his enlistment papers to be buried with an old comrade.[54] Today the Longstreet Society of Gainesville, Georgia, honors the Confederate general for "His skill and valor as a soldier and as commander of the famous old First Corps of the Army of Northern Virginia; His fervent dedication to the *restoration* [emphasis added] of the American Union; His love for his Southern homeland; His advocacy for the ideals of peace and understanding among all peoples; [and] His belief in the brotherhood of man."[55] Susan Rosenvold of the society insists: "*Longstreet was not a scalawag,* although he is commonly seen as one, he was pragmatic. He understood that the best way to control one's future was through participation."[56] William Piston concludes his study of Longstreet's place in southern history by referring to him as a "figure of pity and scorn."[57] Or, as William Richter states, Longstreet's Reconstruction career "was truly a road to hell paved with good intentions."[58]

In the latter half of the twentieth century, the political climate of Louisiana changed. The "southern strategy" initiated by Richard Nixon and Ronald Reagan recruited southern conservative whites into the Republican ranks. Today, Louisiana white southern Republicans are no longer despised "scalawags." They represent the party base for which Longstreet and his associates searched during Reconstruction. In 2011, for example, at the sesquicentennial of the American Civil War, the governor of Louisiana is a Republican, and the Republicans hold six of the seven Louisiana U.S. congressional seats, one U.S. Senate seat, and the majority of the seats in the Louisiana House of Representatives. Longstreet's southern strategy came 150 years too early.

Edward Henry Durell left Louisiana under a cloud of controversy in 1874. Two years previously Durell, then federal circuit judge for the District of Louisiana, had issued an injunction forbidding Warmoth and his Democratic allies from seizing the state government during the heated state elections of 1872. The judge's order effectively made William Pitt Kellogg, Warmoth's carpetbag rival, governor of Louisiana.[59] The order brought on a storm of outrage and led to an investigation by the Judiciary Committee of the United States House of Representatives. The majority report concluded that Durell had exceeded his authority as a federal judge when he intervened in a purely state affair. The majority of the committee, all Republicans, also concluded that Durell was corrupt in his handling of certain bankruptcy cases brought before his court. The committee therefore recommended that Durell "be impeached of high crimes and misdemeanors in office."[60] The impeachment proceedings were not, it seems, entirely politically motivated. Durell had exceeded his authority in supporting the Kellogg-oriented Returning Board, and he had also appointed a close friend, E. W. Norton, as an official assignee in bankruptcy. Norton, it was alleged, charged exorbitant fees for his services. The scalawag judge, however, resigned before the House could vote on the charges, and the impeachment proceedings were stopped.[61]

Following his resignation, Durell retired, or rather retreated, to New York State. But he did not completely sever his ties with the Louisiana Republicans. "I assure you I have not forgotten the great service you have rendered the Republican party of Louisiana," William Pitt Kellogg wrote to Durell in May 1875, "nor am I unmindful of the sacrifices you made in that belief."[62] Durell lived briefly in Newburgh, and then settled in Schoharie, New York, where he married and spent his remaining years working on a manuscript entitled "History of Seventeen Years; from 1860 to the Retiring of the Federal Army from Louisiana and South Carolina." The study, which dealt largely with slavery and the radical years, remained unfinished at his death in March 1887.[63]

In 1878, Rufus Waples, one of the founding fathers of the Louisiana Republican Party and one of the most active Radicals, moved to Ann Arbor, Michigan. He died there in 1902.[64]

State Supreme Court Chief Justice John T. Ludeling remained on the bench until the Democrats ousted him in January 1877. He returned to Monroe in Ouachita Parish, but did not give up hope that his service to the Republican Party during the Reconstruction era would produce some reward. "I would like to have your influence and recommendation," he wrote to his old friend Henry Clay Warmoth in 1881, "to get the appointment as Minister to Mexico, Italy, or Spain. I believe I have the ability to serve the country well in either of these positions; and I am *rusting* here. I do not want anything in Louisiana. Will you help me?"[65] Despite his failure to become a diplomat, Ludeling's law practice in Monroe apparently prospered. He died at Killeden, his plantation estate outside Monroe, on January 21, 1891.[66]

In 1889, H. N. Frisbie, a New Orleans attorney, recommended scalawag William Henry Hire for the position of coiner of the United States Mint at New Orleans. Frisbie recounted Hire's steady devotion to the party: "Therefore Mr. President [Benjamin Harrison], if your policy is to recognize and reward Union men in the South, where it costs something, and where Union Soldiers frequently remark they find their services were on the wrong side of the war 'and' if it is the purpose of your Administration to recognize long tried faithful, honest Republicans and who are such from principle alone, then if such is the case, I ask you to appoint Hire coiner of the New Orleans mint. . . . And by so doing, you will please more Republicans and Union people than you can suppose to be interested in your Southern policy."[67] Hire did not receive the appointment, and he lived his remaining years in obscurity.

Michel Vidal edited the *St. Landry Progress,* a pro-Warmoth newspaper, until Emerson Bently, a young Ohio-born carpetbagger, leased the paper in early 1868. Vidal then moved to New Orleans, where, with the aid of Bently's sixteen-year-old brother, Lincoln, he began publication of a second newspaper, the *Assumption (Parish) Progress.*[68] In 1869, Vidal received an appointment as United States commissioner to Peru. Vidal's duties involved the adjustment of claims on the part of the United States citizens against Peru resulting from the Peruvian-Spanish War of 1866–71.[69] From April 1870 until October 1876, Vidal served as the United

States consul at Tripoli.[70] Nothing is known of Vidal's life after 1876, and he seems to have "dropped out of public life."[71]

Napoleon Underwood's reward for service to the party was less than prestigious. A former Confederate deserter, scalawag delegate to the "Bones and Banjo" constitutional convention of 1868 from St. James Parish, and party functionary, Underwood wound up as a night watchman at the New Orleans Custom House.[72]

9

THE SCALAWAGS IN RETROSPECT

The Aryan Race
—Theme of the parade and ball,
Mistick Krewe of Comus, 1877

Who, then, were the Louisiana scalawags? The "reckless and abandoned" men of Reconstruction legend? "Poor white trash"? "Unprincipled scamps"? What is their legacy? First, they were neither poor nor ignorant. These southern white Republicans were often well educated and well placed professionally. They counted among their ranks men with college educations and professional training and experience: lawyers, physicians, journalists, schoolteachers, ministers, businessmen, bankers, planters, soldiers, and civil servants. They were not poor whites who saw in the disruptive decade after the Civil War a chance to rise above a hardscrabble existence at the expense of the southern aristocrats. They were, more often than not, likely to have been men of education, reputation, and prestige during the antebellum years.

Second, the Louisiana scalawags were not political adolescents. They were frequently men with experience in governing and politics. They brought to the Republican movement political experience gained on the local, state, and federal levels. The scalawag ranks included former judges, district attorneys, city attorneys, school board members, parish office holders, state legislators, and one former United States congressman. They were experienced in party politics as former Democrats, Whigs, Know-Nothings, and Constitutional-Unionists. They had a head for politics and a politician's temperament.

Third, the Louisiana scalawags were often motivated by nationalism. Their Republicanism was an extension of their wartime Unionism.

Michael Hahn, A. P. Dostie, Benjamin Franklin Flanders, James G. Taliaferro, and James Madison Wells, for example, were all outspoken Unionists. The early letters of Durant are exemplary in their reflection of the pro-Union and free-labor arguments of the ideology of the Republican Party before the Civil War.[1] During the wartime occupation of New Orleans, from 1862 until 1865, the local scalawags collaborated with the U.S. Army commanders to stimulate pro-Union feeling in the city. "It is the Union that we are fighting for," Michael Hahn declared in a speech delivered at a review of the first New Orleans Volunteer Infantry in 1864, "the Union as it was when this accursed war was inaugurated by Southern treason."[2] Long after the war, white southern Republicans continued to refer to themselves as Unionists. It is persistent Unionism, with its connection to economic opportunity and the main chance, rather than persistent Whiggery, that is the key to scalawag motivation. There is no evidence to show that the legacy of the Whigism defined Republicanism in Louisiana.

Fourth, the scalawags included men from other states or countries who were attracted to opportunities offered by Louisiana and the unique nature of New Orleans as a southern city in the years before the Civil War. Some scalawags had been born, raised, and educated in the North. Others were European immigrants. This "cosmopolitanism" provides a clue to their nationalist-Unionist principles. Cosmopolitanism broke the mold of southern provincialism, providing some scalawags, at least, with a broader worldview than that of their southern-born-and-raised contemporaries. Although a hotbed of secessionist sympathies, occupied and postwar New Orleans, the focus of Republican political activity during the Reconstruction years was an ideal context for the invention of a new political and social order.[3] The unique atmosphere of the port city of New Orleans encouraged the scalawags to break with Louisiana's conservative political culture and ally themselves with the emerging radical movement.

Fifth, the Louisiana scalawags were most active and influential during the early stages of Reconstruction, beginning with the military occupation in April 1862. It was the scalawags who took the lead in founding the Republican Party in Louisiana. After the bloody New Orleans Riot of 1866, the power and influence of the scalawags gradually declined and gave way to northern newcomers, the carpetbaggers. The scalawag story arc rises from the opportunities offered by wartime collaboration to the climax of 1866, followed by a reversal of fortune and the general decline of scalawag importance.

Sixth, if the Louisiana scalawags were not overtly prejudiced against blacks, they were paternalistic at best. The evidence also indicates that the scalawag leaders considered black men as little more than pawns in the struggle with conservatives, little more than votes to be counted on Election Day. Black suffrage was seen correctly as the necessary foundation of Republican strength. Their support for political equality, however, did not necessarily imply a belief in social equality; rather, it reflected limited rights for blacks as a collateral benefit of Republican office holding. When asked by a congressional committee member whether he thought "that the Negro ought to be made equal with the white man," W. Jasper Blackburn, one of Louisiana's most consistent radicals, replied, "I do, in their political rights; but sir, I am a southern man; I have never been in the north yet, and I will say that there are certain equalities that I do not believe in."[4] R. F. Daunoy, a fellow radical, swore at the same hearings that he had absolutely no prejudice against blacks. "While I was in the college of Louis Philipe [in Paris]," he stated proudly, "there was right alongside of me a great big black negro."[5] In January 1865, New Orleans's black population held a massive rally celebrating the abolition of slavery in Missouri and Tennessee. E. H. Durell, Ezra Hiestand, A. P. Dostie, and Michael Hahn joined in the celebration. "Gov. Hahn's residence on Coliseum Square was the scene of one of the happiest incidents of the day," one newspaper reported, "for there the colored people testified how much they loved and respected [Hahn] for his long continued and arduous labors on behalf of emancipation and civil liberty. The Governor and his guests—among whom were Hon. Judge Durell, Judge Hiestand, Dr. Dostie . . . and one or two others . . . adjourned to the parlor and prepared to receive their visitors." Soon a procession of blacks, preceded by a military band, "filed in until the parlor was densely crowded, and the halls and portico were well filled." A black leader then addressed Hahn, thanking him for his devotion to the cause of black liberty. Then "Mr. Craig, another leader of the colored people, followed, who stated that he had known the Governor from boyhood and knew him always to be a friend of freedom." In response, Hahn thanked the delegation, but he warned them against any "rash and inconsiderate action" in demanding civil liberties. Louisiana's "colored population" had many great obstacles and deep-rooted prejudices to overcome," he stated, and he reminded the black audience that "the Universe is the patrimony of patient men."[6] Only with great reluctance did he later advocate black suffrage. He claimed that although ignorant and uneducated, the blacks were qualified to vote because of their devotion to the Union. Hahn ignored the reality that black leaders in New Orleans were unusually well educated, wealthy, and politically sophisticated. The typical black politician, in fact, was "a young man of unusual ancestry, uncommon wealth, and exceptional ability."[7] Hahn would not admit, or simply omitted, that freeborn blacks in New Orleans constituted "the most sophisticated and exclusive black community in America."[8] This remarkable cluster of men constituted an "educated and well-to-do group [that] included merchants, men of property, lawyers, doctors, journalists, musicians, and skilled workmen."[9] These freeborn "colored Creoles," as they were often called, were "capable, native-born leaders," men not unlike the scalawags themselves in talent and achievement. Additionally, the black people of Louisiana contributed the largest number of black volunteers to the Union army. And the scalawags would suffer from the social ostracism that black people faced. Hahn, of course, did not ignore or dismiss the critical voting bloc that the men of color represented. And shortly before the 1866 riot, A. P. Dostie, Hahn's fellow radical, praised the courage and patriotic devotion of the black people of Louisiana. These people were, Dostie asserted, "black men with white hearts."[10] Throughout Reconstruction, the scalawags and carpetbaggers were, almost without exception, "unwilling to make any concessions towards social equality."[11] Their Unionism and Republicanism did not necessarily equal devotion to black civil rights or a true biracial democracy. They were men of their time, and few white men of that time favored social equality with black people. Their objective was black votes, not black equality. Office holding and the good things associated with patronage came before social change. Although radical social change was promised in the constitution of 1868, including voting, open access to public accommodations, resorts, and schools, the anticipated social order was without real form or foundation. Nevertheless, "the achievements of the Reconstruction period," Dale A. Somers argues, "stand out in brilliant contrast to the Jim Crow policies implemented after 1890." Justin A. Nystrom offers a variation on the theme. Though fatally weakened and devoid of real power after 1877, the Republicans held on to offices for some time after the Redeemer victory. He argues convincingly that Reconstruction in Louisiana ended in two phases: the Redeemer victory in 1877 marked the first stage, but blacks continued to vote, and the Republicans, though greatly reduced in power, held the Custom House and its patronage: a "regime change" whose full consequences were still to be played out. Further, he states, the conservatives were not a monolithic movement. They were as fractured in purpose and organization as the Republicans. The second and final stage of reaction came in 1898 with black disfranchisement led by a "new generation" of white supremacists reared on the Lost Cause ideology. Still, the achievements of Reconstruction in Louisiana (voting rights, office holding, and integrated schools) were ephemeral. And even if some Republicans (black and white) clung to office after 1877, this did not equate to real power. The scalawags were, even with the best of intentions, swimming against the tide. The southern white Republicans of Louisiana within the context of their time and place and despite their manifest faults and limitations attempted to achieve something of value but persistent commitment to social and political reform in Louisiana would have to wait for a hundred years. However Louisiana Reconstruction ended, the limited accomplishments were, in time, eroded in practice and then ignored in the dominant pro-southern historical narrative.[12]

Seventh, the Louisiana scalawags were deeply involved in the self-destructive factional wars over control of the party that sapped the strength of Louisiana Republicanism. They displayed a talent for internecine struggles that served to undermine the party and prepare the way for the triumph of the Redeemers. Factionalism drained the energy of the party, soiled its reputation, and wrecked its achievements.

Eighth, the Louisiana scalawags were typical Gilded Age and Louisiana politicians, often tough, cynical, and unscrupulous spoils men. George Carter did not exaggerate much when he called Henry Clay Warmoth "the Boss Tweed of Louisiana,"[13] for Louisiana politics was not unlike that of New York's Tammany Hall and that notorious Democratic club. Scalawag politicians such as George Carter, George Wickliffe, John Ray, and John T. Ludeling were not above outright stealing, extortion, graft, or shady business deals. Ray and Ludeling, representative spoils men, were involved with the Vicksburg, Shreveport, and Texas Railroad scam. The United States Supreme Court, in ruling on a case involving their scheme, ruled that Ludeling and Ray had deliberately attempted to defraud the original owners and creditors in a conspiracy involving the worthless company.[14] The traditional story of Reconstruction exaggerated corruption but did not invent it. The scalawags were honored guests at what Vernon Louis Parrington calls "the great barbecue."[15] They were not unlike the Tweeds, Belknaps, and Babcocks of the North, but the scalawags were largely beggars at the feast after 1868. "Political bitterness is not so intense here [New Orleans] as a few weeks ago," W. Jasper Blackburn wrote in an editorial published in the *Homer Iliad* in March 1870; "leading men of both parties are constantly freely conferring together—some for the good of the land, and others doubtless for the special consummation of some individual enterprise of class legislation. There is so much of this juggling going on—much more than the unsophisticated honest masses have any idea of." "Nor is it confined," he informed his readers, "to State legislation; it is so in Congress. It is well understood at Washington that no great enterprise involving heavy appropriations can be consummated and no fat office obtained, without the payment of heavy sums—in other words, and in plain English, with bribery."[16] The *New Orleans Republican* summed up the provenance of corruption in Louisiana during Reconstruction best when it replied to an attack from the *New Orleans Bee* (a Democratic newspaper) by stating: "Corruption existed before the war, as now, and the same amount of crime and rampant lawlessness bid defiance to the administration of the laws. It did not require the Radicals to introduce corrupt practices as something new, for if the charges that were made by the political parties that existed here in antebellum times, against one another were true—and we are cognizant of the truth of some of them—a very melancholy condition of society existed here prior to the advent of Radicalism."[17] This is not to say that the scalawag ranks did not include men of genuine virtue: A. P. Dostie, after all, died for his opinions. And until the pressure grew too great, Ernest Breda demonstrated steady principles and real courage in the deadly atmosphere of rural Louisiana. Nevertheless, four years of war had largely exhausted the morale of the nation and, in time, white opposition to Reconstruction in the South eroded the commitment of the North to see the project to a successful end. It proved to be a long hard slog—too long and too hard as it turned out.

Finally, the scalawags in Louisiana were white political leaders without any significant white constituency. Black votes and federal legislation alone or in combination could not sustain meaningful social and political change over time. Reconstruction needed native white support. It was this weakness, as well as the lack of effective or consistent federal intervention, and the continuous resistance of the white population and its commitment to white supremacy amounting to an insurgency—bulldozing—that led eventually to the Redeemer's victory and the end of Reconstruction in Louisiana. Race was the trump that took the trick. Edward King, observing the political and racial climate in Louisiana in 1873, the year of the Colfax massacre, wrote: "it is easy to see how passions, which should have long become extinct, still smolder, and all ready at a moments warning to burst forth at white heat."[18]

If Reconstruction was an "unfinished revolution," the revolution in Louisiana was deformed at birth by factionalism, opposed by vicious, determined paramilitary forces, deeply resented by the white population, tainted by corruption, and poorly led. In many ways, the scalawags, even the best of them, were their own worst enemy. In any event, even a united "revolutionary" front would have faced near impossible odds in Louisiana. Further, without the patience to persist with genuine reform, the failure to effect a quick Reconstruction proved fatal to Louisiana Republicanism.

In 1873, the Mardi Gras theme of the Mystic Krewe of Comus was "The Missing Links to Darwin's Origin of the Species." The parade satirized Reconstruction, the Republican Party, black politicians, and the Metropolitan Police: Ben Butler was pictured as a hyena, President Grant a tobacco grub, and Henry Clay Warmoth a snake. But when the revelers, costumed as mice and monkeys, reached Canal Street, the police stopped their progress. In 1877, the floats of Momus, God of Laughter and Ridicule, celebrating the end of Reconstruction, again poked raucous fun at the Republicans, including the Louisiana scalawags.[19] The Reconstruction years in Louisiana had been a virtual carnival of political turmoil, corruption, and violence. Now, the unreconstructed were not content with a political victory alone. They wanted the last laugh as well. This time no one stopped the parade.

NOTES

Introduction

1. James Gill, *Lords of Misrule: Mardi Gras and the Politics of Race in New Orleans* (Jackson: University Press of Mississippi, 1997), 76. See also Reid Mitchell, *All on a Mardi Gras Day: Episodes in the History of New Orleans Carnival* (Cambridge: Harvard University Press, 1999), 66.

2. Richard L. Hume and Jerry B. Gough, *Blacks, Carpetbaggers, and Scalawags: The Constitutional Conventions of Radical Reconstruction* (Baton Rouge: Louisiana State University Press, 2008), 12.

3. Eric Foner, *Reconstruction: The Unfinished Revolution, 1865–1877* (New York: Harper and Row, 1988), 603.

Chapter One

Note to Epigraph: Gary Rivlin, "Après Le Deluge, Moi: One Man's Flood Is Another Man's Opportunity," *New York Times Magazine,* March 5, 2006.

1. Charles Etienne Gayarré, "The Southern Question," *North American Review* 125 (November–December 1877): 479, 481, 483, 486.

2. Herbert Barnes, "The Scalawag," *Southern Magazine* 15 (November 1874): 303–4, 304, 306, 107.

3. John Rose Ficklen, *History of Reconstruction in Louisiana (through 1868)* (1910; repr., Gloucester, Mass.: Peter Smith, 1966), 214–15.

4. The following five quotations are taken from Ella Lonn, *Reconstruction in Louisiana 1868* (1918; repr., Gloucester, Mass.: Peter Smith, 1967), 16.

5. Ibid., 13–16.

6. Claude G. Bowers, *The Tragic Era: The Revolution after Lincoln* (Cambridge, Mass.: Literary Guild of America and Riverside Press, 1929), 362–67.

7. Carl Van Doren, "Why the Editorial Board Selected *The Tragic Era*," *Wings* 3 (September 1929): 4.

8. Kenneth M. Stampp, *Era of Reconstruction* (New York: Random House, 1965), 4.

9. Quoted in Bruce E. Baker, *What Reconstruction Meant: Historical Memory in the American South* (Charlottesville: University of Virginia Press, 2007), 156.

10. Edwin Adams Davis, *Louisiana: The Pelican State* (Baton Rouge: Louisiana State University Press, 1959), 222–23.

11. Frances FitzGerald, *America Revised: History Schoolbooks in the Twentieth Century* (New York: Vintage, 1980), 85–89.

12. Margaret MacMillan, *Dangerous Games: The Uses and Abuses of History* (New York: Modern Library, 2009), 146. On Reconstruction in textbooks, see ibid., 56.

13. W. E. Burqhardt Du Bois, *Black Reconstruction: An Essay towards a History of the Part Which Black Folk Played in the Attempt to Reconstruct Democracy in America: 1860–1880* (New York: Russell and Russell, 1935).

14. T. Harry Williams, "An Analysis of Some Reconstruction Attitudes," *Journal of Southern History* 12 (November 1946): 474–75.

15. T. Harry Williams, "The Louisiana Unification Movement of 1873," *Journal of Southern History* 11 (August 1945): 349–69.

16. Joe Gray Taylor, *Louisiana Reconstructed, 1863–1877* (Baton Rouge: Louisiana State University Press, 1974), 137.

17. Kenneth M. Stampp, *The Era of Reconstruction* (New York: Random House, 1967), 162–64.

18. Eric Foner, *Reconstruction: The Unfinished Revolution, 1865–1877* (New York: Harper and Row, 1988), 603.

19. William C. Harris, *With Charity for All: Lincoln and the Restoration of the Union* (Lexington: University of Kentucky Press, 1997), 4, 275.

20. James Alex Baggett, *The Scalawags: Southern Dissenters in the Civil War and Reconstruction* (Baton Rouge: Louisiana State University Press, 2003), 7–13.

Chapter Two

1. Alecia P. Long, *The Great Southern Babylon: Sex, Race, and Respectability in New Orleans, 1865–1920* (Baton Rouge: Louisiana State University, 2004), 1.

2. James G. Belden: *New York Times,* April 26, 1864; Willie Malvin Caskey, *Secession and Restoration of Louisiana,* Louisiana State University Studies no. 36 (1938; repr., New York: Da Capo Press, 1970), 108.

3. *New York Times,* April 26, 1864.

4. Caskey, *Secession and Restoration,* 108.

5. William Jasper Blackburn: *Biographical Directory of the American Congress, 1774–1971,* rev. ed. (Washington, D.C.: Government Printing Office, 1971), s.v. "Blackburn, William Jasper"; James Grant Woods and John Fiske, eds., *Appleton's Cyclopaedia of American Biography,* 8 vols. (1901; repr., Farmington Hills, Mich.: Gale Research, 1968), s.v. "Blackburn, William Jasper."

6. For evidence of Blackburn's Unionist convictions, see the letters of recommendation from Michael Hahn to [Department of the Treasury], February 18, 1867, and Thomas J. Durant to [Department of the Treasury], February 18, 1867, Applications and Letters of Recommendation for Collectors of Internal Revenue, General Records of the Department of the Treasury, Record Group 56, Box 73, National Archives. Biographical data and further evidence of Blackburn's Unionist convictions are found in U.S. Congress, House, *New Orleans Riots of July 30, 1866,* 39th Cong., 2nd sess., 1867, H. Dept. 16 (repr., New York: Arno Press and New York Times, 1969), 421–24.

7. George Washington Carter: Henry Clay Warmoth, *War, Politics and Reconstruction: Stormy Days in Louisiana* (New York: Macmillan, 1930), 109; James K. Hogue, *Uncivil War: Five New Orleans Street Battles and the Rise and Fall of Radical Reconstruction* (Baton Rouge: Louisiana State University Press), 79, quoted in James Alex Baggett, *The Scalawags: Southern Dissenters in the Civil War and Reconstruction* (Baton Rouge: Louisiana State University Press, 2003), 255–56.

8. Thomas Green Davidson: See E. Russ Williams, "Tom Green Davidson: Southern Statesman or Louisiana Scalawag?" *Louisiana Studies* (Spring 1971): 15–21.

9. Anthony Paul (A. P.) Dostie: Emily Hazen Reed, *Life of A. P. Dostie or The Conflict in New Orleans* (New York: William P. Tomlinson, 1868), 13–30; *New York Times,* April 26, 1864; "Who Is A. P. Dostie?," copy of *True Delta* editorial, n.d., handwritten copy in the commonplace book of E. H. Durell, Durell Family Papers, New York Historical Society (hereafter cited as NYHS); Hans L. Trefousse, "Anthony Paul Dostie," in *Historical Dictionary of Reconstruction* (New York: Greenwood Press, 1991).

10. Thomas Jefferson Durant: H. W. Howard Knott, "Thomas Jefferson Durant," in *Dictionary of American Biography* (hereafter cited as *DAB*), ed. Allen Johnson and Dumas Malone (New York: Scribner's, 1959), 5:543–44; Joseph G. Tregle Jr., "Thomas J. Durant, Utopian Socialism, and the Failure of Presidential Reconstruction in Louisiana," *Journal of Southern History* 45, no. 4 (November 1979): 485–512; Letter Press Copies of Outgoing Correspondence, 1844–1847, 1857, 1860–1865, Thomas Jefferson Durant Papers, NYHS. For an authoritative summary of Fourier's ideas, see Nicholas V. Riasonovsky, "Francois Marie Charles Fourier," in *Encyclopedia of Philosophy,* ed. Paul Edwards (New York: Macmillan and Free Press, 1967), 3:215–16. Whitelaw Reid, *After the War: A Tour of the Southern States, 1865–1866* (1866; repr., New York: Harper and Row, 1965), 232. Durant to John D. Wilkins, November 14, 1844; Durant to Robert Wilson, June 4, 1847; Durant to Albert Brisbane, June 6, 1847; Durant to the editors of the *Harbinger,* January 13, 1847; Durant to John D. Wilkins, December 8, 1844; Durant to Robert Dale Owen, February 10, 1847; Durant to Robert Dale Owen, June 1, 1847; Durant to Albert Brisbane, June 6, 1847; Durant to Henry G. Langley, December 27, 1844; Durant to Joseph Walker, October 24, 1844, all in Durant Papers, NYHS. Perry Howard, *Political Tendencies in Louisiana,* rev. ed. (Baton Rouge: Louisiana State University Press, 1971), 53. Durant to John D. Wilkins, December 8, 1844; Durant to Sarah Hyeliger Durant, January 1, 1846; Durant to J. J. MacCougham, February 16, 1847, all in Durant Papers, NYHS.

11. Edward Henry Durell: H. W. Howard Knott, "Edward Henry Durell," in *DAB,* 3:545–46; *Appleton's Cyclopaedia of American Biography,* 8 vols. (1901; repr., Farmington Hills, Mich.: Gale Research, 1968), s.v. "Durell, E. H."; "Hon. Edward Henry Durell," *Granite Monthly* 4 (April 1888): 115–29; Edward C. Billings, *The Struggle between the Civilization of Slavery and That of Freedom Recently and Now Going on in Louisiana* (1873; repr., Freeport, N.Y.: Books for Libraries Press, 1971), 29–31. For information on the Wentworth family, see *Appleton's Cyclopaedia,* s.v. "Wentworth, William."

12. Benjamin Franklin Flanders: *Biographical Directory of the American Congress,* s.v. "Flanders, Benjamin Franklin"; *National Cyclopaedia of American Biography* (New York: J. T. White, 1898–1965), s.v. "Flanders, Benjamin Franklin"; *Jewell's Crescent City Illustrated* (1872), 39. Rufus Waples to Rutherford B. Hayes, May 8, 1877, Applications for Assistant Treasurer and Mint Officers, New Orleans, General Records of the Department

of the Treasury, Box 13, Record Group 56, National Archives; N. S. Berry to Flanders, March 25, 1862, Benjamin F. Flanders Papers, Department of Archives, Louisiana State University. The majority of the material in the Flanders Papers deals with his duties as special agent for the Treasury Department. On Flanders's Unionism, see Benjamin F. Butler to President, November 28, 1862, *Private and Official Correspondence of Gen. Benjamin F. Butler: During the Period of the Civil War,* vol. 2, *Benjamin Franklin Butler, Jessie Ames Marshall* (privately issued: Plimpton Press, 1917), digitized, August 10, 2006. http://books.google.com/books.

13. Michael Hahn: Amos E. Simpson and Vaughn B. Baker, "Michael Hahn: Steady Patriot," *Louisiana History* 13, no. 3 (Summer 1972): 229–52; *Appleton's Cyclopaedia,* s.v. "Hahn, Michael"; *National Cyclopaedia of American Biography,* s.v. "Hahn, Michael"; *Biographical Directory of the American Congress,* s.v. "Hahn, Michael"; *Memorial Addresses on the Life and Career of Michael Hahn* (Washington, D.C.: Government Printing Office, 1886). See also Frank J. Wetta, "Michael Hahn," in *The Louisiana Governors: From Iberville to Edwards,* ed. Joseph G. Dawson (Baton Rouge: Louisiana State University Press, 1990), 148–52.

14. William Henry Hire: Secretary to the Librarian, Royal College of Surgeons of England, London, to the author, January 13, 1976; *New Orleans Riots of July 30, 1866,* 64–68. H. N. Frisbee to Benjamin Harrison, September 7, 1889; Hire to William Window, March 15, 1890; Headquarters, General Council, Association of Union Veterans, New Orleans, to Chester Arthur, November 16, 1881; see also C. H. Williams to Rutherford B. Hayes, June 5, 1880; and Hire to Rutherford B. Hayes, June 9, 1880, all at Applications for Assistant Treasurer and Mint Officers, New Orleans, General Records of the Department of the Treasury, Box 14, Record Group 56, National Archives.

15. James Longstreet: Donald Bridgman Sanger and Thomas Robson Hay, *James Longstreet* (Baton Rouge: Louisiana State University Press, 1952), 8–20; Douglas Southall Freeman, "James Longstreet," in *DAB,* 6:391–93; William B. Hesseltime, *Confederate Leaders in the New South* (Baton Rouge: Louisiana State University Press, 1950), 110–14; William Garrett Piston, *Lee's Tarnished Lieutenant: James Longstreet and His Place in Southern History* (Athens: University of Georgia Press, 1987); William L. Richter, "'The Road to Hell Is Paved with Good Intentions': James Longstreet in War and Peace," in *Lee and His Generals: Essays in Honor of T. Harry Williams,* ed. Lawrence Lee Hewitt and Thomas E. Schott (Knoxville: University of Tennessee Press, 2012).

16. Douglas Southall Freeman, *Lee's Lieutenants: A Study in Command,* vol. 2, *Manassas to Malvern Hill* (New York: Scribner's, 1942), xiiv.

17. Michael Shaara, *The Killer Angels: A Novel* (New York: McKay, 1974), xi.

18. Douglas Southall Freeman, *Lee's Lieutenants: A Study in Command,* vol. 3, *Gettysburg to Appomattox* (New York: Scribner's, 1944), xxix.

19. David W. Blight, *Race and Reunion: The Civil War in American Memory* (Cambridge: Harvard University Press, 2001), 293.

20. John Theodore Ludeling: Melvin J. White, "John Theodore Ludeling," in *DAB,* 6:489–90; *Catalogue of the Officers and Students of the St. Louis University,* Missouri, August 14, 1839 (St. Louis: Chambers & Knapp, 1839). Ludeling's name also appears in the university catalogue for the years 1840, 1840–41, 1842, and 1843.

21. White, "John Theodore Ludeling," in *DAB,* 6:490.

22. Philip Hickey Morgan: *Dictionary of Louisiana Biography,* s.v. "Philip Hickey Morgan; Baggett, *The Scalawags,* 55; Dennis C. Rousey, *Policing the Southern City: New Orleans, 1805–1889* (Baton Rouge: Louisiana State University Press, 1996), 103.

23. John Ray: E. Russ Williams, "John Ray, A Northeast Louisiana Scalawag," typescript of unpublished article generously provided by the author, 1–3; *Appleton's Cyclopaedia,* s.v. "Ray, John."

24. Williams, "John Ray," 1.

25. *Appleton's Cyclopaedia,* s.v. "Ray, John," 192.

26. James Govan Taliaferro: Wynona Gillmore Mills, "James Govan Taliaferro, 1798–1876: Louisiana Unionist and Scalawag" (master's thesis, Louisiana State University, 1968); *National Cyclopaedia of American Biography,* s.v. "Taliaferro, James Govan." See also James G. Taliaferro and Family Papers, Department of Archives, Louisiana State University. The political makeup of Catahoula Parish is described in Howard, *Political Tendencies,* 60, 61, 81, and 98; and Mills, "Taliaferro," 7.

27. Michel Vidal (some sources spell his first name as Michael): Michel Vidal to Benjamin Perly, December 1868, Michel Vidal Papers, Department of Archives, Louisiana State University; *Biographical Directory of the American Congress,* s.v. "Vidal, Michael."

28. Rufus Waples: Christian Roselius to Abraham Lincoln, August 5, 1864, Records Relating to the Appointment of Federal Judges, Marshalls, and Attorneys, 1853–1901, Louisiana, 1853–1869, General Records of the Department of Justice, Box 333, Record Group 60, National Archives; *Who Was Who in America: Historical Volume, 1607–1896,* rev. ed. (St. Louis: Von Hoffman Press and A. N. Marquis Co., 1967), s.v. "Waples, Rufus"; Ninth U.S. Census (1870), New Orleans, Tenth Ward.

29. James Madison Wells: Walter Lowrey, "The Political Career of James Madison Wells," *Louisiana Historical Quarterly* 21 (October 1948): 995–1003; Ella Lonn, "James Madison Wells," in *DAB,* 10:641–42; *Biographical and Historical Memoirs of Northwest Louisiana Comprising a Large Fund of Biography of Actual Residents, and an Interesting Historical Sketch of the Thirteen Counties* (Nashville: Southern, 1890), 660–61; *National Cyclopaedia of American Biography,* s.v. "Wells, James Madison"; *Who Was Who, 1607–1896,* s.v. "Wells, James Madison"; Lowrey, "Political Career of James Madison Wells," 996, 999, 1003, 1007.

30. James Belden: *New Orleans Daily Picayune,* January 28, 1872; Ninth U.S. Census (1870), New Orleans, Fifth Ward. The geographic and political classification of Natchitoches Parish and all other parishes described in the section on geographic origins is based on Howard, *Political Tendencies,* 3–17. Breda brothers: *Biographical and Historical Memoirs of Northwest Louisiana,* 325–26. Cooley: *New Orleans Daily Picayune,* January 21, 1872. Oscar Jeffrion: Oscar Jeffrion to Rutherford B. Hayes, December 7, 1878, Applications . . . Collectors of Internal Revenue, Box 73, Record Group 56, National Archives. Delery: *Monroe Ouachita Telegraph,* May 18, 1872. Robert J. Caldwell: Robert J. Caldwell to the Senate and House of Representatives, March 29, 1868, Papers of the (Senate) Select Committee on Political Disabilities, Petitions & Memorials, Tray № 110, Record Group 46, National Archives. The petition is endorsed by John Ray. "The undersigned," Ray wrote, "has known Mr. Robert J. Caldwell since infancy." Commagere: Ninth U.S. Census (1870), New Orleans, Sixth Ward.

31. Bloomfield: Petition to the Senate and House of Representatives (1868), Papers of

the (Senate) Select Committee on Reconstruction, Records of the United States Senate, Box 46, Record Group 46, National Archives. Those who endorsed the petition included W. Jasper Blackburn, Henry Clay Warmoth, George Kelse, G. M. Wickliffe, C. C. Antoine, and James Madison Wells. Daunoy: *New Orleans Riots of July 30, 1866,* 135. Leaumont: *New Orleans Daily Picayune,* January 28, 1872; Ninth U.S. Census (1870), New Orleans, Seventh Ward. Pitkin: Michael Hahn to Schuyler Colfax, August 26, 1868, William Eaton Chandler Papers, Manuscript Division, Library of Congress. S. R. Snaer: *New Orleans Riots of July 30, 1866,* 171. Eugene Staes: *New Orleans Riots of July 30, 1866,* 118.

32. Napoleon Underwood and Gilderoy Sneider: Hume and Gough, *Blacks, Carpetbaggers, and Scalawags*, appendix B. Richard C. Downes: Downes to J. S. Harris, January 7, 1869 (Senate) Select Committee on Political Disabilities, Record Group 46, National Archives.

33. Ray brothers: *Appleton's Cyclopaedia,* s.v. "Ray, John." Robert Ray: *Richland Beacon News,* October 28, 1899. Rufus Waples: *Who Was Who, 1607–1896,* s.v. "Waples, Rufus." L. W. Baker, Thomas Crawford, and John Dinkard: Hume and Gough, *Blacks, Carpetbaggers, and Scalawags*, appendix B.

34. Peter Kolchin, "Scalawags, Carpetbaggers, and Reconstruction: A Quantitative Look at Southern Congressional Politics, 1868–1872," *Journal of Southern History* 45, no. 1 (February 1979): 66.

35. Fletcher M. Green, *The Role of the Yankee in the Old South* (Athens: University of Georgia Press, 1972), 5–6, 4.

36. Crane: *New Orleans Tribune, May 30, 1867;* Ninth U.S. Census (1870), New Orleans, First Ward; 13. Fisk: Two specific references to Fisk as a "scalawag" appear in U.S. Congress, House, *Use of the Army in Certain of the Southern States,* Ex. Doc. 30, 44th Cong., 2nd sess., 1877 (repr.; New York: Arno Press and New York Times, 1969), 224–25. Faulkner: U.S. Congress, *House Miscellaneous Document* 154, pt. 1, 41st Cong., 2nd sess., 1870, 711. Veazie: James H. Veazie to George S. Boutwell, April 8, 1863, Applications and Letters of Recommendation for Collectors of Internal Revenue, General Records of the Department of the Treasury, Box 74, Record Group 56, National Archives.

37. Green, *Role of the Yankee,* 5.

38. Bonzano: *Goodspeed's Biographical and Historical Memoir of Louisiana* (Chicago: Goodspeed, 1892), 303.

39. Gerald M. Capers Jr., "Confederates and Yankees in Occupied New Orleans, 1862–1865," *Journal of Southern History* 30 (November 1964): 412.

40. Alexander Breda: *Biographical and Historical Memoirs of Northwest Louisiana,* 325.

41. Simeon Belden: *New York Times,* April 26, 1864. Charles Leaumont: *New Orleans Daily Picayune*, January 28, 1872. M. F. Bonzano: *Goodspeed's Biographical and Historical Memoirs of Louisiana,* 303–4.

42. Robert J. Caldwell: Caldwell to the Senate and House of Representatives, March 29, 1869, Senate Committee on Political Disabilities, Tray № 110, Record Group 46, National Archives. William R. Crane: Ninth U.S. Census (1870), New Orleans, First Ward. Josiah Fisk: *Use of the Army,* 224. Ezra Hiestand: Louis Janan to R. R. Hoar, March 23, 1869, Records Relating to the Appointments of Federal Judges, Marshals, and Attorneys, 1853–1901, Louisiana, 1865–1877, Packard-Billings, General Records of the Department of Justice, Record Group 60, Box 334 , National Archives; Wade H. Hough, John Ray, et

al., Petition to (House Select Committee on Reconstruction), June 23, 1868, Papers of the (House) Select Committee on Reconstruction, 40th and 41st Cong., H. Dept. 40A-H21.10, *Louisiana,* Nos. 13550–13559 and unnumbered Box 8, Record Group 68, National Archives. G. S. Lacey: J. Calhoun, Thomas R. Brady to Ulysses S. Grant, Appointment of Federal Judges, Marshals and Attorneys, Box 335, Record Group 60, National Archives. James H. Veazie: James H. Veazie to William Pitt Fessenden, March 2, 1869, Correspondence of William Pitt Fessenden, vol. 7, Library of Congress. George Wickliffe: Joe Gray Taylor, *Louisiana Reconstructed, 1863–1877* (Baton Rouge: Louisiana State University Press, 1974), 149.

43. For the occupations of the white southern members of the 1868 Louisiana constitutional convention, see Richard L. Hume and Jerry B. Gough, *Blacks, Carpetbaggers, and Scalawags: The Constitutional Conventions of Radical Reconstruction* (Baton Rouge: Louisiana State University Press, 2008), appendix B. See also specific references to the Louisiana scalawags, including William Crane, James G. Taliaferro, Napoleon Underwood, Rufus Waples, and George Wickliffe on economic, racial, suffrage, and other issues, 158–167 and 194–197.

44. Simeon Belden: *New Orleans Daily Picayune,* January 28, 1872; Ninth U.S. Census (1870), Fifth Ward. James K. Belden: *New Orleans Riots of July 30, 1866,* 466; Ninth U.S. Census (1870), Fifth Ward. This is James K. Belden and not to be confused with James G. Belden. J. Ernest Breda: *Biographical and Historical Memoirs of Northwest Louisiana,* 325; John Barrett: Hume and Gough, *Blacks, Carpetbaggers, and Scalawags,* appendix B. Robert J. Caldwell: Caldwell to the Senate and House of Representatives, March 29, 1869 (Senate) Select Committee on Political Disabilities, Tray № 110, Record Group 56, National Archives. William H. Cooley: *New Orleans Daily Picayune,* January 21, 1872. William R. Crane: Ninth U.S. Census (1870), New Orleans, First Ward. Thomas Crawford: Hume and Gough, *Blacks, Carpetbaggers, and Scalawags,* appendix B. Wade H. Hough: John Ray (Petition June 28, 1868), (House) Select Committee on Reconstruction, Box 8. Hough had twenty years of experience as an attorney, according to Ray. Chauncey S. Kellogg: Schmidt Ziegler to Benjamin Harrison, Petition on behalf of Chauncey S. Kellogg, August, 1889, Applications . . . New Orleans, Record Group 56, Box 14, National Archives. Lacey had thirty years' experience in the state and federal courts as of 1875. George S. Lacey: J. Calhoun, Thomas R. Brady to Ulysses S. Grant, Petition on behalf of George S. Lacey, December 18, 1875, Appointment of Federal Judges, Marshals, and Attorneys, Box 335, Record Group 60, National Archives. Charles Leaumont: *New Orleans Daily Picayune,* January 28, 1872; *New Orleans Riots of July 30, 1866,* 255. In 1866, Lacey was a judge of the Fifth District Court of the City of New Orleans. James K. Lewis: Hume and Gough, *Blacks, Carpetbaggers, and Scalawags,* appendix B. B. L. Lynch: B. L. Lynch to N. P. Banks, February 2, 1869 (House) Select Committee on Reconstruction, Box 8. James Veazie: Veazie claimed to have twenty years of experience as a lawyer (see James H. Veazie to William Pitt Fessenden, March 2, 1869, Correspondence of William Fessenden, vol. 7, LC. 47).

45. James G. Belden: *New York Times,* April 26, 1864. Alexander Breda: *Biographical and Historical Memoirs of Northwest Louisiana,* 325. William Henry Hire: Hire to William Windom, April 2, 1899, Applications . . . New Orleans, Box 14, Record Group 56, National Archives. John Vandergriff: Hume and Gough, *Blacks, Carpetbaggers, and Scalawags,* ap-

pendix B. George M. Wickliffe: Taylor, *Louisiana Reconstructed,* 149. A. P. Dostie: Reed, *Life of A. P. Dostie,* 17, 28.

46. Charles Delery: *Monroe Ouachita Telegraph,* May 18, 1872. W. E. Maples: Maples to John Sherman, April 13, 1877, Applications . . . Collectors of Internal Revenue, Box 74, Record Group 56, National Archives. Frederick Otto: Michael Hahn to George S. Boutwell, March 27, 1869, Applications Assessors of Internal Revenue, Box 11, Record Group 56, National Archives. S. R Snaer: *New Orleans Riots of July 30, 1866,* 171. John Walton: Erastus and Fanny Clark to Benjamin Franklin Flanders, July 21, 1862, Flanders Papers, Department of Archives, Louisiana State University. Walton "has been engaged in business more or less directly connected with shipping for nearly 30 years" (*New Orleans Republican,* March 27, 1870). Oglesby had also been involved in "the western produce commission business" (see *New Orleans Riots of July 30, 1866,* 316). L. H. Panza: *New Orleans Riots of July 30, 1866,* 247. Nathan Schwab, Gelderoy Snider, Andrew Demarest, John Dinkard, William Phillips, Charles Dearing, Edward Fielding: Hume and Gough, *Blacks, Carpetbaggers, and Scalawags,* appendix B.

47. J. G. Beauchamp: Emerson Bently to Henry Clay Warmoth, June 12, 1868, Henry Clay Warmoth Papers, Southern Historical Collection, University of North Carolina. Alexander P. Breda: *Biographical and Historical Memoirs of Northwest Louisiana,* 325. Chauncey Kellogg: *Biographical and Historical Memoirs of Northwest Louisiana,* 325. Robert Ray: *Richland Beacon News,* October 28, 1899. Louis Dupleix: *Biographical and Historical Memoirs of Northwest Louisiana,* 342.

48. *Goodspeed's Biographical and Historical Memoirs of Louisiana,* 304.

49. *Speech of Hon. Aaron A. Sargent of California in the Senate of the United States, February 15, 16, and 17, 1875* (Washington, D.C.: Government Printing Office, 1875), 35.

50. *New Orleans Riots of July 30, 1866,* 140.

51. *Andrew Hero, Jr., Chairman, Republican Congressional Committee, Second Congressional District* (n.p., n.d.), pamphlet contained in Applications . . . New Orleans, Record Group 56, Box 14, National Archives.

52. Caldwell to The Senate and House of Representatives, March 29, 1869 (Senate) Select Committee on Political Disabilities, Tray № 110, Record Group 46, National Archives.

53. Downes to J. H. Harris, January 7, 1869 (Senate) Select Committee on Political Disabilities, Ky.-Miss., Sen. 41A-H 27, Record Group 46, National Archives.

54. J. Calhoun, Thomas R. Brady to Ulysses S. Grant, December 18, 1875, Appointment of Federal Judges, Marshals, and Attorneys, Box 335, Record Group 60, National Archives.

55. Emerson Bently, Henry Clay Warmoth, G. Donato to the President, Members of the Senate, the Speaker and Members of the House of Representatives (Petition on behalf of James Monroe Porter), February 1869, Tray № 110, Papers of the (Senate) Select Committee on Political Disabilities, Record Group 46, National Archives. "He further sheweth that in the month of November, 1845, [Porter] was elected a member of the Legislature of the State of Louisiana, and as such served two years."

56. J. G. Watkins to the Senate and House of Representatives of the Congress of the United States, 1868, Papers of the (House) Select Committee on Reconstruction, 40th and 41st Cong., unnumbered, HR 40A-F29, 21, Box 2. This petition for removal of Watkins's political disabilities was endorsed by James G. Taliaferro, Michael Hahn, and Rufus K.

Howell. "Petitioner [Watkins] shows that before the war he acted as Dist. Atty. for several years commissioned by the State."

57. Thomas R. Dye and L. Harmon Zeigler, *The Irony of Democracy: An Uncommon Introduction to American Politics* (Belmont, Calif.: Wadsworth, 1970), 91; Joel Williamson, *After Slavery: The Negro in South Carolina during Reconstruction 1861–1877* (Chapel Hill: University of North Carolina Press, 1965), 362.

58. Edward Pessen, "How Different from Each Other Were the Antebellum North and South," *American Historical Review* 85 (December 1980): 1149.

Chapter Three

1. Joe Gray Taylor, *Louisiana Reconstructed, 1863–1877* (Baton Rouge: Louisiana State University Press, 1974), 71.

2. J. R. G. Pitkin, *To the Whigs* (Republican State Central Committee, March 1, 1876), 1–8.

3. Kellogg to W. H. H. Miller, April 8, 1899, Applications . . . New Orleans, Box 14, Record Group 56, National Archives.

4. Bullitt to John W. Noble, May 1, 1889, Applications . . . New Orleans, Box 15, Record Group 56, National Archives.

5. Taylor, *Louisiana Reconstructed,* 481.

6. James O. Fuqua to James G. Kilbourne, June 8, 1865, James G. Kilbourne Correspondence, Department of Archives, Louisiana State University.

7. Ray to The Senate and House of Representatives, endorsement appended to a petition for removal of political disabilities, Caldwell to The Senate and House of Representatives, March 29, 1869, Papers of the (Senate) Select Committee on Removal of Political Disabilities, Tray № 110, Record Group 46, National Archives.

8. Ibid.

9. U.S. Congress, House, *New Orleans Riots of July 30, 1866,* 39th Cong., 2nd sess., 1867, H. Dept. 16 (repr., New York: Arno Press and New York Times, 1969), 136.

10. Ray to (Congress), June 23, 1868, Papers of the (House) Select Committee on Reconstruction, 40th and 41st Cong. HR 40A-H21.10, Applications for Removal of Political Disabilities, *Louisiana,* Nos. 13550–13559 and unnumbered, Box 8, Record Group 233, National Archives.

11. Hahn to (Congress), 1868 (no month or day), Papers of the (House) Select Committee on Reconstruction, 40th and 41st Cong. HR 40A-H21.10, Applications for Removal of Political Disabilities, *Louisiana,* Nos. 13550–13559 and unnumbered, Box 8, Record Group 233, National Archives.

12. Hough to Ulysses S. Grant, August 20, 1871, Appointment of Federal Judges, Marshals, and Attorneys, Box 344, Record Group 60, National Archives.

13. Lynch to B. F. Butler, March 25, 1868, Papers of the (House) Select Committee on Reconstruction, 40th and 41st Cong., HR 40A-H21.10, Applications for Removal of Political Disabilities, *Louisiana,* № 13519, Record Group 233, National Archives.

14. Lynch to B. F. Butler, December 9, 1869, Papers of the (House) Select Committee on Reconstruction, 40th and 41st Cong., HR 40A-H21.10, Applications for Removal of Political Disabilities, *Louisiana,* № 13519, Record Group 233, National Archives.

15. Porter to The President & Members of the Senate & the Speaker and members of the House of Representatives of the U.S. of America in Congress Assembled, n.d., Senate 41A-H27, Petitions & Memorials, Papers of the Select Committee on the Removal of Political Disabilities, Tray № 110, Record Group 46, National Archives.

16. *Richland Beacon News,* October 28, 1899.

17. Rovee to Ulysses S. Grant, April 1, 1869, Letters of Application and Recommendation, Internal Revenue, Assessors, Louisiana, 1st–3rd Districts, General Records of the Department of the Treasury, Box 11, Record Group 56, National Archives.

18. Watkins to the Senate and House of Representatives, July 22, 1868, Papers of the (House) Select Committee on Reconstruction, 40th and 41st Cong., Various Louisiana Affairs, 41st Cong., unnumbered, HR 40A-F29.21, Box 2, Record Group 233, National Archives.

19. *Biographical and Historical Memoirs of Northwest Louisiana Comprising a Large Fund of Biography of Actual Residents, and an Interesting Historical Sketch of the Thirteen Counties* (Nashville: Southern, 1890), 325.

20. J. Ernest Breda to Eliza Blanchard, July 25, 1864, J. P. Breda and Family Papers, Department of Archives, Louisiana State University.

21. J. Ernest Breda to Eliza Blanchard, November 28, 1864, J. P. Breda and Family Papers, Department of Archives, Louisiana State University.

22. *Biographical and Historical Memoirs of Northwest Louisiana,* 326.

23. Henry Clay Warmoth, *War, Politics and Reconstruction: Stormy Days in Louisiana* (New York: Macmillan, 1930), 2.

24. Mark Mayo Boatner, *The Civil War Directory* (New York: McKay, 1959), s.v. "Washington Artillery."

25. *New Orleans Daily Picayune,* April 22, 1866.

26. *Louisiana Standard,* April 22, 1888.

27. Oath of Eligibility, September 9, 1868, Andrew J. and George Hero Papers, Department of Archives, Louisiana State University.

28. Graham to Henry Clay Warmoth, June 30, 1868, Andrew J. and George Hero Papers, Department of Archives, Louisiana State University.

29. Mader to William Pitt Kellogg, November 25, 1868, Papers of the (Senate) Select Committee on the Removal of Political Disabilities, Petitions & Memorials 41A-H27, Tray № 110, Record Group 46, National Archives.

30. *New Orleans Republican,* March 22, 1870.

31. Magee to Captain G. B. Halsted, November 4, 1863, contained among the Letters of Application and Recommendation, Internal Revenue, Assessors, Louisiana, 1st–3rd Districts, General Records of the Department of the Treasury, Box 11, Record Group 56, National Archives.

32. Hahn to George S. Boutwell, March 27, 1868, contained among the Letters of Application and Recommendation, Internal Revenue, Assessors, Louisiana, 1st–3rd Districts, General Records of the Department of the Treasury, Box 11, Record Group 56, National Archives.

33. David H. [last name illegible] to Ulysses S. Grant (1869?), Letters of Application and Recommendation for Collectors of Internal Revenue, General Records of the Department of the Treasury, Box 73, Record Group 56, National Archives.

34. Pendleton to Ulysses S. Grant, March 4, 1869, Letters of Application and Recommendation for Collectors of Internal Revenue, General Records of the Department of the Treasury, Box 73, Record Group 56, National Archives.

35. A. P. Banks to George S. Boutwell, July 6, 1869, Letters of Application and Recommendation, Internal Revenue, Assessors, Louisiana, 1st–3rd Districts, General Records of the Department of the Treasury, Box 11, Record Group 56, National Archives.

36. Ready to George S. Boutwell, March 15, 1869, Letters of Application and Recommendation, Internal Revenue, Assessors, Louisiana, 1st–3rd Districts, General Records of the Department of the Treasury, Box 11, Record Group 56, National Archives.

37. General William Hemsley Emory confirmed Ready's account in a letter to President Andrew Johnson on April 10, 1866, Letters of Application and Recommendation, Internal Revenue, Assessors, Louisiana, 1st–3rd Districts, General Records of the Department of the Treasury, Box 11, Record Group 56, National Archives.

38. *New Orleans Riots of July 30, 1866,* 421.

39. Appointment of Federal Judges, Marshals and Attorneys, Record Group 60, Box 334, National Archives.

40. E. Russ Williams, "John Ray, A Northeast Louisiana Scalawag," typescript of unpublished article generously provided by the author, 2–3.

41. U.S. Congress, House, *Use of the Army in Certain of the Southern States,* Ex. Doc. 30, 44th Cong., 2nd sess., 1877 (repr., New York: Arno Press and New York Times, 1969), 349.

42. Amos E. Simpson and Vaughn B. Baker, "Michael Hahn: Steady Patriot," *Louisiana History* 13, no. 3 (Summer 1972): 232.

43. H. W. Howard Knott, "Thomas Jefferson Durant," in *DAB,* 5:543.

44. Benjamin F. Butler to Edwin M. Stanton, June 10, 1862, *Butler Correspondence,* vol. 1.

45. H. W. Howard Knott, "Edward Henry Durell, in *DAB,* 3:545.

46. Ibid.

47. Quoted in Wynona Gillmore Mills, "James Govan Taliaferro, 1798–1876: Louisiana Unionist and Scalawag" (master's thesis, Louisiana State University, 1968), 25–26.

48. Ibid., 32.

49. A copy of the broadside in Applications . . . New Orleans, Box 14, Record Group 56, National Archives.

50. Quoted in Mills, "James Govan Taliaferro," 42.

51. Ibid., 46.

52. Bonzano to Salmon P. Chase, May 5, 1862, Applications . . . New Orleans, Box 14, Record Group 56, National Archives.

53. *Goodspeed's Biographical and Historical Memoirs of Louisiana,* 304–5.

54. C. C. Chaffee to Maj. Gen. B.F. Butler, May 19, 1862, *Butler Correspondence,* vol. 1.

55. Quoted in Emily Hazen Reed, *Life of A. P. Dostie or The Conflict in New Orleans* (New York: William P. Tomlinson, 1868), 29–30.

56. Willie Malvin Caskey, *Secession and Restoration of Louisiana,* Louisiana State University Studies no. 36 (1938; repr., New York: Da Capo Press, 1970), 108.

57. Whitelaw Reid, *After the War: A Tour of the Southern States, 1865–1866* (New York: Harper and Row, 1968), 268.

58. Applications . . . New Orleans, Box 13, Record Group 56, National Archives.

59. Undated clipping from the *New York Tribune* contained in the Flanders Papers, Department of Archives, Louisiana State University.

60. Christian Roselius to Abraham Lincoln, August 5, 1864, Appointment of Federal Judges, Marshals, and Attorneys, Box 333, Record Group 60, National Archives.

61. Joel Williamson, *After Slavery: The Negro in South Carolina during Reconstruction 1861–1877* (Chapel Hill: University of North Carolina Press, 1965), 360.

62. Fay Welton, *Introduction to the Epistles of Paul the Apostle to the Corinthians* (New York: Grove, 1998), vii.

63. Gary Gallagher, *The Union War* (Cambridge: Harvard University Press, 2011), 2.

Chapter Four

1. Quoted in James Marten, "The Making of a Carpetbagger: George S. Denison and the South, 1854–1866," *Louisiana History* 34, no. 2 (Spring 1993): 133–60.

2. George S. Denison to Salmon P. Chase, November 29, 1862, "Diary and Correspondence of Salmon P Chase, Part IV: Letters from George S. Denison to Salmon P. Chase, May 15, 1862, to March 21, 1865," in *American Historical Association, Annual Report* (1902).

3. Ibid.

4. Quoted in Willie Malvin Caskey, *Secession and Restoration of Louisiana,* Louisiana State University Studies no. 36 (1938; repr., New York: Da Capo Press, 1970), 55–56.

5. Ibid.

6. Ibid.

7. *New Orleans True Delta,* August 20, 1862, quoted in Emily Hazen Reed, *Life of A. P. Dostie or The Conflict in New Orleans* (New York: William P. Tomlinson, 1868), 41.

8. Quoted in Reed, *Life of A. P. Dostie,* 41–42. Reed's volume must be used with extreme caution. The book is eulogistic and presents Dostie in only the most favorable light.

9. Ibid., 46.

10. Quoted ibid., 46–48.

11. Fred H. Harrington, *Fighting General: Major General N. P. Banks* (Philadelphia: University of Pennsylvania Press, 1948), 95.

12. Quoted in Reed, *Life of A. P. Dostie,* 47, 48, 49, 49–50.

13. Harrington, *Banks,* 95.

14. Quoted in Reed, *Life of A. P. Dostie,* 50–59.

15. For a description of the Varieties Theater demonstration, see ibid., 59–60; *New Orleans True Delta,* April 24, 1863; and Harrington, *Banks,* 97.

16. Harrington, *Banks,* 63–64.

17. Ibid., 64.

18. Denison to Salmon P. Chase, November 29, 1862, Denison Letters, *AHA, Annual Report* (1902).

19. Denison to Salmon P. Chase, December 4, 1862, Denison Letters, *AHA, Annual Report* (1902).

20. Michael Hahn, *Speech of Hon. M. Hahn of Louisiana on the Louisiana Election Delivered in the House of Representatives, February 17, 1863* (Washington, D.C.: L. Towers & Co., 1863), 2–4. This is a reprint of Hahn's speech published in pamphlet form.

21. McCrary, "Lincoln and the Failure of Reconstruction in Louisiana," 77.

22. Joe Gray Taylor, *Louisiana Reconstructed, 1863–1877* (Baton Rouge: Louisiana State University Press, 1974), 13.

23. Caskey, *Secession and Restoration of Louisiana,* 57.

24. Gerald M. Capers, *Occupied City: New Orleans under the Federals, 1862–1865* (Lexington: University of Kentucky Press, 1965), 128.

25. Ibid., 125.

26. Harrington, *Banks,* 100.

27. Hutchins to Chase, December 6, 1863, Salmon P. Chase Papers 84 (November 14–December 7, 1863), no. 12303–12304, Manuscript Division, Library of Congress.

28. Durant to Wrotroski, December 14, 1863, Durant Papers, NYHS.

29. Capers, *Occupied City,* 128.

30. The speech was published in pamphlet form (see Michael Hahn, *What Is Unconditional Unionism?* [New Orleans: New Orleans Era Office, 1863], 4–12).

31. Simpson and Baker, "Michael Hahn," 231.

32. *The Political Career of Hon. Michael Hahn* (New Orleans: New Orleans Era Office, January 31, 1864), 2.

33. For the text of the speech, see Michael Hahn, *Ex-Governor Hahn on Louisiana Legislation Relating to Freedmen* (Washington, D.C.: W. H. Moore, Printer, 1866).

34. Capers, *Occupied City,* 130.

35. McCrary, "Lincoln and the Failure of Reconstruction in Louisiana," 156. McCrary claims that Harrington and Capers overemphasized the moderate-radical split before 1864. The weight of the evidence balances in favor of McCrary's thesis (James Payton McCrary. "Moderation in a Revolutionary World: Lincoln and the Failure of Reconstruction in Louisiana," Ph.D. diss., Princeton University, 1972).

36. Capers, *Occupied City,* 125.

37. Harrington, *Banks,* 100.

38. Roy P. Basler, ed., *The Collected Works of Abraham Lincoln,* vol. 6, *1862–1863* (New Brunswick, N.J.: Rutgers University Press, 1953), editor's note, 288.

39. Ibid., 5:287.

40. Ibid., 6:288–89.

41. Caskey, *Secession and Restoration of Louisiana,* 76.

42. The activities of the General Committee are recorded in the Minute Book of the General Committee Union Associations of New Orleans and Jefferson, Louisiana, 1863, NYHS.

43. Ibid., 14–17.

44. Shepley to Durant and Graham, May 25, 1863, *War of the Rebellion: Official Records of the Union and Confederate Armies* (Washington, D.C.: Government Printing Office, 1880–1901), ser. 3, 3:234–35.

45. McCrary, "Lincoln and the Failure of Reconstruction in Louisiana," 140–41.

46. Lincoln to Banks, August 5, 1863, *Works of Lincoln,* 4:364–65.

47. Ibid.

48. Ibid., November 5, 1863, *Works of Lincoln,* 7: 1.

49. Ibid.

50. Ready, Dostie, and Hire to Banks, January 25, 1863, Nathaniel P. Banks Papers, Manuscript Division, Library of Congress.

51. Durant to Chase, February 21, 1864, Salmon P. Chase Papers, Manuscript Division, Library of Congress.

52. Hahn to Banks, October 3, 1863, Box 44, Nathaniel P. Banks Papers, Manuscript Division, Library of Congress.

53. Durant to Chase, February 21, 1864, Salmon P. Chase Papers, Manuscript Division, Library of Congress.

54. The most complete analysis of the 1864 state elections is in McCrary, "Lincoln and the Failure of Reconstruction in Louisiana," 267, 273–75.

55. Reed, *Life of A. P. Dostie,* 97–98.

56. Roger W. Shugg, *Origins of Class Struggle in Louisiana: A Social History of White Farmers and Laborers during Slavery and After, 1840–1875,* 2nd ed. (Baton Rouge: Louisiana State University Press, 1966), 196–211; Taylor, *Louisiana Reconstructed,* 49–52. See also McCrary, "Lincoln and the Failure of Reconstruction in Louisiana," 300–322.

57. Michael Hahn, *Message of the Governor of the State of Louisiana, Delivered October 7, 1864* (New Orleans: W. R. Fish, State Printer, 1864).

58. Denison to Hugh McCulloch, May 6, 1865, George S. Denison Papers, Manuscript Division, Library of Congress.

59. N. P. Banks to Montgomery Blair, May 6, 1865, Blair Family Papers, Manuscript Division, Library of Congress.

60. Walter Lowrey, "The Political Career of James Madison Wells," *Louisiana Historical Quarterly* 21 (October 1948): 995–1003, 1014–15.

61. Taylor, *Louisiana Reconstructed,* 58–59.

62. Ibid., 59.

63. Lowrey, "Political Career of James Madison Wells," 1025.

64. Taylor, *Louisiana Reconstructed,* 60–61.

65. George S. Denison to Hugh McCulloch, May 6, 1865, George S. Denison Papers, Manuscript Division, Library of Congress.

66. *New Orleans Tribune,* June 4, 1865.

67. N. P. Banks to Montgomery Blair, May 6, 1865, Blair Family Papers, Manuscript Division, Library of Congress.

68. Reed, *Life of A. P. Dostie,* 194–98.

69. Ibid., 191.

70. John A. Rozier to A. P. Field, June 16, 1865, in Reed, *Life of A. P. Dostie,* 203.

71. *New Orleans Tribune,* June 1, 1865.

72. *Proceedings of the Convention of the Republican Party of Louisiana, held at Economy Hall, New Orleans, September 25, 1865 and the Central Executive Committee of the Friends of Universal Suffrage of Louisiana now the Central Executive Committee of the Republican Party of Louisiana* (n.p., n.d.), 1–8. See also Philip D. Uzee, "The Beginnings of the Louisiana Republican Party," *Louisiana History* 7 (Summer 1971): 204–5.

73. *Proceedings of the Convention of the Republican Party,* 2.

74. *New Orleans Tribune,* June 23, 1865.

75. Ibid., June 18, 1865.

76. George S. Denison to D. C. Denison, June 2, 1865, in James A. Padgett, ed., "Some Letters of George Stanton Denison, 1856–1866: Observations of a Yankee on Conditions in Louisiana and Texas," *Louisiana Historical Quarterly* 23 (October 1940): 1225.

77. Uzee, "Beginnings of the Louisiana Republican Party," 204.

78. *New Orleans Tribune,* June 18, 1865.

79. Ibid., June 23, 1865.

80. Ibid., 20.

81. The debates and voting records are from the *Proceedings of the Convention of the Republican Party,* 14–27.

82. Donald Bruce Johnson and Kirk H. Porter, eds., *National Party Platforms, 1840–1972* (Urbana: University of Illinois Press, 1973), 35–36.

83. *Proceedings of the Convention of the Republican Party,* 16.

84. Michael W. Fitzgerald, *Splendid Failure: Postwar Reconstruction in the American South* (Chicago: Dee, 2007), 120.

Chapter Five

Note: This chapter, here retitled and revised, was originally published as "Bloody Monday: The Louisiana Scalawags and the New Orleans Riot of 1866," *Southern Studies: An Interdisciplinary Journal of the South* 2 (Spring 1991): 5–15. I am indebted to the publisher, who holds the copyright, for permission to reprint the essay in this modified form.

1. Morton Keller, ed., *The Art and Politics of Thomas Nast* (New York: Oxford University Press, 1968), plate 17.

2. Taken from the minority (Democratic) report of the congressional committee that investigated the riot (see U.S. Congress, House, *New Orleans Riots of July 30, 1866,* 39th Cong., 2nd sess., 1867, H. Dept. 16 [repr., New York: Arno Press and New York Times, 1969], 60).

3. Gilles Vandal, *The New Orleans Riot of 1866: Anatomy of a Tragedy* (Lafayette: Center for Louisiana Studies at the University of Southwestern Louisiana, 1983), vii–viii.

4. James G. Hollandsworth Jr., *An Absolute Massacre: The New Orleans Race Riot of July 30, 1866* (Baton Rouge: Louisiana State University Press, 2001), 4.

5. James K. Hogue, *Uncivil War: Five New Orleans Street Battles and the Rise and Fall of Radical Reconstruction* (Baton Rouge: Louisiana State University Press, 2006), 30.

6. Donald E. Reynolds, "New Orleans Riot of 1866, Reconsidered," *Louisiana History* 5 (Winter 1964): 6–8.

7. Ibid., 7–8.

8. Joe Gray Taylor, *Louisiana Reconstructed, 1863–1877* (Baton Rouge: Louisiana State University Press, 1974), 81.

9. For Edward H. Durell testimony, U.S. Congress, House, *New Orleans Riots of July 30, 1866,* 39th Cong., 2nd sess., 1867, H. Dept. 16 (repr., New York: Arno Press and New York Times, 1969), 262–63; John T. Monroe testimony, 44; Absalom Baird testimony, 442–43; Andrew Johnson telegram, 443.

10. Emily Hazen Reed, *Life of A. P. Dostie or The Conflict in New Orleans* (New York: William P. Tomlinson, 1868), 292–93.

11. Ibid, 293–97. Reed makes no mention of Dostie's speech within the institute.

12. Reynolds, "New Orleans Riot . . . Reconsidered," 10–13.

13. *New Orleans Riots of July 30, 1866,* 17.

14. Ibid., 12.

15. Reynolds, "New Orleans Riot . . . Reconsidered," 13.

16. *New Orleans Picayune,* July 31, 1866.

17. *New Orleans Times* (n.d.), reprinted in *New York Times,* August 5, 1866.

18. Ibid.

19. *New Orleans Riots of July 30, 1866,* 17.

20. *New York Times,* July 4, 1866.

21. Ibid., July 14, 1866.

22. Ibid., July 31, 1866.

23. Ibid.

24. See the minority report, *New Orleans Riots of July 30, 1866,* 60; and Ficklen, *History of Reconstruction in Louisiana,* 173.

25. Walter L. Fleming, ed., *Documentary History of Reconstruction, Political Military, Social, Religious, Educational and Industrial, 1865 to 1906* (New York: McGraw-Hill, 1966), 232.

26. Ficklen, *History of Reconstruction in Louisiana,* 161; Bowers, *The Tragic Era,* 128.

27. For Richard L. Shelly testimony, *New Orleans Riots of July 30, 1866,* 475, 476, 483, 485, 47.

28. Ibid., 476.

29. For John L. Anden testimony, *New Orleans Riots of July 30, 1866,* 15–16.

30. For Stephen A. Fish testimony, *New Orleans Riots of July 30, 1866,* 38–39.

31. Ibid.

32. *New York Times,* August 1, 1866.

33. *New Orleans Riots of July 30, 1866,* 61.

34. Ficklen, *History of Reconstruction in Louisiana,* 173.

35. Bowers, *The Tragic Era,* 128.

36. Ibid.

37. For Eugene Tisdale testimony, *New Orleans Riots of July 30, 1866,* 259–60; for Joint Committee denials, 486–504; for Rufus K. Howell testimony, 56; for Edward [?] H. Durell testimony, 56.

38. Reynolds, "New Orleans Riot . . . Reconsidered," 20.

39. Taylor, *Louisiana Reconstructed,* 111.

40. Reynolds, "New Orleans Riot . . . Reconsidered," 17.

41. The following testimony is found in *New Orleans Riots of July 30, 1866:* Ezra Hiestand, 1–3, 5; Rufus King Cutler, 32, 28, 29, 30; Rufus Waples, 23, 24, 26; William Henry Hire, 66, 67, 64, 65, 66; James Madison Wells, 438, 440; Thomas Jefferson Durant, 8–9.

42. A. P. Dostie deposition, *Proceedings of the Military Board of Investigation on the New Orleans Riots from August 10 to September 5, 1866; Exhibits, and Correspondence Relating to the Riots, 1866–1867,* Microfilm, roll 477, Office of the Adjutant General, Record Group 94, National Archives.

43. J. B. Jourdain testimony, *New Orleans Riots of July 30, 1866,* 205.

44. Ibid., 177–78.

45. William Hanksworth testimony, *New Orleans Times,* August 8, 1866.

46. *New Orleans Daily Picayune,* August 6, 1866.

47. *New Orleans Tribune,* September 2, 1866.

48. *New York Times,* August 8, 1866.

49. *New Orleans Riots of July 30, 1866,* 478.

50. *New York Times,* August 1, 1866.

51. Ibid., August 8, 1866.

52. *New Orleans Riots of July 30, 1866,* 478.

53. *New Orleans Times,* July 31, 1866, reprinted in *New York Times,* August 5, 1866.

54. "The New Orleans Riot: Report of the Grand Jury," *New York Times,* August 17, 1866.

55. See George Rable, *But There Was No Peace: The Role of Violence in the Politics of Reconstruction* (Athens: University of Georgia Press, 1984).

Chapter Six

1. Eric L. McKitrick, *Andrew Johnson and Reconstruction* (Chicago: University of Chicago Press, 1960), 428.

2. Quoted in *Trial of Andrew Johnson, President of the United States, Before the Senate of the United States on Impeachment by the House of Representatives for High Crimes and Misdemeanors I* (1868; repr., New York: Da Capo Press, 1970), 340–41.

3. McKitrick, *Andrew Johnson,* 427.

4. *New Orleans Tribune,* September 11, 1866.

5. See U.S. Congress, House, *New Orleans Riots of July 30, 1866,* 39th Cong., 2nd sess., 1867, H. Dept. 16 (repr., New York: Arno Press and New York Times, 1969) for testimony by the following: James K. Belden, 466; Rufus King Cutler, 33; William Henry Hire, 67; Rufus Howell, 50; B. L. Lynch, 239; James K. Belden, 467; Rufus King Cutler, 33; Rufus Waples, 27; R. F. Daunoy, 138; James Madison Wells, 440; Thomas Jefferson Durant, 11.

6. For an analysis of the testimony given at these hearings, see also Hans Trefousse, ed., *Background for Radical Reconstruction* (Boston: Little, Brown, 1970).

7. Ibid., xvi.

8. Walter L. Fleming, ed., *Documentary History of Reconstruction, Political Military, Social, Religious, Educational and Industrial, 1865 to 1906* (New York: McGraw-Hill, 1966), 402–19.

9. This account of Sheridan and Louisiana Reconstruction is drawn from Joe Gray Taylor, *Louisiana Reconstructed, 1863–1877* (Baton Rouge: Louisiana State University Press, 1974), 140–44.

10. *New Orleans Times,* December 10, 1867, December 19, 1867, and February 26, 1868.

11. Richard L. Hume and Jerry B. Gough, *Blacks, Carpetbaggers, and Scalawags: The Constitutional Conventions of Radical Reconstruction* (Baton Rouge: Louisiana State University Press, 2008), appendix B.

12. The unsuccessful candidates included Crane, Waples, Smith, and Belden (see Wynona Gillmore Mills, "James Govan Taliaferro, 1798–1876: Louisiana Unionist and Scalawag" [master's thesis, Louisiana State University, 1968], 60–61).

13. For the scalawag voting record, see Richard L. Hume, "The 'Black and Tan' Constitutional Conventions of 1867–1868 in Ten Former Confederate States: A Study of Their Membership" (Ph.D. diss., University of Washington, 1969), 111–14.

14. The constitution was adopted by the delegates by a vote of 61 to 6 (Taylor, *Louisiana Reconstructed,* 151).

15. The following account of the Republican factional wars is taken from F. Wayne Binning, "Carpetbaggers' Triumph: The Louisiana State Election of 1868," *Louisiana History* 14, no. 1 (Winter 1973): 21, 26, 28, 26, 27–31, 32, 36. Hahn would continue to edit the *Republican* for the next four years (see *Appleton's Cyclopaedia of American Biography,* 8 vols. [1901; repr., Farmington Hills, Mich.: Gale Research, 1968], s.v., "Michael Hahn," and *Memorial Address,* 18).

16. "Tabular Statement of the vote for and against the Constitution at an election held in the State of Louisiana on the 17th and 18th days of April pursuant to special orders Nos. 55 and 63, Current Series, Headquarters, Fifth Military District," Louisiana Constitution Document № 1718, Department of Archives, Louisiana State University, Baton Rouge. The ratification votes were counted and substantiated by three Federal officers (L. P. Graham, G. Norman Lieber, and B. Johnson).

17. For a history of the "Tabular Statement," see Donald W. Davis, "Ratification of the Constitution of 1868—Record of Voters," *Louisiana History* 6 (Summer 1965): 301–5.

18. This and all other references to the ratification vote are taken from the "Tabular Statement." The regional classifications and descriptions used throughout this section are drawn from Howard, *Political Tendencies in Louisiana,* 3–17.

19. Taylor, *Louisiana Reconstructed,* 160.

20. Mills, "Taliaferro," 56–57; Taylor, *Louisiana Reconstructed,* 156; Binning, "Carpetbaggers' Triumph," 34.

21. Taylor, *Louisiana Reconstructed,* 156; Binning, "Carpetbaggers' Triumph," 34.

22. Taylor, *Louisiana Reconstructed,* 157.

23. *New Orleans Daily Picayune,* April 2, 1868, quoted in Mills, "Taliaferro," 78.

24. Ibid., April 10, 1868, quoted in Mills, "Taliaferro," 78.

25. Mills, "Taliaferro," 82; Taylor, *Louisiana Reconstructed,* 156; Binning, "Carpetbaggers' Triumph," 38.

26. Binning, "Carpetbaggers' Triumph," 38.

27. James Alex Baggett, *The Scalawags: Southern Dissenters in the Civil War and Reconstruction* (Baton Rouge: Louisiana State University Press, 2003), 266.

28. Henry Clay Warmoth, *War, Politics and Reconstruction: Stormy Days in Louisiana* (New York: Macmillan, 1930), 270.

29. Richard Nelson Current, *Those Terrible Carpetbaggers: A Reinterpretation* (New York: Oxford University Press, 1988), ix.

30. Joe Gray Taylor, "Henry Clay Warmoth," in *The Louisiana Governors: From Iberville to Edmonds* (Baton Rouge: Louisiana State University Press, 1990), 168. See also Hume and Gough, *Blacks, Carpetbaggers, and Scalawags,* for Warmoth's classification as a carpetbagger, 183.

31. Edward King, "The Great South: Old and New Louisiana," *Scribner's Monthly,* December 1873, 159, http://ebooks.library.cornell.edu/s/scmo/index.html.

32. Simeon Belden: Taylor, *Louisiana Reconstructed,* 156. "He is of small stature. His complexion is rather pale, has mild blue eyes, small features, and chestnut hair. He dresses elegantly" (*New Orleans Daily Picayune,* January 28, 1872). W. Jasper Blackburn: *Appleton's Cyclopaedia,* s.v. "Blackburn, William Jasper"; *Biographical Directory*

of the American Congress, 1774–1971, rev. ed. (Washington, D.C.: Government Printing Office, 1971), s.v. "Blackburn, William Jasper." As a delegate to the teachers convention, Blackburn complained about corruption in the public school system and lashed out at the Republican state administration as "utterly worthless, serving no purpose whatever except to provide salaries for the higher ups" (quoted in Davis, "Ratification of the Constitution of 1868," 226). M. F. Bonzano: *Goodspeed's Biographical and Historical Memoirs of Louisiana,* 305–6; *Edward's New Orleans Directory 1870* (1871). J. Ernest Breda: *Biographical and Historical Memoirs of Northwest Louisiana Comprising a Large Fund of Biography of Actual Residents, and an Interesting Historical Sketch of the Thirteen Counties* (Nashville: Southern, 1890), 326. Mortimer Carr: *Annual Cyclopaedia* (1870); Taylor, *Louisiana Reconstructed,* 212–13. George W Carter: Warmouth, *Stormy Days,* 110, 118. Valentine Chase: U.S. Congress, House, *Use of the Army in Certain of the Southern States,* Ex. Doc. 30, 44th Cong., 2nd sess., 1877 (repr., New York: Arno Press and New York Times, 1969), 224–25; Warmoth, *Stormy Days,* 69; Allen W. Trelease, *White Terror: The Ku Klux Klan Conspiracy and Southern Reconstruction* (New York: Harper and Row, 1971), 128; Armand Commagere, *Edward's New Orleans Directory (1870),* 746; Ninth U.S. Census (1870), Sixth Ward. Thomas Green Davidson: E. Russ Williams, "Tom Green Davidson: Southern Statesman or Louisiana Scalawag?," *Louisiana Studies* (Spring 1971): 21–24. Richard C. Downes: "I supported Governor Warmoth and the regular Republican ticket at the late Election [1868] and I was elected Parish Judge for [Madison Parish] by an almost unanimous vote at that time." Downes to J. S. Harris, January 7, 1869 (Senate) Select Committee on Political Disabilities, KY-MS., Sen. Y1A-H27, Record Group 46. Louis Dupleix held the registrar's position throughout the Reconstruction era (*Biographical and Historical Memoirs of Northwest Louisiana,* 342). E. H. Durell: Lincoln appointed Durell for judge of the Eastern District of Louisiana in 1863. In 1866, Durell's jurisdiction was extended to cover the entire state (Knott, "Edward Henry Durell," in *DAB,* 3:545). A. W. Faulkner: Document 154, House Miscellaneous Documents, 41st. Cong., 2nd. sess., 1870, Part I; "Lists of state senators and representatives," Henry Clay Warmoth Papers, Southern Historical Collection, University of North Carolina. Benjamin Franklin Flanders: *Biographical Directory of the American Congress,* s.v. "Flanders, Benjamin Franklin"; see also Frank J. Wetta, "Benjamin Franklin Flanders," in *The Louisiana Governors: From Iberville to Edwards,* ed. Joseph G. Dawson (Baton Rouge: Louisiana State University Press, 1990), 155–64. James Graham: Ninth U.S. Census (1870), New Orleans First Ward. Michael Hahn: *Appleton's Cyclopaedia,* s.v., "Hahn, Michael." Andrew Hero: *Gardner's New Orleans Directory* (1866, 1867, 1868, 1869); *Edward's New Orleans Directory* (1870). Ezra Hiestand: *Gardner's New Orleans Directory* (1868), 520. William Henry Hire: *Gardner's New Orleans Directory* (1868), 520; *Edward's New Orleans Directory* (1870, 1871, 1872, 1873). Rufus K. Howell: Henry Planche Dart, "The Celebration of the Centenary of the Supreme Court of Louisiana," *Louisiana Historical Quarterly* 4 (January 1921): 120. Oscar Jeffrion: Jeffrion to Rutherford B. Hayes, December 4, 1878, Applications . . . Collectors of Internal Revenue, Box 73, Record Group 56, National Archives. Charles Leaumont: *New Orleans Daily Picayune,* January 28, 1872; Ninth U.S. Census (1870), Seventh Ward. James Longstreet: Donald Bridgman Sanger and Thomas Robson Hay, *James Longstreet* (Baton Rouge: Louisiana State University Press, 1952), 345–77. Hogue states that Longstreet resigned his commission in the state militia in 1875.

John Theodore Ludeling: Dart, "Supreme Court [of Louisiana]," 120. George W. Mader: "We congratulate the Republicans of Louisiana on the reappointment of that sterling, consistent and influential Republican, Mr. George W. Mader, to the position of Inspector of Customs under Colonel [James F.] Casey. Mr. Mader, without whom the Republican Party would be a feeble organization, resigned a similar position in the Customhouse early in January, and served with fidelity and marked ability as clerk of seven committees of the [State] House of Representatives until the session closed" (*New Orleans Republican,* March 22, 1870). William G. Phillips: *Use of the Army,* 401. E. L. Pierson: *Speech of . . . Aaron A. Sargent,* 19. R. G. Pitkin: *Gardner's New Orleans Directory* (1868); Taylor, *Louisiana Reconstructed,* 484. John Ray: *Appleton's Cyclopaedia,* s.v. "Ray, John." Robert Ray: *Richard Beacon News,* October 28, 1899. James Ready: *Gardner's New Orleans Directory* (1868). Charles Smith: Ninth U.S. Census (1870), Third Ward. Eugene Staes: J. L. Dupont and Walter L. Cohen to H. D. Coleman, n.d., Applications . . . New Orleans, Box 14, Record Group 56, National Archives. James Govan Taliaferro: Dart, "Supreme Court of Louisiana," 120. James Veazie: *Edward's New Orleans Directory* (1871, 1872). Michel Vidal: *Biographical Directory of the American Congress,* s.v. "Vidal, Michael"; Louis Clinton Nolan, "The Relations of the United States and Peru with Respect to the Claims," *American Historical Review* 17 (February 1937): 30–66. Rufus Waples: *Edward's New Orleans Directory* (1871, 1872); *Who Was Who,* s.v. "Waples, Rufus." James Madison Wells: *Appleton's Cyclopaedia of American Biography,* s.v. "Wells, James Madison"; Lowrey, "Political Career of James Madison Wells," 1093–110. George M. Wickliffe: Cortez A. M. Ewing, "Five Early Louisiana Impeachments," *Louisiana Historical Quarterly* 31 (July 1948): 688.

33. For a comprehensive study of the factional struggles in Louisiana from 1868 to 1876, see Taylor, *Louisiana Reconstructed,* 165–313, 480–505.

34. Baggett, *The Scalawags,* 255.

35. John Rose Ficklen, *History of Reconstruction in Louisiana (through 1868)* (1910; repr., Gloucester, Mass.: Peter Smith, 1966), 194; Taylor, *Louisiana Reconstructed,* 156.

36. Ewing, "Louisiana Impeachments," 688.

37. *American Annual Cyclopaedia and Register of Important Events of the Year 1869* (New York: D. Appleton and Co., 1871), 9:389.

38. Wickliffe to John Harris, April 14, 1869, Henry Clay Warmoth Papers, Southern Historical Collection, University of North Carolina.

39. *Annual Cyclopaedia* (1869), 398.

40. Miriam G. Reevis, *The Governors of Louisiana* (Gretna, La,: Pelican, 1972), 76; Baggett, *The Scalawags* 255.

41. Wickliffe to Harris, April 14, 1869, Henry Clay Warmoth Papers, Southern Historical Collection, University of North Carolina.

42. *Annual Cyclopaedia* (1869), 398; Ewing, "Louisiana Impeachments," 689.

43. Quoted in *Annual Cyclopaedia* (1869), 398.

44. *Annual Cyclopaedia* (1870), 456, 695–97.

45. Taylor, *Louisiana Reconstructed,* 198; Ewing, "Louisiana Impeachments," 698.

46. For this account of Carter's opposition to Warmoth, see Warmoth, *Stormy Days,* 109–10.

47. Ibid., 111; See also Taylor, *Louisiana Reconstructed,* 212–13.

48. Althea D. Pitre, "The Collapse of the Warmoth Regime, 1870–72," *Louisiana History* 6 (Spring 1965): 166.

49. Warmoth, *Stormy Days,* 118.

50. Taylor, *Louisiana Reconstructed,* 213.

51. Warmoth, *Stormy Days,* 111.

52. Taylor, *Louisiana Reconstructed,* 213.

53. Warmoth, *Stormy Days,* 111.

54. Pitre, "Collapse of the Warmoth Regime," 167.

55. Taylor, *Louisiana Reconstructed,* 216.

56. Ibid., 163.

57. Pitre, "Collapse of the Warmoth Regime," 167–68; Taylor, *Louisiana Reconstructed,* 216–17.

58. *Official Report of the Proceedings, Addresses and Resolutions of the Republican State Convention of Louisiana, Held in Turner Hall, New Orleans, August 9 and 10, 1871* (New Orleans: Printed at the Office of the Republican, 1871), 1–16.

59. *Annual Cyclopaedia* (1871), 473.

60. This account of Republican factionalism is taken from Taylor, *Louisiana Reconstructed,* 217–23.

61. *Annual Cyclopaedia* (1872), 471.

62. Taylor, *Louisiana Reconstructed,* 223.

63. *Annual Cyclopaedia* (1872), 471.

64. Taylor, *Louisiana Reconstructed,* 223–24.

65. *Annual Cyclopaedia* (1872), 471.

66. Taylor, *Louisiana Reconstructed,* 223–24.

67. *Annual Cyclopaedia* (1872), 472.

68. Taylor, *Louisiana Reconstructed,* 225.

69. *New Orleans Daily Picayune,* January 21, 1872.

70. *Annual Cyclopaedia* (1872), 472–73.

71. Taylor, *Louisiana Reconstructed,* 227.

72. Quoted in Justin A. Nystrom, New Orleans: *After the Civil War: Race, Politics, and a New Birth of Freedom* (Baltimore: John Hopkins University Press, 2010), 112.

73. The Davidson-Warmoth story comes from Williams, "Tom Green Davidson," 21–24. Davidson to Taliaferro, April 25, 1868, Taliaferro Papers, Department of Archives, Louisiana State University. Parish of Livingston, Republican Ticket; Davidson to Walker, October 23, 1870; Walker to Davidson, October 28, 1870; Charles E. Kemmon to Tim Ellis, November 11, 1870, all in Ellis Family Papers, Department of Archives, Louisiana State University. E. Russ Williams, "Tom Green Davidson," 21–22; *East Feliciana Democrat,* March 1, 1871, quoted in Williams, "Tom Green Davidson," 22, see also 23–24.

74. *New Orleans Times,* March 11, 17, 1867.

75. Ibid., March 19, 1867.

76. Ibid., April 7, 1867.

77. Quoted in William Garrett Piston, *Lee's Tarnished Lieutenant: James Longstreet and His Place in Southern History* (Athens: University of Georgia Press, 1987), 105.

78. William Richter, "'The Road to Hell Is Paved with Good Intentions': James Longstreet in War and Peace," in *Lee's Generals: Essays in Honor of T. Harry Williams* (Knoxville: University of Tennessee Press, 2012).

79. For Longstreet's July 4, 1867, letter and its impact, see Piston, *Lee's Tarnished Lieutenant,* 106–7.

80. *New Orleans Tribune,* June 9, 1867.

81. *New Orleans Republican,* June 5, 6, 1867.

82. *New Orleans Daily Picayune,* June 9, 1867.

83. Quoted in Jeffery D. Wert, *General James Longstreet: The Confederacy's Most Controversial Soldier* (New York: Touchstone, 1994), 412.

84. *New Orleans Times,* June 7, 1867, reprinted in *New York Times,* June 13, 1867.

85. This account of the Warmoth-Longstreet connection and the militia is taken from James K. Hogue, *Uncivil War: Five New Orleans Street Battles and the Rise and Fall of Radical Reconstruction* (Baton Rouge: Louisiana State University Press, 2006), 69, 73, 70–71, 89, 88, 139.

86. William L. Richter, "James Longstreet; From Rebel to Scalawag," *Louisiana History* 11, no. 3 (Summer 1970): 230; William B. Hesseltine, *Confederate Leaders in the New South* (Baton Rouge: Louisiana State University, 1950), 110–15.

87. *New Orleans Daily Picayune,* May 31, 1866.

88. James Longstreet to Ulysses S. Grant, March 31, 1869, *Papers of Ulysses S. Grant.*

89. Sanger and Hay, *James Longstreet,* 345–46.

90. Taylor, *Louisiana Reconstructed,* 241–52; Pitre, "Collapse of the Warmoth Regime," 178–82.

91. Sanger and Hay, *James Longstreet,* 365.

92. King, "The Great South," 148. King was influenced by conversations with the Charles Gayarré anti-Reconstruction opinions.

93. Taylor, *Louisiana Reconstructed,* 201.

94. Hume and Gough, *Blacks, Carpetbaggers, and Scalawags,* 263.

Chapter Seven

Note: This chapter, here retitled and revised, was originally published as "Bulldozing the Scalawags: Some Examples of the Persecution of Southern White Republicans in Louisiana during Reconstruction." *Louisiana History* 21 (Winter 1980): 43–58. I am indebted to the publisher, who holds the copyright, for permission to reprint the essay in its modified form.

Note to Epigraph: Henry O'Connor, comp., "History of Former Elections in Louisiana," in *Republican Political Handbook for Speakers and Local Committees* (New York: Evening Post Steam Press, 1880).

1. Hudnall affidavit, U.S. Congress, House, *Use of the Army in Certain of the Southern States,* Ex. Doc. 30, 44th Cong., 2nd sess., 1877 (repr., New York: Arno Press and New York Times, 1969), 351.

2. Fisk affidavit, *Use of the Army,* 224–25.

3. Henry Clay Warmoth, *War, Politics and Reconstruction: Stormy Days in Louisiana* (New York: Macmillan, 1930), 69.

4. See esp. *Use of the Army,* 150–546; and Allen W. Trelease, *White Terror: The Ku Klux Klan Conspiracy and Southern Reconstruction* (New York: Harper and Row, 1971), 127–36.

5. See James K. Hogue, *Uncivil War: Five New Orleans Street Battles and the Rise and Fall of Radical Reconstruction* (Baton Rouge: Louisiana State University Press); Charles Lane, *The Day Freedom Died: The Colfax Massacre, the Supreme Court, and the Betrayal of Reconstruction* (New York: Holt, 2008); and LeeAnna Keith, *The Colfax Massacre: The Untold Story of Black Power, White Power, and the Death of Reconstruction* (New York: Oxford University Press, 2008).

6. Lewis to Warmoth, November 4, 1868, Henry Clay Warmoth Papers, Southern Historical Collection, University of North Carolina.

7. Lewis to Warmoth, July 10, 1868, in *Use of the Army,* 267.

8. W. L. Muefitt? to Warmoth, April 29, 1868, Henry Clay Warmoth, Southern Historical Collection, University of North Carolina.

9. Goodwin to Stephen B. Packard, September 17, 1871, Henry Clay Warmoth Papers, Southern Historical Collection, University of North Carolina.

10. Elcey Breda to J. Ernest Breda, April 11, 1873, J. P. Breda and Family Papers, Department of Archives, Louisiana State University.

11. Quoted in Lane, *The Day Freedom Died,* 142–43.

12. J. Ernest Breda to Elcey Breda, November 14, 1874, J. P. Breda and Family Papers, Department of Archives, Louisiana State University.

13. Edward King, "The Great South: Old and New Louisiana," *Scribner's Monthly,* December 1873, 156, http://ebooks.library.cornell.edu/s/scmo/index.html.

14. Joe Gray Taylor, *Louisiana Reconstructed, 1863–1877* (Baton Rouge: Louisiana State University Press, 1974), 291.

15. Ibid., 291–93.

16. Quoted in Stuart Owen Landry, *The Battle of Liberty Place* (New Orleans: Pelican, 1955), 126.

17. Ibid., 126–27.

18. Donald Bridgman Sanger and Thomas Robson Hay, *James Longstreet* (Baton Rouge: Louisiana State University Press, 1952), 370–71.

19. Taylor, *Louisiana Reconstructed,* 295.

20. Ibid., 296.

21. Ibid., 295.

22. L. C. James to Packard, October 10, 1874, in *Use of the Army,* 370.

23. J. A. Brookshire and Carl G. Schneider to Packard, October 30, 1874, reprinted in *Use of the Army,* 302–3.

24. Richard Talbot to Packard, October 15, 1874, reprinted in *Use of the Army.*

25. *New Orleans Daily Picayune,* September 20, 1868.

26. *Alexandria Caucasian,* April 18, 1874.

27. Quoted in *The White League of Louisiana* (n.p., n.d.), 15.

28. Ibid., 19.

29. Ibid., 20.

30. J. Ernest Breda to Elcey Breda, November 14, 1874, J. P. Breda and Family Papers, Department of Archives, Louisiana State University.

31. Quoted in Bill Tunnard to J. Ernest Breda, November 21, 1876, J. P. Breda and Family Papers, Department of Archives, Louisiana State University.

32. J. Ernest Breda to Elcey Breda, November 30, 1878, J. P. Breda and Family Papers, Department of Archives, Louisiana State University.

33. O'Connor, comp., *Republican Political Handbook for Speakers and Local Committees,* 77.

Chapter Eight

Note to Epigraph: Edward L. Ayers, "The First Occupation: What the Reconstruction Period after the Civil War Can Teach Us about Iraq," *New York Times Magazine,* May 29, 2005.

1. Stephen Hahn, *A Nation under Our Feet: Black Political Struggles in the Rural South from Slavery to the Great Migration* (Cambridge: Harvard University Press, 2003), 251.

2. *Memorial Addresses on the Life and Career of Michael Hahn* (Washington, D.C.: Government Printing Office, 1886), 7, 10, 18; Amos E. Simpson and Vaughn B. Baker, "Michael Hahn: Steady Patriot," *Louisiana History* 13, no. 3 (Summer 1972): 230; *National Cyclopaedia of American Biography* (New York: J. T. White, 1898–1965), s.v., "Hahn, Michael."

3. E. Russ Williams, "Tom Green Davidson: Southern Statesman or Louisiana Scalawag?" *Louisiana Studies* (Spring 1971), 25; *Biographical Directory of the American Congress, 1774–1971,* rev. ed. (Washington, D.C.: Government Printing Office, 1971), s.v., "Davidson, Thomas Green."

4. Snow to Hiscock (1880?), Applications . . . New Orleans, Record Group 56, Box 14, National Archives. For other recommendations and evidence of Kellogg's Republicanism, see Kellogg file, Applications . . . New Orleans, Box 14, Record Group 56, National Archives.

5. Neuman to William Windom, Secretary of the Treasury, March 22, 1889, Applications . . . New Orleans, Box 13, Record Group 56, National Archives; Fontelieu supplied letters of recommendation from William Pitt Kellogg and Henry Clay Warmoth. See Fontelieu file, Applications . . . New Orleans, Box 13, Record Group 56, National Archives.

6. Jeffrion to Hayes, December 4, 1878, Applications . . . Collectors of Internal Revenue, Box 73, Record Group 56, National Archives.

7. A. A. Braver to Harrison, June 1, 1899, Applications . . . New Orleans, Box 15, Record Group 56, National Archives.

8. H. Dudley Coleman to Benjamin Harrison, May 31, 1889, Applications . . . New Orleans, Box 14, Record Group 56, National Archives.

9. E. J. Barrett to Benjamin Harrison (1889?), Applications . . . New Orleans, Box 14, Record Group 56, National Archives; *Andrew Hero, Jr. Chairman, Republican Congressional Committee, Second Congressional District* (n.p., n.d.), passim.

10. Merchant to Benjamin Harrison, February 14, 1889, Applications . . . New Orleans, Box 14, Record Group 56, National Archives. Hero's son, Andrew Hero Jr., attended Tulane and Columbia Universities and was graduated from West Point in 1891. He served in the United States Army for forty years and retired in 1930 with the rank of major general (see *Who Was Who in America: Historical Volume, 1607–1896,* rev. ed. [St. Louis: Von Hoffman Press and A. N. Marquis Co., 1967], s.v., "Hero, Andrew, Jr.").

11. Philip D. Uzee, "Republican Politics in Louisiana, 1877–1900" (Ph.D. diss., Louisiana State University, 1950), vii–viii.

12. Walter Lowrey, "The Political Career of James Madison Wells," *Louisiana Historical Quarterly* 21 (October 1948): 1092–97; Joe Gray Taylor, *Louisiana Reconstructed, 1863–1877* (Baton Rouge: Louisiana State University Press, 1974), 303.

13. Lowrey, "Political Career of James Madison Wells," 1097–98.

14. Ibid., 1099.

15. For a detailed history of the board proceedings, see Taylor, *Louisiana Reconstructed,* 491–93; Lowrey, "Political Career of James Madison Wells," 1102–8; *Appleton's Cyclopaedia of American Biography,* 8 vols. (1901; repr., Farmington Hills, Mich.: Gale Research, 1968), s.v. "Wells, Thomas Jefferson."

16. Lowrey, "Political Career of James Madison Wells," 1108–18.

17. Ibid., 1108.

18. Ibid., 1111–13.

19. Ibid., 1113; H. W. Howard Knott, "James Madison Wells," in *DAB,* s.v. "James Madison Wells."

20. *Biographical and Historical Memoirs of Northwest Louisiana Comprising a Large Fund of Biography of Actual Residents, and an Interesting Historical Sketch of the Thirteen Counties* (Nashville: Southern, 1890), 342.

21. *Biographical Directory of the American Congress, 1774–1971,* rev. ed. (Washington, D.C.: Government Printing Office, 1971), s.v., "Flanders, Benjamin Franklin." According to *The National Cyclopaedia of American Biography* (New York: J. T. White, 1898–1965), Flanders remained as United States treasurer at New Orleans until 1885 (s.v. "Flanders, Benjamin Franklin").

22. *Goodspeed's Biographical and Historical Memoir of Louisiana* (Chicago: Goodspeed, 1892), 306.

23. "Philip Hickey Morgan," Dictionary of Louisiana Biography, www.lahistory.org/site16.php.

24. See Robert Ray's obituary in Louisiana's *Richland Beacon News,* October 28, 1899.

25. Quoted in E. Russ Williams, "John Ray, A Northeast Louisiana Scalawag," typescript of unpublished article generously provided by the author, 24.

26. Ibid., 25. For references to B. H. Dinkgrave, see Henry O'Connor, comp., *Republican Political Handbook for Public Speakers and Local Committees* (New York: Evening Post Steam Press, 1880), 79. Ouachita Parish Biographies, http://genealogytrails.com/lou/ouachita/biographies.html.

27. *Appleton's Cyclopaedia,* s.v., "Ray, John."

28. Ibid.

29. Durant to Flanders, February 10, 1867, Benjamin Franklin Flanders Papers, Department of Archives, Louisiana State University; see also Durant to Warmoth, February

12, 1867; Durant to Warmoth, April 9, 1867; Durant to Warmoth, June 10, 1867; Durant to Warmoth, October 11, 1867, all in Henry Clay Warmoth Papers, Southern Historical Collection, University of North Carolina.

30. In a long, detailed letter, Durant advised Flanders on international law and constitutional history and theory as they applied to the writing of the new constitution (Durant to Flanders, November 18, 1867, Benjamin Franklin Flanders Papers, Department of Archives, Louisiana State University).

31. Durant to Flanders, December 7, 1867, Benjamin Franklin Flanders Papers, Department of Archives, Louisiana State University.

32. Durant to Benjamin F. Butler, March 12, 1869, Applications and Letters of Recommendation for Assessors of Internal Revenue, General Records of the Department of the Treasury, Box 11, Record Group 56, National Archives.

33. Durant to Warmoth, March 28, 1868, Warmoth Papers, Southern Historical Collection, University of North Carolina.

34. *New Orleans Tribune,* December 10, 1867.

35. Graham to Oscar J. Dunn, June 24, 1868, Taliaferro Papers, Department of Archives, Louisiana State University. This was an open letter addressed to Dunn and distributed as a broadside.

36. H. W. Howard Knott, "Thomas Jefferson Durant," *DAB,* 5:543–44.

37. Robert F. Cushman, *Leading Constitutional Decisions,* 14th ed. (New York: Appleton-Century-Crofts, 1971), 185. See also Paul A. Freund, ed., *History of the Supreme Court of the United States,* vol. 6, *Reconstruction and Reunion,* by Charles Fairman (New York: Macmillan, 1971), 1301–88.

38. Fairman, *Reconstruction and Reunion,* 1346.

39. Quoted ibid., 1376.

40. Fairman, *Reconstruction and Reunion,* 1375.

41. *Boston Daily Advertiser,* April 27, 1867, quoted in Knott, "Thomas Jefferson Durant," in *DAB,* 5:544.

42. Hans L. Trefousse, *Historical Dictionary of Reconstruction* (New York: Greenwood Press, 1991), s.v., "Thomas Jefferson Durant."

43. *Biographical Directory of the American Congress,* s.v. "Blackburn, William Jasper"; *Appleton's Cyclopaedia of American Biography,* s.v. "Blackburn, William Jasper."

44. *Little Rock Republican,* August 24, 1889.

45. Bussey to Blackburn, June 20, 1889, Benjamin Harrison Papers, Presidential Papers Microfilm, Series 2, Reel 65, Louisiana State University.

46. *Biographical Directory of the American Congress,* s.v. "Blackburn, William Jasper."

47. Longstreet to General Benjamin Alvord, March 17, 1877, quoted in Donald Bridgman Sanger and Thomas Robson Hay, *James Longstreet* (Baton Rouge: Louisiana State University Press, 1952), 378.

48. Longstreet settled his family in Gainesville sometime in 1876 (Sanger and Hay, *James Longstreet,* 377).

49. Longstreet to Hayes, April 26, 1877, quoted in Sanger and Hay, *James Longstreet,* 379.

50. Douglas Southall Freeman, "James Longstreet," *DAB,* 6:392; Grady McWhiney, "James Longstreet," in *Encyclopedia of American Biography,* ed. John A. Garraty (New York: Harper and Row, 1974), 687.

51. Glen LaFantasie "Considering Longstreet's Legacy," in *With My Face to the Enemy: Perspectives on the Civil War,* ed. Robert Crowley (New York: Putnam's, 2001), 347.

52. Thomas L. Connelly and Barbara L. Bellows, *God and General Longstreet* (Baton Rouge: Louisiana State University Press, 1982), 37.

53. Jeffery D. Wert, *General James Longstreet: The Confederacy's Most Controversial Soldier* (New York: Touchstone, 1994), 426.

54. Ibid, 427.

55. Longstreet Society, www.longstreet.org/open1.html.

56. Susan Rosenvold, "A Question," e-mail to Frank J. Wetta, June 18, 2011.

57. William Garrett Piston, *Lee's Tarnished Lieutenant: James Longstreet and His Place in Southern History* (Athens: University of Georgia Press, 1987), 165.

58. William Richter, "'The Road to Hell Is Paved with Good Intentions': James Longstreet in War and Peace," in *Lee and His Generals: Essays in Honor of T. Harry Williams,* ed. Lawrence Lee Hewitt and Thomas E. Schott (Knoxville: University of Tennessee Press, 2012).

59. For the details of the controversy, see Taylor, *Louisiana Reconstructed,* 244–45; and Lonn, *Reconstruction in Louisiana,* 193–98.

60. House Reports, 43th Cong., 1st sess., no. 732, 1–13.

61. Fairman, *History of the Supreme Court,* 837.

62. Kellogg to Durell, May 12, 1875, Durell Papers, NYHS.

63. Knott, "Edward Henry Durell," in *DAB,* 3:546; *Appleton's Cyclopaedia of American Biography,* s.v. "Durell, Edward Henry"; Fortier, *Louisiana* 2:341. See also Durell Papers, NYHS.

64. *Who Was Who, 1607–1896,* s.v. "Waples, Rufus."

65. Ludeling to Warmoth, January 31, 1881, Henry Clay Warmoth Papers, Southern Historical Collection, University of North Carolina.

66. White, "John Theodore Ludeling," 490.

67. Frisbie to Harrison, September 7, 1889, Applications . . . New Orleans, Box 14, Record Group 56, National Archives.

68. Emerson Bently to Warmoth, June 12, 1868, Henry Clay Warmoth Papers, Southern Historical Collection, University of North Carolina.

69. Nolan, "The Relations of the United States and Peru with Respect to Claims," 30–66.

70. *Biographical Directory of the American Congress,* s.v. "Vidal, Michel."

71. Fortier, *Louisiana,* 2:573.

72. Thomas Anderson to Secretary of the Treasury, April 30, 1878, Custom House Nominations, General Records of the Department of the Treasury, Box 116, Record Group 56, National Archives.

Chapter Nine

1. See Eric Foner, *Free Soil, Free Labor, Free Men: The Ideology of the Republican Party before the Civil War* (New York: Oxford University Press, 1970).

2. *New Orleans Era,* September 20, 1865.

3. Charles L. Dufour, "The People of New Orleans," 41.

4. *New Orleans Riots of July 30, 1866,* 423.

5. Ibid., 138.

6. Quoted in Michael Hahn, *Pamphlets,* untitled newspaper clipping, January 25, 1865, Louisiana State University Rare Book Room.

7. See David R. Rankin, "The Origins of the Black Leadership in New Orleans during Reconstruction," *Journal of Southern History* 11, no. 3 (August 1974): 440.

8. Ibid.

9. Dale A Somers, "Black and White in New Orleans: A Study of Urban Race Relations, 1865–1900." *Journal of Southern History* 40 (February 1974): 22.

10. "Speeches of a Radical Agitator," in *Documentary History of Reconstruction, Political Military, Social, Religious, Educational and Industrial, 1865 to 1906,* ed. Walter L. Fleming (New York: McGraw-Hill, 1966), 234.

11. Taylor, *Louisiana Reconstructed,* 438.

12. Charles Vincent, *Black Legislators in Louisiana during Reconstruction* (1976; rev. ed., Carbondale and Edwardsville: Southern Illinois Press, 2011). Vincent recounts the frustrations faced by black legislators in enacting even modest change.

13. Quoted in Ella Lonn, *Reconstruction in Louisiana 1868* (1918; repr., Gloucester, Mass.: Peter Smith, 1967), 92.

14. E. Dale Odom, "The Vicksburg, Shreveport and Texas: The Fortunes of a Scalawag Railroad," *Southwestern Social Science Quarterly* 12 (December 1973): 284.

15. Vernon Louis Parrington, *Main Currents in American Thought: An Interpretation of American Literature from the Beginning to 1920* (New York: Harcourt, Brace and World, 1958), 2:23.

16. *Homer Iliad,* March, 1870, reprinted in *New Orleans Republican,* March 20, 1870.

17. *New Orleans Republican,* March 12, 1870.

18. King, "The Great South, pt. 2, 150. King's view of Reconstruction Louisiana was influenced by conversations with Charles Etienne Gayarré.

19. Michael Taylor, "What Do Charles Darwin, Ulysses S. Grant and Mardi Gras Have in Common?" Archive for the "Cabinet of Curiosities" Category, Louisiana State University Libraries Special Collections. http://hill.blogs.lib.lsu.edu/category/cabinet-of-curiosities; Laurraine Goreau, "Mardi Gras," in *The Past as Prelude: New Orleans, 1718–1968,* ed. Hodding Carter (New Orleans: Pelican, 1968), 352. According to James Gill, "The scions of the old plutocracy in Cosus, Monus, and Proteus were . . . still capable [long after Reconstruction] of rejecting otherwise respectable candidates for membership if their forebears had been 'scalawags'" (Gill, *Lords of Misrule: Mardi Gras and the Politics of Race in New Orleans* [Jackson: University Press of Mississippi, 1997], 7).

BIBLIOGRAPHY

Primary Sources

Manuscript Collections

LIBRARY OF CONGRESS, MANUSCRIPT DIVISION

Banks, Nathaniel P., Papers. 1863–68.
Blair Family. Papers. 1865.
Chandler, William Eaton. Papers. 1868.
Chase, Salmon P., Papers. 1863–64.
Denison, George S., Papers. 1865.
Fessenden, William Pitt. Correspondence. 1869.
Stevens, Thaddeus. Papers. 1865–67.

LOUISIANA STATE UNIVERSITY, DEPARTMENT OF ARCHIVES

Breda, J. P., and Family. Papers. 1840–95.
Ellis Family. Papers. 1870.
Flanders, Benjamin Franklin. Papers. 1864–75.
Hero, Andrew and George. Papers. 1868.
Kilbourne, James G., Correspondence. 1865.
"Tabular Statement of the vote for and against the Constitution at an election held in the State of Louisiana on the 17th and 18th days of April pursuant to special orders Nos. 55 and 63, Current Series, Headquarters, Fifth Military District." Louisiana Constitutional Document № 1718.
Taliaferro, James Govan, and Family. Papers. 1865–68.
Vidal, Michel. Papers. 1868.

NATIONAL ARCHIVES, WASHINGTON, D.C.

Applications for Assistant Treasurer and Mint. 1862–1900. General Records of the Department of the Treasury. Record Group 56.
Custom House Nominations. New Orleans. 1862–1900. General Records of the Department of Treasury. Record Group 56.

Letters of Application and Assessors. Recommendation. Internal Revenue. Assessors. Louisiana. 1862–1900. General Records of the Department of the Treasury. Record Group 56.

Letters of Application Internal Revenue. The Department of and Recommendation for Collectors of 1862–1900. General Records of the Department of the Treasury. Record Group 56.

Papers of the (House) Select Committee on Reconstruction. 40th and 41st Cong. Applications for Removal of Political Disabilities, Louisiana. 1868–69. Records of the United States House of Representatives. Record Group 233.

Papers of the (House) Select Committee on Reconstruction. 40th and 41st Cong. Various Louisiana Affairs. Records of the United States House of Representatives. Record Group 233.

Papers of the (Senate) Select Committee on Political Disabilities, Petitions and Memorials. Louisiana. 1868–69. Records of the United States Senate. Record Group 46.

Proceedings of the Military Board of Investigation on the New Orleans Riots from August 10 to September 5, 1866; Exhibits and correspondence 1866–67 relating to the riots. 1866–67. Microfilm roll 477. Records of the Adjutant General's office, 1780s–1917. Record Group 94.

Records Relating to the Appointment of Federal Judges, Marshals, and Attorneys, 1853–1901, Louisiana. General. Records of the Department of Justice. Record Group 60.

NEW YORK HISTORICAL SOCIETY, NEW YORK CITY

Durant, Thomas Jefferson. Papers. 1844–65.

Durell Family. Papers. 1847–87.

Minute Book of the General Committee. Union Associations and Jefferson, Louisiana. 1863.

SOUTHERN HISTORICAL COLLECTION, UNIVERSITY OF NORTH CAROLINA

Warmoth, Henry Clay. Papers. 1868–81. Microfilm.

U.S. Government Publications

U.S. Congress. House. *House Miscellaneous Document* № 154. 41th Cong, 2nd sess., 1870. Part I.

——. House. *New Orleans Riots of July 30, 1866.* H. Rpt. 16, 39th Cong., 2nd sess. 1867. Reprint, New York: Arno Press and *New York Times,* 1969.

——. House. *Report of the Committee on the Judiciary on Judge E. H. Durell.* H. Rept. 732, 43th Cong., 1st sess., 1874.

——. House. *Use of the Army in Certain of the Southern States.* Ex. Doc. 30, 44th Cong., 2nd sess., 1877. Reprint, New York: Arno Press and New York Times, 1969.

——. Senate. *Trial of Andrew Johnson, President of the United States, Before the Senate of the United States on Impeachment the House of Representatives for Crimes and Misdemeanors.* Washington D.C.: Government Printing Office, 1868. Reprint, New York: Da Capo Press, 1970.

War of the Rebellion: Official of the Union and Confederate Armies. 128 vols. Washington, D.C.: Government Printing Office, 1880–1901.

Census Materials, City Directories, and References

Edward's New Orleans Directory. 1870, 1871, 1872, and 1873.

Gardner's New Orleans Directory. 1866, 1867, 1868, and 1869.

Jewell's Crescent City Illustrated. 1872.

Ninth United States Census.1870. First-Twelfth Wards.

Miscellaneous

Basler, Roy P., ed. *The Collected Works of Abraham Lincoln.* New Brunswick, N.J.: Rutgers University Press, 1953.

Harrison, Benjamin. Papers. Presidential Papers Microfilm series 2, reel 65. 1889. Louisiana State University.

Papers of Ulysses S. Grant. Volume 19, *July 1, 1868–October 31, 1869.* The Ulysses S. Grant Digital Collection. http://digital.library.msstate.edu/collections.

Private and Official Correspondence of Gen. Benjamin F. Butler: During the Period of the Civil War. Vol. 2, *Benjamin Franklin Butler, Jessie Ames Marshall.* Privately issued: Plimpton Press, 1917. Digitized, August 10, 2006. http://books.google.com/books.

Newspapers

Alexandria Caucasian, April 18, 1874, June 6, 1874.

Little Rock Republican, November 3, 1888, August 24, 1889.

Louisiana Standard, April 22, 1888.

Monroe Ouachita Telegraph, May 18, 1872.

New Orleans Daily Picayune, 1862–77.

New Orleans Era, 1863–65.

New Orleans Republican, 1862.

New Orleans Tribune, 1864–68.

New York Times, 1864–67.

New York Tribune, 1866–1867.
Richland Beacon News, October 28, 1899.

Contemporary Books, Pamphlets, References, and Articles

American Annual Cyclopaedia and Register of Important Events. New York: D. Appleton and Co., 1871–88.

Andrew Hero, Jr., Chairman, Republican Congressional Committee, Second Congressional District, n.p., n.d.

Barnes, Herbert. "The Scalawag," *Southern Magazine* 15 (November 1874): 302–7.

Billings, Edward C. *The Struggle between the Civilization of Slavery and That of Freedom Recently and Now Going on in Louisiana.* 1873. Reprint, Freeport, N.Y.: Books for Libraries Press, 1971.

Biographical and Historical Memoirs of Northwest Louisiana Comprising a Large Fund of Biography of Actual Residents , and an Interesting Historical Sketch of Thirteen Counties. Nashville and Chicago: Southern Publishing Co., 1890.

Catalogue of the Officers and Students of the St. Louis University, Missouri. St. Louis, Mo.: Chambers and Knapp, 1839.

"Diary and Correspondence of Salmon P. Chase. Part IV: Letters from George S. Denison to Salmon P. Chase, May 15, 1862, to March 21, 1865." *American Historical Association. Annual Report* (1902): 297–22.

Durell, Edward Henry (H. Didimus). *New Orleans as I Found It.* New York: Harper and Row, 1845.

Gayarré, Charles Etienne. "The Southern Question." *North American Review* 125 (November–December 1877): 472–98.

Goodspeed's Biographical and Historical Memoirs of Louisiana. Chicago: Goodspeed Publishing Co., 1892.

Hahn, Michael. *Ex-Governor Hahn on Louisiana Legislation Relating to Freedman.* Washington. D.C.: W. H. Moore Printer, 1866.

———. *Manhood the Basis of Suffrage.* Washington, D.C.: L. Pearson, 1865.

———. Pamphlets. N.p., n.d. Louisiana State University Rare Book Room.

———. *Speech of Hon. M. Hahn of Louisiana on the Louisiana Election.* Washington, D.C.: L. Towers and Co. Printers, 1863.

———. *What Is Unconditional Unionism?* New Orleans: Era Office, 1863.

"Hon. Edward Durell." *Granite Monthly* 4 (April 1888): 115–29.

King, Edward. "The Great South: Old and New Louisiana." *Scribner's Monthly,* December 1873, 129–60. http://ebooks.library.cornell.edu.

Memorial Address on the Life and Career of Michael Hahn. Washington, D.C.: Government Printing Office, 1886.

O'Connor, Henry, comp. *Republican Political Handbook for Public Speakers and Local Committees.* New York: Evening Post Steam Press, 1880.

Official Report of the Proceedings, Addresses and Resolutions of the Republican State Convention of Louisiana, Held in Turner Hall, New Orleans, August 9 and 10, 1871. New Orleans: Office of the Republican, 1871.

Padgett, James A., ed. "Some Letters of George Stanton Denison, 1856–1866: Observations of a Yankee on Conditions in Louisiana and Texas." *Louisiana Historical Quarterly* 23 (October 1940): 1132–240.

Pitkin, J. R. G. *To the Whigs.* New Orleans: Republican State Central Committee, 1876.

Proceedings of the Convention of the Republican Party of Louisiana Held at Economy Hall, New Orleans, September 25, 1865 and the Central Executive Committee of the Friends of the Universal Suffrage of Louisiana now the Central Executive Committee of the Republican Part of Louisiana. N.p., n.d.

Secondary Sources

Books

Baggett, James Alex. *The Scalawags: Southern Dissenters in the Civil War and Reconstruction.* Baton Rouge: Louisiana State University Press, 2003.

Blight, David W. *Race and Reunion: The American Civil War in American Memory.* Cambridge: Harvard University Press, 2001.

Bowers, Claude G. *The Tragic Era: The Revolution after Lincoln.* Cambridge, Mass.: Riverside Press, 1929.

Capers, Gerald M. *Occupied City: New Orleans under the Federals, 1862–1865.* Lexington: University of Kentucky Press, 1965.

Carter, Dan T. *When the War Was Over: The Failure of Self-Reconstruction in the South, 1865–1867.* Baton Rouge: Louisiana State University Press, 1985.

Caskey, Willie Malvin. *Secession and Restoration of Louisiana.* Louisiana State University Studies no. 36. 1938. Reprint, New York: Da Capo Press, 1970.

Connley, Thomas L., and Barbara L. Bellows. *God and General Longstreet: The Lost Cause and the Southern Mind.* Baton Rouge: n.p., 1982.

Current, Richard N. *Those Terrible Carpetbaggers.* New York: Oxford University Press, 1988.

Cushman, Robert F. *Leading Constitutional Decisions.* 14th ed. New York: Appleton-Century-Crofts, 1971.

Davis, Edwin Adams. *Louisiana: The Pelican State.* Baton Rouge: Louisiana State University Press, 1959.

———. *Louisiana: The Pelican State.* Baton Rouge: Louisiana State University Press, 1979.

Du Bois, W. E. Burqhardt. *Black Reconstruction: An Essay towards a History of the Part Which Black Folk Played in the Attempt to Reconstruct Democracy in America, 1860–1880.* New York: Russell and Russell, 1935.

Dunning, William Archibald. *Reconstruction, Political and Economic, 1865–1877.* 1907. Reprint, New York: Harper and Row, 1962.

Ficklen, John Rose. *History of Reconstruction in Louisiana (through 1868).* 1910. Reprint, Gloucester, Mass.: Peter Smith, 1966.

Fischer, Roger A. *The Segregation Struggle in Louisiana, 1862–1877.* N.p., 1974.

FitzGerald, Frances. *America Revised: History Textbooks in the Twentieth Century.* New York: Vintage, 1979.

Fitzgerald, Michael W. *Splendid Failure: Postwar Reconstruction in the American South.* Chicago: Ivan R. Dee, 2007.

Fleming, Walter L. ed. *Documentary History of Reconstruction, Political Military, Social, Religious, Educational and Industrial, 1865 to 1906.* New York: McGraw-Hill, 1966.

Foner, Eric. *Free Soil, Free Labor, Free Men: The Ideology of the Republican Party before the Civil War.* New York: Oxford University Press, 1970.

———. *Reconstruction: America's Unfinished Revolution, 1863–1877.* New York: Harper and Row, 1988.

Fortier, Alcee. *A History of Louisiana.* Vol. 4, pt. 2, *The American Dominion, 1861–1903.* New York: Goupil, 1904.

Freeman, Douglass Southall. *Lee's Lieutenants.* Vol. 1, *Manassas to Malvern Hill.* New York: Scribner's, 1942.

Freund, Paul A., ed. *History of the Supreme Court of the United States.* Vol. 6, *Reconstruction and Reunion,* by Charles Fairman. New York: Macmillan, 1971.

Gallagher, Gary. *The Union War.* Cambridge: Harvard University Press, 2011.

Gill, James. *Lords of Misrule: Mardi Gras and the Politics of Race in New Orleans.* Jackson: University Press of Mississippi, 1997.

Green, Fletcher M. *The Role of the Yankee in the Old South.* Athens: University of Georgia Press, 1972.

Hahn, Stephen. *A Nation Under Our Feet: Black Political Struggles in the Rural South from Slavery to the Great Migration.* Cambridge: Harvard University Press, 2003.

Harris, William C. *Presidential Reconstruction in Mississippi.* Baton Rouge: Louisiana State University Press, 1967.

———. *With Charity for All: Lincoln and the Restoration of the Union.* Lexington: University Press of Kentucky, 1997.

Hesseline, William B. *Confederate Leaders in the New South.* Baton Rouge: Louisiana State University Press, 1950.

Hogue, James K. *Uncivil War: Five New Orleans Street Battles and the Rise and Fall of Radical Reconstruction.* Baton Rouge: Louisiana State University, 2006.

Hollandsworth, James G., Jr. *An Absolute Massacre: The New Orleans Race Riot of July 30, 1866.* Baton Rouge: Louisiana State University Press, 2001.

Howard, Perry H. *Political Tendencies in Louisiana.* Rev. ed. Baton Rouge: Louisiana State University Press, 1967.

Hume, Richard L., and Jerry B. Gough. *Blacks, Carpetbaggers, and Scalawags: The Constitutional Conventions of Radical Reconstruction.* Baton Rouge: Louisiana State University Press, 2008.

Johnson, Donald Bruce, and Kirk H. Porter, eds. *National Party Platforms, 1840–1972.* Urbana: University of Illinois Press, 1973.

Keller, Morton, ed. *The Art and Politics of Thomas Nast.* New York: Oxford University Press, 1968.

Kieth, LeeAnna. *The Colfax Massacre: The Untold Story of Black Power, White Terror, and the Death of Reconstruction.* New York: Oxford University Press, 2008.

Landry, Stuart Owen. *The Battle of Liberty Place.* New Orleans: Pelican, 1955.

Lane, Charles. *The Day Freedom Died: The Colfax Massacre, the Supreme Court, and the Betrayal of Reconstruction.* New York: Holt, 2008.

Lonn, Ella. *Reconstruction in Louisiana after 1868.* 1918. Reprint, Gloucester, Mass.: Peter Smith, 1967.

MacMillan, Margaret. *Dangerous Games: The Uses and Abuses of History.* New York: Modern Library, 2009.

McCrary, Peyton. *Abraham Lincoln and Reconstruction: The Louisiana Experiment.* Princeton: Princeton University Press, 1978.

McKitrick, Eric L. *Andrew Johnson and Reconstruction.* Chicago: University of Chicago Press, 1960.

McPherson, James H. *The Struggle for Equality: Abolitionists and the Negro in the Civil War and Reconstruction.* Princeton: Princeton University Press, 1964.

Mitchell, Reid. *All on a Mardi Gras Day: Episodes in the History of New Orleans Carnival.* Cambridge: Harvard University Press, 1999.

Nystrom, Justin. *New Orleans after the Civil War: Race, Politics, and a New Birth of Freedom.* Baltimore: John Hopkins University Press, 2010.

Parrington, Vernon Louis. *Main Currents in American Thought: An Interpretation of American Literature from the Beginning to 1920.* New York: Harcourt, Brace and World, 1958.

Patrick, Rembert. *The Reconstruction of the Nation.* New York: Oxford University Press, 1967.

Perman, Michael. *Reunion without Compromise: The South and Reconstruction, 1865–1868.* Cambridge: n.p., 1973.

Piston, William Garrett. *Lee's Tarnished Lieutenant: James Longstreet and His Place in Southern History*. Athens: University of Georgia Press, 1987.

Rable, George C. *But There Was No Peace: The Role of Violence in the Politics of Reconstruction*. Athens: University of Georgia Press, 1984.

Reevis, Mirian G. *The Governors of Louisiana*. Gretna, La.: Pelican, 1972.

Rousey, Dennis C. *Policing the Southern City: New Orleans, 1805–1889*. Baton Rouge: Louisiana State University Press, 1996.

Sanger, Donald Bridgman, and Thomas Robson Hay. *James Longstreet*. Baton Rouge: Louisiana State University Press, 1952.

Shugg, Roger W. *Origins of Class Struggle in Louisiana: A Social History of White Farmers and Laborers during Slavery and After, 1848–1875*. 2nd ed. Baton Rouge: Louisiana State University Press, 1966.

Stampp, Kenneth M. *The Era of Reconstruction*. New York: Random House, 1965.

Taylor, Joe Gray. *Louisiana Reconstructed, 1863–1877*. Baton Rouge: Louisiana State University Press, 1974.

Trefousse, Hans L., ed. *Background for Radical Reconstruction*. Boston: Little, Brown, 1970.

———. *The Radical Republicans: Lincoln's Vanguard for Social Justice*. New York: Knopf, 1969.

Trelease, Allen W. *White Terror: The Ku Klux Klan Conspiracy and Southern Reconstruction*. New York: Harper and Row, 1971.

Tunnell, Ted. *Crucible of Reconstruction: War, Radicalism and Race in Louisiana, 1862–1877*. Baton Rouge: Louisiana University Press, 1984.

Vandal, Gilles. *New Orleans Riot of 1866: Anatomy of a Tragedy*. Lafayette, La.: Center for Louisiana Studies, 1983.

Vincent, Charles. *Black Legislators in Louisiana during Reconstruction*. 1976. Rev. ed., Carbondale and Edwardsville: Southern Illinois Press, 2011.

Warmoth, Henry Clay. *War, Politics, and Reconstruction: Stormy Days in Louisiana*. New York: Macmillan, 1930.

Williamson, Joel. *After Slavery: The Negro in South Carolina during Reconstruction, 1861–1877*. Chapel Hill: University of North Carolina Press, 1965.

Articles, Book Chapters, Reference Entries

Alexander, Thomas B. "Persistent Whiggery in Alabama and the Lower South, 1860–1877." *Alabama Review* 12 (January 1959): 35–52.

———. "Persistent Whiggery in Mississippi: The Hinds County Gazette." *Journal of Southern History* 23 (August1961): 71–93.

———. "Persistent Whiggery in the Confederate South, 1860–1877." *Journal of Southern History* 27 (August 1961): 305–29.

———. "Whiggery and Reconstruction in Tennessee." *Journal of Southern History* 16 (August 1950): 291–305.

Binning, F. Wayne. "Carpetbaggers' Triumph: The Louisiana State Elections of 1868." *Louisiana History* 14 (Winter 1973): 21–40.

Bloomfield, Maxwell. "Dixon's *The Leopard's Spots:* A Study in Popular Racism." *American Quarterly* 3 (Fall 1964): 387–401.

Capers, Gerald M., Jr. "Confederates and Yankees in Occupied New Orleans, 1862–1865." *Journal of Southern History* 30 (November 1964): 405–26.

Connor, William P. "The *New Orleans Tribune* in Post-War Louisiana." *Louisiana History* 21 (Spring 1980):159–81.

Curry, Richard O. "The Civil War and Reconstruction, 1861–1877: A Critical Overview of Recent Trends and Interpretations." *Civil War History* 20 (September 1974): 215–38.

Dart, Henry Planche. "The Celebration of the Centenary of the Supreme Court [of Louisiana]." *Louisiana Historical Quarterly* 4 (January 1921): 1–125.

Dauphine, James G. "The Knights of the White Camellia and the Election of 1868." *Louisiana History* 30 (Spring 1989): 173–90.

Davis, Donald W. "Ratification of the Constitution of 1868—Record of Votes." *Louisiana History* 6 (Summer 1965): 301–5.

Delatte, Carolyn E. "The St. Landry Riot: A Forgotten Incident of Reconstruction Violence." *Louisiana History* 17 (Winter 1976): 41–49.

Donald, David. "The Scalawag in Mississippi Reconstruction." *Journal of Southern History* 10 (November 1944): 447–60.

Dufour, Charles L. "The People of New Orleans." In *The Past as Prelude: New Orleans, 1718–1968,* edited by Hodding Carter, 20–41. New Orleans: Pelican, 1968.

Ewing, Cortez A. M. "Five Early Louisiana Impeachments." *Louisiana Historical Quarterly* 31 (July 1948): 567–97.

Freeman, Douglas Southall. "James Longstreet." In *Dictionary of American Biography,* edited by Dumas Malone. New York: Scribner's, 1959.

Goreau, Laurraine. "Mardi Gras." In *The Past As Prelude: New Orleans, 1718–1968,* edited by Hodding Carter. New Orleans: Pelican, 1968.

Harris, William C. "The Creed of the Carpetbaggers: The Case of Mississippi." *Journal of Southern History* 40 (May 1974): 199–224.

Hennessey, Melinda Meek. "Race and Violence in New Orleans: The 1868 Riot." *Louisiana History* 20 (Winter 1979): 77–91.

King, Edward. "The Great South: Old and New Louisiana, I." *Scribner's Monthly: An Illustrated Magazine for the People,* November 1873. http://ebooks.library.cornell.edu/s/scmo/index.html.

———. "The Great South: Old and New Louisiana, II." *Scribner's Monthly: An*

Illustrated Magazine for the People, December 1873. http://ebooks.library.cornell.edu/s/scmo/index.html.

Kolchin, Peter. "Scalawags, Carpetbaggers, and Reconstruction: A Quantitative Look at Southern Congressional Polities, 1868–1872." *Journal of Southern History* 45 (1979): 63–76.

Knott, H. W. Howard. "Edward Henry Durell." In *Dictionary of American Biography,* edited by Allen Johnson and Dumas Malone. New York: Scribner's, 1959.

———. "Thomas Jefferson Durant." In *Dictionary of American Biography,* edited by Allen Johnson and Dumas Malone. New York: Scribner's, 1959.

LaFantasie, Glen. "Considering Longstreet's Legacy." In *With My Face to the Enemy: Perspectives on the Civil War,* edited by Robert Crowley, 332–47. New York: Putnam's, 2001.

Lonn, Ella. "James Madison Wells." In *Dictionary of American Biography,* edited by Dumas Malone. New York: Scribner's, 1936.

Lowrey, Walter M. "The Political Career of James Madison Wells." *Louisiana Historical Quarterly* 31 (October 1948): 995–1123.

Marten, James. "The Making of a Scalawag: George S. Dennison and the South." *Louisiana History* 34 (Spring 1993): 133–60.

McWhiney, Grady. "James Longstreet." In *Encyclopedia of American Biography,* edited by John A. Garraty. New York: Harper and Row, 1974.

Mering, John Vollmer. "Persistent Whiggery in the Confederate South: A Reconsideration." *South Atlantic Quarterly* 69 (Winter 1970): 124–34.

Nolan, Louis Clinton. "The Relations of the United States and Peru with Respect to the Claims." *American Historical Review* 17 (February 1937): 30–66.

Odom, E. Dale. "The Vicksburg, Shreveport and Texas: The Fortunes of a Scalawag Railroad." *Southwestern Social Science Quarterly* 64 (December 1963): 277–85.

Olsen, Otto H. "Reconsidering the Scalawags." *Civil War History* 12 (December 1966): 304–20.

Pessen, Edward. "How Different from Each Other Were the Antebellum North and South." *American Historical Review* 85 (December 1980): 1119–49.

Pitre, Althea D. "The Collapse of the Warmoth Regime, 1870–72." *Louisiana History* 6 (Spring 1965): 161–87.

Rable, George C. "Republican Albatross: The Louisiana Question, National Politics, and the Failure of Reconstruction." *Louisiana History* 23 (Spring 1982): 109–30.

Rankin, David. "The Origins of Black Leadership in New Orleans during Reconstruction." *Journal of Southern History* 40 (August 1974): 417–40.

Reynolds, Donald E. "New Orleans Riot of 1866, Reconsidered." *Louisiana History* 5 (Winter 1964): 5–27.

Riasonovsky, Nicholas V. "Francois Marie Charles Fourier." In *The Encyclopedia of Philosophy,* edited by Paul Edwards. New York: Macmillan and Free Press, 1967.

Richter, William L. "James Longstreet: From Rebel to Scalawag." *Louisiana History* 11 (Summer 1970): 215–30.

———. "'The Road to Hell Is Paved with Good Intentions': James Longstreet in War and Peace." In *Lee and His Generals: Essays in Honor of T. Harry Williams,* edited by Lawrence Lee Hewitt and Thomas E. Schott. Knoxville: University of Tennessee Press, 2012.

Simpson, Amos E., and Vaughn B. Barker. "Michael Hahn: Steady Patriot." *Louisiana History* 13 (Summer 1972): 229–52.

Somers, Dale A. "Black and White in New Orleans: A Study of Urban Race Relations, 1865–1900." *Journal of Southern History* 40 (February 1974): 19–42.

Summer, Mark W. "The Moderates' Last Chance: The Louisiana Election of 1865." *Louisiana History* 24 (Winter 1983): 49–69.

Tregle, Joseph G., Jr. "Thomas J. Durant, Utopian Socialism and the Failure of Presidential Reconstruction in Louisiana." *Journal of Southern History* 45 (1979): 485–512.

Trelease, Allen W. "Who Were the Scalawags?" *Journal of Southern History* 24 (November 1963): 445–68.

Tunnell, Ted. 2011. "Carpetbaggers and Scalawags." KnowLA Encyclopedia of Louisiana. www.www.knowla.org.

———. "Creating 'the Propaganda of History': Southern Editors and the Origins of 'Carpetbagger' and 'Scalawag." *Journal of Southern History* 72 (November 2006): 789–822.

Uzee, Philip D. "The Beginnings of the Louisiana Republican Party." *Louisiana History* 12 (Summer 1971): 197–211.

Vandal, Gilles. "The Origins of the New Orleans Riot of 1866, Revisited." *Louisiana History* 22 (Spring 1981): 135–65.

Wetta, Frank J. "Benjamin Franklin Flanders." In *The Louisiana Governors: From Iberville to Edwards,* edited by Joseph G. Dawson, 155–64. Baton Rouge: Louisiana State University Press, 1990.

———. "Michael Hahn." In *The Louisiana Governors: From Iberville to Edwards,* edited by Joseph G. Dawson, 148–52. Baton Rouge: Louisiana State University Press. 1990.

Wharton, Vernon L. "Reconstruction." In *Writing Southern History: Essays in Historiography in Honor of Fletcher Green,* edited by Arthur S. Link and Rembert W. Patrick, 295–315. Baton Rouge: Louisiana State University Press, 1967.

White, Melvin J. "John Theodore Ludeling." *Dictionary of American Biography,* edited by Dumas Malone, 489–90. New York: Scribner's, 1959.

Williams, E. Russ. "John Ray: Forgotten Scalawag." *Louisiana Studies* 8 (Fall 1974): 240–62.

———. "Tom Green Davidson: Southern Statesman or Louisiana Scalawag?" *Louisiana Studies* (Spring 1971): 15–27.

Williams, T. Harry. "An Analysis of Some Reconstruction Attitudes." *Journal of Southern History* 12 (November 1946): 469–86.

———. "The Louisiana Unification Movement of 1873." *Journal of Southern History* 11 (August 1945): 349–69.

Woolfolk, Sara Van Voorhies. "Five Men Called Scalawags." *Alabama Review* 17 (January 1964): 45–55.

Dissertations and Theses

McCrary James Payton. "Moderation in a Revolutionary World: Lincoln and the Failure of Reconstruction in Louisiana." Ph.D. diss., Princeton University, 1972.

Mills, Wynona Gillmore. "James Govan Taliaferro (1798–1876): Louisiana Unionist and Scalawag." Master's thesis, Louisiana State University, 1968.

Uzee, Philip D. "Republican Politics in Louisiana, 1877–1900." Ph.D. diss., Louisiana State University, 1950.

Biographical References

Biographical Directory of the American Congress, 1774–1971. Washington, D.C.: Government Printing Office, 1971.

Dictionary of Louisiana Biography. Louisiana Historical Association, 2008. www.lahistory.org/site16.php.

National Cyclopaedia of American Biography. New York: J. T. White, 1898–1965.

Ouachita Parish Biographies. http://genealogytrails.com/lou/ouachita/biographies.html.

Wilson, James Grant, and John Fiske, eds. *Appleton's Cyclopaedia of American Biography*. 1888. Reprint. Detroit: Gale, 1968.

Who Was Who in America: Historical Volume, 1607–1869. Rev. ed. St. Louis: Von Hoffman Press and A. N. Marquis Co., 1967.

Historical Dictionaries and References

Johnson, Donald Bruce, and Kirk H. Porter, eds. *National Party Platforms, 1840–1972*. Urbana: University of Illinois Press, 1973.

Sperber, Hans, and Travis Truttschuh, eds. *American Political Terms: An Historical Dictionary*. Detroit: Wayne State University Press, 1962.

Trefousse, Hans L. *Historical Dictionary of Reconstruction.* New York: Greenwood Press, 1991.

INDEX